D1086003

Basic Income

Also available from Bloomsbury

The Precariat, Guy Standing
A Precariat Charter, Guy Standing
The Rediscovery of India, Meghnad Desai

Basic Income

A Transformative Policy for India

Sarath Davala, Renana Jhabvala,
Soumya Kapoor Mehta and Guy Standing

Bloomsbury Academic
An imprint of Bloomsbury Publishing Plc

B L O O M S B U R Y
LONDON • NEW DELHI • NEW YORK • SYDNEY

Bloomsbury Academic

An imprint of Bloomsbury Publishing Plc

50 Bedford Square	1385 Broadway
London	New York
WC1B 3DP	NY 10018
UK	USA

www.bloomsbury.com

BLOOMSBURY and the Diana logo are trademarks of Bloomsbury Publishing Plc

First published 2015

© Sarath Davala, Renana Jhabvala, Soumya Kapoor Mehta and Guy Standing, 2015

This work is published subject to a Creative Commons Attribution Non-Commercial Licence. You may share this work for non-commercial purposes only, provided you give attribution to the copyright holder and the publisher. For permission to publish commercial versions please contact Bloomsbury Academic.

Sarath Davala, Renana Jhabvala, Soumya Kapoor Mehta and Guy Standing have asserted their right under the Copyright, Designs and Patents Act, 1988, to be identified as Authors of this work.

No responsibility for loss caused to any individual or organization acting on or refraining from action as a result of the material in this publication can be accepted by Bloomsbury Academic or the Authors.

British Library Cataloguing-in-Publication Data
A catalogue record for this book is available from the British Library.

ISBN: PB: 978-1-4725-8311-6
HB: 978-1-4725-8310-9
ePDF: 978-1-4725-8313-0
ePub: 978-1-4725-8312-3

Library of Congress Cataloguing-in-Publication Data
A catalog record for this book is available from the Library of Congress.

Typeset by Fakenham Prepress Solutions, Fakenham, Norfolk NR21 8NN
Printed and bound in India

Contents

Abbreviations   vi

Prologue   viii

1   The Transformative Challenge   1
2   Launching Basic Income in Madhya Pradesh   31
3   Basic Income's Emancipatory Value   47
4   The Impact on Living Conditions   71
5   The Impact on Nutrition   83
6   From Ill-Health to Regular Medicine   99
7   Schooling: Loosening Constraints, Boosting Education?   115
8   Work, Productivity and Growth   137
9   Women's Status: Empowerment, Identity and Citizenship   157
10 No Longer Last nor Least ... The Elderly and the Disabled   181
11 The Transformative Potential   195

Appendix: Variables Used in Regressions   215
Bibliography   217
Index   227

Abbreviations

AAY	Antyodaya Anna Yojana
ANM	Auxiliary Nurse Midwife
APL	Above Poverty Line
ASHA	Accredited Social Health Activist
AWW	Anganwadi Worker
BPL	Below Poverty Line
CCT	Conditional Cash Transfer
DBT	Direct Benefit Transfer
FES	Final Evaluation Survey
HIV/AIDS	Human Immunodeficiency Virus/ Acquired Immuno-Deficiency Syndrome
ICDS	Integrated Child Development Scheme
ID Card	Identity Card
IES	Interim Evaluation Survey
LKG	Lower Kindergarten
LMP	Local Medical Practitioner
MGNREGS	Mahatma Gandhi National Rural Employment Guarantee Scheme
MPUCT	Madhya Pradesh Unconditional Cash Transfer Pilot
NBA	Nirmal Bharat Abhiyan (Total Sanitation Campaign)
NCAER	National Council of Applied Economic Research
NSS	National Sample Survey
PDS	Public Distribution System
PFES	Post-Final Evaluation Survey
PHC	Primary Health Centre
PL	Poverty Line
RBI	Reserve Bank of India

Rs.	Rupees
SC	Scheduled Caste
SEWA	Self-Employed Women's Association
ST	Scheduled Tribe
TB	Tuberculosis
TVCT	Tribal Village Cash Transfer Pilot
TV-FES	Tribal Village Final Evaluation Survey
TV-IES	Tribal Village Interim Evaluation Survey
UKG	Upper Kindergarten
UNDP	United Nations Development Programme
UNICEF	United Nations Children's Fund
UPA	United Progressive Alliance (Congress-led coalition government)
WHO	World Health Organization

Note on statistics in text

Most statistics from the evaluation surveys that are cited in the text are rounded to the nearest complete number, with the exception of values that are half (.5), which are rounded to the nearest one decimal point. All statistics are given to one decimal point in the report to UNICEF cited in the text as Jhabvala et al., 2014.

Prologue

The main proposition underpinning this book is that a modest basic income, paid monthly in cash, individually and without conditions, would be a means of achieving three development objectives that taken together would be *transformational*.

Although we believe that a basic income along these lines is affordable and technically feasible, we do not go into the arguments in any depth in this book. Resolving those issues is for other occasions, and will depend ultimately on political decisions on priorities. All we set out to do in this book is assess the results of what has been in several respects a unique experiment or set of pilots.

As far as we are aware, there has been no pilot anywhere that has considered the impact of a basic income cash transfer and a collective organization, both separately and in combination. The reasoning behind the decision to design the pilots in this way was that the positive effects of a basic income would be enhanced if a collective body was operational in the community at the same time.

In total, about 6,000 men, women and children in nine villages in Madhya Pradesh received a basic income, most paid every month for about a year and a half. Many opened bank or cooperative accounts for the first time. The exact figures and the methods used are described in the course of the book. The point here is to emphasize the three complementary development objectives.

Any social policy should be assessed by whether or not it contributes to the recipients' personal development, that is, their well-being or welfare, by whether or not it contributes to economic growth in a sustainable way, and by whether or not it contributes to emancipation, that is, personal and societal freedom. And in doing so, any social policy should be assessed by ethical principles, which are defined in Chapter 1.

It is our contention, first, that a basic income has the potential to promote a substantial improvement in welfare, and is therefore consistent with the best traditions of Indian policy since 1947, however patchy actual achievements in practice might have been. Improved welfare means improved living standards, in health, access to healthcare, sanitation, schooling, nutrition and so on. And it should mean most improvement for the most disadvantaged and improvement for communities as well as for individuals.

However, a policy of this kind should not be judged or assessed solely or even predominantly in terms of welfare. It is the underlying hypothesis that a basic income could also contribute powerfully to growth, by raising productivity, incomes, and work and labour. As such, it would be wrong and unfair to describe it as simply a welfare policy, to be contrasted with alternative uses of spending that might be presented as promoting economic growth. It is a growth-enhancing measure in its own right, and one that would be beneficial for ordinary Indians of all social categories.

The conventional juxtaposition of welfare and growth is too crude, and should be avoided. The contention is that a basic income would be a means of stimulating economic production, raising the quality and quantity of work, and doing so in an inclusive, sustainable and relatively equitable manner.

The third aspect of social policy tends to be overlooked in societies where the privileged are materially and psychologically distant from the disadvantaged. Great inequalities of wealth, income, status and opportunity invariably produce disdain by the privileged for the plight of the disadvantaged and vulnerable. The proposition that unfolds through the following is that a basic income is emancipatory.

It is a means of enhancing – and in some cases reclaiming – personal freedom, particularly of women and those who normally receive lower priority in social policymaking, including all those with disabilities and the elderly. For some, it is a means of reclaiming a degree of freedom that they had lost years ago. This is the case with the notorious *naukar* system, the pattern of debt bondage prevalent in Madhya Pradesh.

The several forms of emancipation are diverse, and are both individual and collective in character. Freedom evolves through the actions of structurally free people, so the emancipatory effects comprise a powerful argument for moving in the direction of a basic income, a road to be taken. Another way of looking at it is that any policy that is not emancipatory in some ways should be shunned.

Taken together, policies that promote personal development, growth and emancipation are, potentially at least, transformational. The idea of transformation encompasses a surge of hope, at the level of individual women and men, at the level of families and households, and at wider levels of community.

Transformation means setting a new course with different structures of decision-making and different types of aspirations and expectations. It means altering states of mind as much as material conditions, altering consciousness of what is possible and what is desirable, and defining anew what is normal.

Social policies also operate in several time dimensions. The pilots that are the core of the book were time-bound, for practical reasons. So are all pilots. So it is sensible to be aware of the limitations and the dynamics that such experiments invariably entail. An impact on some spheres of behaviour and some attitudes may be almost immediate. Others take time to unfold. Effects on some attitudes may take quite a long time. In some cases, a short-term effect may wear off. In others, an effect may be shown for a few individuals or families, leading to demonstration effects, whereby others copy or even surpass those early pioneers.

Many social scientists have mused over cumulative deprivation and cumulative benefits. We all experience these phenomena in one way or another. A basic income is particularly likely to have a series of effects, direct and indirect. The human condition is such that we should have faith that if an intervention succeeds in breaking a cycle of impoverishment and deprivation, it could unleash the capacities of ordinary people in wonderful ways.

Transformation derives from uplifting hope and awakening a sense of imagining, a sense that new initiatives are feasible and desirable. It remains to be seen whether this faith is borne out and in what ways. We merely assert at this point that transformation depends on an integrated balance of welfare, growth and emancipation. They fall together or they rise together.

The pilots on which this book is based could only have been conducted with the generous financial assistance from UNICEF. Its role went well beyond that of providing the essential money. Its officials were supportive and in several cases also enthusiastic and well-informed participants in the many meetings and workshops held during the project. We have great pleasure in thanking them, particularly Louis-Georges Arsenault, the Country Representative, Joaquin Gonzalez-Aleman and Ramya Subramanian. All those inside UNICEF and in other organizations who contributed in one way or another are thanked in the technical report cited in the course of the book.

We also thank Mirai Chatterjee and Shiv Kumar, whose advice, wisdom and encouragement were always welcome. We have so many others to thank that it is almost invidious to single out a few of them. However, we cannot let the opportunity pass to thank, in alphabetical order, Nina Badgaiyan, Seema Grover, Y. P. Gupta, Dipjyoti Konwar, Santosh Malviya and László Zsoldos.

The implementation of the project was coordinated by SEWA Bharat, SEWA's All-India Federation, whose task is to promote new SEWA organizations, strengthen existing ones and advocate for national policies. Again, those who were involved are thanked by name in the technical report produced by the project team that is available through SEWA and UNICEF.

Why was SEWA interested in a basic income? It is essentially a union organization, with over 1.9 million members in ten states of India. It tries to help its members improve income and work security, social security and self-reliance. It seeks to advise government on policies, mobilizes women to take advantage of government schemes and seeks to help government agencies to implement them.

Although government funding for social security has grown, the multiplicity of schemes and the 'clogged pipes' in the delivery system have blocked the flow of benefits to intended beneficiaries. SEWA has tried to improve the flow by advising its members and by lobbying. It is also active in microfinance, and believes it can help members manage cash well through its Cooperative, encouraging the use of cash for the betterment of families.

In that context, a reason for selecting Madhya Pradesh for the pilots was SEWA's deep-rooted presence there. A project of this nature requires an understanding of local realities and also a network of people capable of efficient implementation and an ability to engage with the local community, banks and government.

SEWA Madhya Pradesh was established in Indore in 1985. At first, it worked to organize *bidi* workers in the city, primarily to make them aware of their rights. After 1992, its work spread to other areas, reaching out to women doing other activities. Today it has over 600,000 members, engaged in diverse activities, ranging from *bidi* making, *aggarbatti* (incense stick) making, stitching ready-made clothes and tendu leaf (used to make *bidis*) collection to farming and working as casual wage labourers. We thank its leaders for their involvement and encouragement.

It remains to be stated that although this is an attempt to present a fairly comprehensive description and evaluation of the impact of the basic incomes, it is actually a work-in-progress. The data gathered in the course of the project are rich and complex, requiring years of more research to tease out many of the more nuanced findings.

We hope the book provides a reasonable overview, and that the results will be valuable for social scientists wishing to improve India's social policy and for policymakers wishing to develop and implement better policies. Too often, in the face of failing social policies, apologists attribute the failing to faults of implementation, without questioning the scheme's fundamentals, without considering that there may need to be a paradigm shift, a need to take a new road.

We believe strongly that much more could and should be done, with current resources. Nobody should be remotely satisfied by the extent of poverty and economic insecurity in India today. Nothing less than a transformative policy is needed.

Disclaimer

The research on which this book is based was made possible by the generous support of UNICEF, the United Nations Children's Fund. While we are extremely grateful for their support, all opinions and data interpretations are entirely the responsibility of the authors, and should not be attributed to either UNICEF or SEWA.

1

The Transformative Challenge

Introduction

The Indian economy has grown and changed considerably in recent years. Yet poverty and deprivation are visible everywhere. Successive governments have spent a lot, but the problems seem intractable. Literally thousands of schemes have been launched – over 1,000 at national level alone – in a vast patchwork of wonderful names, which taken together promise so much, and deliver so little.

Villages and towns across the country are a paradox of growth and poverty existing side by side. While wealth has expanded, with roads, bridges, buildings, shopping malls and consumer goods of all types, most villages, especially where scheduled castes or tribes live, seem almost left behind. Yet the residents are working and striving, hoping for a better future for their children, and they look to government to help them achieve that.

What if we went back to basics? Suppose people were provided with a basic income, enough to cover their food needs and basic accommodation. The country's rulers are committed to that by the Constitution. It is affordable. It is a matter of spending priorities. It might be a matter of switching expenditures, but imagine giving people basic economic security, some cash to use, so they could try to improve their lives themselves. It would be 'something more', a little more, not necessarily a replacement for other means of assistance, particularly public services such as infrastructure, free public schooling and free healthcare.

This book is about two pilot basic income schemes. But to set the scene we start by reviewing the standard approaches to poverty alleviation in India, because the debate on what have been called 'cash transfers' has been clouded by comparisons with those alternatives.

Policy evaluation principles

How should the success or failure of any social policy be judged? Although policies are generally judged by whether the outcomes match the stated objectives, evaluations need to be more holistic and take into account fundamental principles of equity and social justice.

Thus a policy or scheme that makes entitlement conditional on families sending their children to school might be judged a success simply if the school registration rate rises. But if the poverty and use of time of the family worsen, then overall that policy might not be judged a success. Similarly, a scheme might reduce poverty simply because a lot of money is spent. But unless it is shown that the spending was more effective than feasible alternatives, we should be wary about declaring it a success.

However, to evaluate policies properly one should go beyond measuring trade-offs of particular benefits and go beyond economic criteria. Social policies should be judged by ethical principles. Merging different ethical values is often difficult. But one can fairly easily blend perspectives into a coherent set of principles (Standing, 2009). Principles drawn from the ethical system of progressive liberalism could be:

- The *Security Difference Principle*, drawing on John Rawls' liberal theory of social justice (1971): This states that a policy is socially just only if it lessens the insecurity of the most insecure groups in society. If a policy helps others but does not help the most insecure, it is unlikely to be socially just.
- The *Paternalism Test Principle*: It is socially unjust to impose controls or directives on some groups that are not imposed on the most-free groups in society.
- The *Rights-not-Charity Principle*: A policy that extends the discretionary power of bureaucrats or other intermediaries while limiting the rights of recipients is socially unjust.
- The *Dignified Work Principle*: A policy is socially just only if it enables recipients to pursue a more dignified working life.
- The *Ecological Constraint Principle*: No policy should create externalities that result in pollution or environmental damage affecting the recipients or the communities in which they live.

To those should be added principles drawn from a Gandhian perspective, as adapted by SEWA for practical application:

- The *Swadeshi Local Production Principle*: As far as possible, products and services required to meet basic needs should be produced locally. This ensures that wealth grows within villages and that communities are strengthened.
- The *Swaraj and Self-Reliance Principle*: Literally meaning self-rule, this has been interpreted by SEWA to mean self-reliance of individuals, families, communities and villages.
- The *Non-Violence and Harmony Principle*: This Gandhian value emphasizes a way of life in which cooperation rather than competition is the norm, and where people can live in harmony with nature.
- The *Weakest at the Centre Principle*: This states that the most vulnerable should be strengthened first and any policy must ensure their economic and social security.

Clearly, the final Gandhian principle is another way of expressing the Security Difference Principle. However, all these principles merge into an ethical framework for evaluating any policy. And as such, they link back to what we will be calling a policy's transformative potential.

What is in a name?

A welfare state plays a key role in protecting and promoting economic and social well-being. It is supposed to promote equality of opportunity, an equitable distribution of wealth and public responsibility for those unable to obtain the minimal provisions for a good life. The government can pursue these goals by providing public goods and services, including infrastructure, healthcare and schools, and by direct benefits, universal or means-tested.

While the Indian state has long provided public services, such as health and education, and targeted social assistance, such as subsidized food through the Public Distribution System (PDS), cash transfers have been marginal in social policy. The most common have been 'cash benefits', notably pensions for the elderly, widows and the disabled.

In 2009, the Indian debate on cash transfers sharpened, stemming from the view that conditional cash transfers (CCTs) in Latin America were successful. These were cash transfer schemes conditional on recipients sending their children to school regularly and on attending medical clinics. The Indian debate was initiated by commentators (Kapur et al., 2008a) whose concern was the immense wastage in existing schemes and the belief that cash transfers could cut through barriers blocking intended beneficiaries from their entitlements.

This fanned opposition by economists on the left, suspecting it was a ruse to cut public services. As some on the political right evidently did have that objective, the debate rapidly became clouded by ideological posturing. This continued through 2011 and 2012, crystallizing in acrimonious exchanges that became over-simplified in claims around 'cash' versus 'food'.

In 2013, two initiatives were launched by the UPA (United Progressive Alliance) government that left the conflict unresolved. While 'direct benefit transfer' (DBT) pilots were launched, the Food Security Act was passed. Both were presented as 'game-changers', even though pulling in opposite directions.

DBT proponents said it would reduce fiscal leakages, allow portability of benefits and spread financial inclusion, incidentally enabling migrants to send back remittances to deprived local communities. Proponents of the Food Security Act claimed that leakages would remain high even if the food subsidy were monetized, because of problems in targeting through using Below Poverty Line (BPL) lists known to be riddled with errors of exclusion and inclusion.

Their preferred solution was to universalize India's Public Distribution System (PDS) and to reduce leakages, for instance, by reducing food prices so sellers did not have an incentive to hoard subsidized grain and sell in the open market, or by adopting information and communications technology to streamline PDS procedures. In turn, sceptics remained convinced that rolling out a complex, inefficient subsidy scheme would merely intensify the bureaucratic raj. But in any case the general election of early 2014 changed the context.

One drawback of the debate around cash transfers has been that commentators have used the term rather loosely with different ideas in mind. There are four types of 'cash transfer' – incentives, subsidies, bonuses and benefits. Cash incentives are sums given to individuals if they do something the state wishes to encourage (such as giving birth in public hospitals rather than at home); cash subsidies are paid to cut the cost of consumer or producer commodities, as in the PDS; cash bonuses are lump-sums given to particular communities; cash benefits are sums paid regularly, such as pensions.

All may or may not be targeted (for the poor only), selective (for designated groups), and conditional (paid only if the person does something specific in return). Old age pensions, for example, are unconditional cash benefits targeted and paid to selective groups (in the case of India, those above the age of 60 and in possession of a BPL card); but they do not require the beneficiary to do something specific in return. The *Janani Suraksha Yojana,* on the other hand, is a conditional cash incentive that requires a selective group, in this case pregnant women, to give birth in hospital to be able to qualify for the incentive.

Given the acrimonious debate around cash versus subsidies in India, we decided on an alternative name for unconditional cash transfers, a name that could be seen as compatible with either ideological position and did not have the baggage that cash transfers have acquired. Perhaps 'basic income' or 'citizen's income' is the goal to pursue.

Basic income is defined as a sum paid regularly, in money, to individuals, without conditions, as a universal or rights-based payment, paid as an equal amount to all adults, as citizens.[1] It does away with means-testing and the exclusion and inclusion errors of measuring poverty lines. It thus removes poverty traps, in which anybody going from a low income to a slightly higher income would lose as much or more in benefits. A basic income would be a modest additional payment. That is how we have piloted it. And that is what this book is about.

Before reviewing the claims and counter claims made about cash transfers, it is appropriate to recall those made about the main alternatives to alleviating economic insecurity. These can be called the Commodity Line (providing food or other commodities for free or at subsidized rates for those designated as 'the poor') and the Labour Line (provision of labour, in return for monetary payment or food). Together with cash, they present the main ways by which governments try to reduce poverty or economic insecurity. There is no need to see the three approaches as alternatives, but they have very different qualities. The big question is which offers the most promising way to achieve a trans-formative set of outcomes.

The subsidy or commodity line

We spend far too much money funding subsidies in the name of equity, with neither equity objectives nor efficiency objectives being met.
Manmohan Singh, Prime Minister (2007)[2]

The primary mechanism by which India has tried to ensure food security to its poor is the PDS. Managed jointly by the central and state governments, the PDS is a targeted scheme that is meant to provide subsidized staple food – wheat, rice and sugar – and kerosene through a network of fair price shops, commonly known as ration shops. In coverage and public expenditure, the PDS is the main subsidy offered to help the economically insecure.

The PDS has attracted many criticisms, not least of which is that it does not reach its intended target groups. In 2009, the Deputy Chairman of the Planning Commission, Montek Singh Ahluwalia, said that only 16 per cent of the food allocated to it reached the poor.[3] At the same time, the Planning Commission estimated that only 27 per cent of PDS expenditure reached low-income groups, and the Finance Minister described it as 'an albatross around our neck and an opportunity for rent seekers to enrich themselves'.

That the subsidized items do not reach the poor partly reflects poor targeting. The mechanism used is the BPL list, which has vast inclusion and exclusion errors, as numerous studies have shown (Sundaram, 2003; Hirway, 2003; Jain, 2004; Mukherjee, 2005; Jalan and Murgai, 2007; Alkire and Seth, 2008; Saxena, 2009; Jhabvala and Standing, 2010; Roy, 2011; Mahamalik and Sahu, 2011; Alkire and Seth, 2012).

There have also been differences between the caps on 'officially poor' set by the Planning Commission and the number with such cards, as identified by the states. In Bihar for instance, the Government of India capped the number of BPL families at 7.3 million, whereas the state BPL figure was 12.6 million families (Government of Bihar, 2011). So, over five million were automatically excluded. In short, targeting was seriously faulty over many years.

Another flaw is inadequate availability of food and non-food items in ration shops. This is largely due to the dual price system the government uses in making commodities available to shopkeepers. There has been a huge difference in the price at which a staple such as wheat is sold in fair price shops (Rs.2 per kg) and the average market price (Rs.20 per kg). That gives shopkeepers an incentive to hoard the food in order to sell it in the black market, leaving consumers who queue at these shops without the subsidized items.

An argument for transferring the PDS into a DBT scheme is that it would undermine this dual pricing. Consumers could approach the ration shop with Rs.2 and their Unique Identification Card, and the shop would sell a kilo of wheat at the market rate, having received the balance (Rs.18 per kg) through a government transfer. A concern is that fair price shop owners, who sell PDS items, would run out of business, unable to make any gains and pay their licences and the onerous bribes. They might self-select out of the system, leaving the government with the task of selling about 60 million tonnes of grain in the market, with considerable risk of corruption. The DBT would not solve the problems of poor targeting, faulty selection of beneficiaries and arbitrary capping of beneficiaries at state level.

Besides long queues, consumers often receive poor quality food. Many opt out of the PDS because of stigma associated with buying such items and the cost involved in fetching them (Himanshu and Sen, 2013; Shrinivasan, 2011). As the poor have the most onerous labour, they are left with inconvenient time schedules to trek to ration shops and wait in queues in the hope that items will have arrived. That they still do so speaks of their reliance on the PDS, despite its flaws, as a source of food security. But aiming for self-selection is scarcely a laudable objective.

A fourth concern is inefficiency. As the Finance Minister told the National Development Council in December 2007, the Planning Commission estimated that one rupee of food cost Rs.3.65 to administer. The inefficiency of the Food Corporation of India (FCI) that is tasked with procuring and distributing food grains is well documented. Supporters of the system whereby government procures food grains at minimum support prices through the FCI say it provides income support to farmers, while creating buffer stocks. But many believe state procurement helps large-scale farmers to the detriment of smallholders (Misra and Ramnath, 2011).

It also means the FCI is a monopoly, removing any incentive to provide quality food, on time and in adequate amounts. There has been uproar about how food rots in decrepit FCI warehouses and does not reach the fair price shops. Between 2008 and 2012, 36,000 tonnes of grain had rotted in the FCI facilities, enough to feed 80 million people 440 grams each. That was due mainly to stocks being kept in the open (*Hindustan Times*, 2012). Yet in a country where 60 per cent of the population still depends on agriculture, moving away from state procurement may be politically difficult.

Linked to inefficiency is how subsidies distort markets. Subsidized food acts as a disincentive to producing local food (Besley and Kanbur, 1988). At the time of drafting of the Food Security Act, critics noted that the extra procurement needed to meet the target of providing subsidized food to over half the Indian population would denude the open market, driving up urban food prices (*The Hindu*, 2013; Winterbottom and Bhardwaj, 2013).

Defenders of the PDS claimed that states that had universalized their PDS, such as Tamil Nadu and Chhattisgarh, had reduced leakages, and that the PDS could work optimally (Khera, 2011a). This view lay behind the Food Security Act, broadening entitlement to subsidized food to two-thirds of the rural population and 50 per cent of the urban, and leading to a vast increase in public expenditure on food subsidies, of 45 per cent according to the UPA government's estimates. The FSA was to make the consumer's cost of grain about 10 per cent of the market price. Predictably, there were conflicting estimates of the likely cost (Bhalla, 2013; Ramaswami et al., 2013).

Defenders of the PDS have also claimed it has provided the poor with food and income security, enabling them to spend on non-food essentials while protecting them from food price fluctuations. This was also claimed by the activist group Rozi-Roti Adhikar Abhiyan Delhi in their protest against our Delhi pilot cash transfer scheme in 2011. To the extent it reaches the intended beneficiaries, the PDS frees up purchasing power. We will consider this in the course of analysing the impact of the basic income.

Finally, PDS supporters argue that complaints about subsidies are more common among those outside their net, citing a 2010 study by the National Council of Applied Economic Research (NCAER) that showed 80 per cent satisfaction among beneficiaries in most states, other than Bihar. They also argue that it helps reduce poverty and improve nutrition. Himanshu and Sen (2013), using consumption data, claimed that the PDS accounted for a substantial part of poverty reduction in India between 2004–5 and 2009–10. They claimed that 'those consuming from the PDS are the only group of households that have seen an increase in calorie consumption'. But they admitted that 'there is no counterfactual to test it with what would have happened with cash transfers'.

It is this opportunity cost argument that should trouble even the most adamant defenders of the PDS and should make policymakers wonder if there is a better way to improve the lives of those at the bottom of Indian society.

The labour line

A second route to tackling poverty and economic insecurity is provision of labour for the designated poor. In India, this is done primarily through the Mahatma Gandhi National Rural Employment Guarantee Scheme (MGNREGS) and public works.

Advocates of the labour line, and public works in general, claim they (i) are targeted to the poor, (ii) create jobs, (iii) lead to construction of public infrastructure, (iv) supplement other incomes, (v) reduce seasonal income variability and (vi) are equitable because they are self-selecting.

While public works have been an important component of safety net programmes since the 1970s, the MGNREGS was hailed as an important shift to a rights-based approach to poverty alleviation by providing a legislatively backed 100-day employment guarantee. Unlike previous public works programmes which also had a food component, wage payments under the MGNREGS are entirely in cash, payable into a worker's post office or bank account.

Proponents claim the scheme has strengthened workers' bargaining. Its wage often exceeds the local wage for manual labour. There have been complaints by farmers that they cannot obtain labour or must pay more. It also promised equal wages to men and women. MGNREGS defenders claim it has reduced seasonal income and consumption variability (Ravi and Engler, 2008). Further, and while coverage of the scheme has been low and the 100-day employment guarantee rarely met, the scheme has included scheduled castes and tribes, and women (Khera and Nayak, 2009). There is also evidence that it has curbed distress migration and improved use of barren areas for cultivation (Kumar and Prasanna, 2010; Kareemulla et al., 2010; CSE, 2008; Sanyal, 2012).

However, MGNREGS has faced criticism around the quality and sustainability of assets created under it (Bassi and Kumar, 2010). There is evidence that public works result in poor output, as in 'washed-away-roads' and flimsy bridges. The cost of monitoring is also high, which is one reason why schemes are rarely evaluated. And while the choice of assets is supposed to be decided collectively by the village in the *gram sabha* (village assembly), this rarely happens. So, the labour tends to be 'make-work' activities without economic justification, undertaken just to spend budgets and give people something to do (McCord and Farrington, 2008).

Although anyone can request labour, the scheme discriminates against labour-constrained households, i.e. those without members available to take such jobs. The poorest households often have people who are ill, aged or disabled. Drawing one person away may leave others more vulnerable. And the labour is particularly onerous for women, who are under time pressure owing to household and other work. The energy-draining labour means the calories used in the labour may exceed the calorific value of food that could be purchased as a result.

Rationing also occurs because of discretion of local officials in responding to labour demands. In an evaluation in Bihar, Dutta et al. (2014) found that controlling for other household and village characteristics, richer households obtained more days of labour if they participated. Connections to the *mukhiya* or *sarpanch* (village headman) also mattered. This resulted in unmet demand in that not everyone who wanted labour obtained it, or they obtained fewer days than they wanted.

Yet another argument against the labour line is that it emphasizes unskilled labour. Although the MGNREG Act mandates that the programme also provide for, as far as possible, training and upgrading of skills, this has not been implemented. As MGNREGS is restricted to unskilled labour – like digging – it weakens the incentives to learn skills. India's demographic transition means that millions are being added to the workforce with low skills, and as constituted MGNREGS will have to continue to provide labour to an 'army of unskilled workers' (Hirway, 2004). And as it has not generated skills, it has not helped the non-farm part of the rural economy.

The cash line

If the subsidy and labour lines are flawed, what about the cash line? All countries have some cash transfers. But the debate is about addressing poverty and economic insecurity through *non-contributory* transfers. Social insurance schemes, such as unemployment insurance benefits, are inadequate in open, flexible labour markets, since they do not reach those working informally, those outside the labour market, the precariat, or those moving between diverse forms of labour and work (Standing, 2011b).

In India, the main non-contributory cash transfers are pensions for the elderly, widows and the disabled. But here targeting problems arise. In most states, pensions are limited to those who have a BPL card or who feature on an official BPL list. Some states allow for self-declared income as proof of poverty but require that eligibility be attested by a local politician or official.

With this in mind, let us consider the criteria that cause policymakers difficulty in designing cash transfer schemes – whether they should be targeted (for the poor only) or universal (paid to everybody), selective (for designated groups), conditional (paid only if the person does something specific in return), and who should be the recipient (the household or the individual).

In India, there have been instances of all types of social policy – universal, targeted and selective. Public health services and schooling, for instance, have been universal. The PDS was also universal until targeting became the vogue. Since the 1990s targeting has been the dominant approach.

Targeting

Although there are several forms of targeting – household means-testing, proxy means-testing, geographical targeting, community-based targeting and so-called self-targeting – the objective has been to focus benefits on the poor by using the notion of a poverty line.

In India, there are three ways of identifying the poor: people below the state-specific poverty lines set by the Planning Commission of India, people on so-called BPL lists based on periodic surveys by the Ministry of Rural Development (for rural areas), and people who have a BPL ration card issued by the state Food and Civil Supplies Department, which determines the amount and price of grains households can buy from the PDS.

There has been a divergence across departments, states and programmes in defining the terms 'poor' or 'below the poverty line'. Exclusion and inclusion errors in BPL lists are well known. But the 'poverty line' is arbitrary, as many in or near poverty experience fluctuating incomes (Narayan et al., 2009). They may be just above in one week, just below in another. Procedures are so cumbersome that determining whether a household is poor is often done years before entitlement to a benefit is put into effect.

Targeting presumes policy should address *yesterday*'s not *tomorrow*'s poverty in helping those who have fallen into poverty rather than those in danger of doing so (Krishna, 2007). To reduce poverty most effectively, one should prevent it, since it costs less to prevent than to help people recover.

Targeting involves high administrative costs. That is inherent to means-testing (Caldes et al., 2004). When evaluations measure a scheme's cost, they should take account of the fact that funds spent on administration could be used to give recipients more money.

Actual targeting has been riddled with errors. Since 1992, the Ministry of Rural Development has conducted censuses to identify the poor, and procedures have become steadily more complex (Mehrotra and Mander, 2009). The resultant chaos has been subject to withering criticism (Saith, 2007) and led to the Saxena Committee report in 2009. As its chairman later observed, the failure of targeting was revealed by the National Sample Survey, which showed that vast numbers of the poor were excluded from having a BPL card, while many non-poor were allocated one (Saxena, 2010). In Gujarat, we found that a huge proportion of those in need did not have cards or had been denied one for some spurious reason (Standing et al., 2010). Possession is often regressive, with the poorest being the least likely to have one.

Because of inclusion and exclusion errors, elaborate attempts have been made to develop proxy means-tests (sets of indicators correlated with income poverty). But they are no better; they identify the poor inaccurately, at great expense and with long lags between the gathering of data and classification of households (Development Pathways, 2011). Proxy means-tests were recommended by the Saxena Committee (2009) for identifying those deserving a BPL card. But that route is as cumbersome and as prone to exclusion and inclusion errors as similar schemes have proven elsewhere. In sum, targeting in reality is neither efficient nor equitable.

Outside India, studies have considered whether targeted or universal schemes have more effect in reducing poverty. Due to exclusion errors, targeting has fared worse. In the four largest Latin American countries, targeted schemes on average reached less than half of the poorest 20 per cent. Similar failings emerged in Brazil's *Bolsa Família* and Mexico's *Oportunidades* (Lindert et al., 2006; Soares et al., 2007). And in China, cities that used more targeting were less likely to reduce poverty (Ravallion, 2007).

Selectivity

A second distinction made in social policy is between selective and non-selective payments, where selectivity means providing the benefit for particular groups, either regardless of their income or through means-testing as well. To highlight

Table 1.1 Common ways of determining benefit entitlement

Targeting	Universal	Selective
• Means-testing • Proxy means-test • Geographical/ locational • Social categories	• All citizens • All legal residents • All long-term residents • All contributors	• Mothers of young children • Girl children • Tribals • Pregnant women • Disabled • Unemployed, seeking jobs • Schoolchildren • Elderly/widows/ widowers • Marginal farmers • Urban 'informal' workers

the differences between targeting and selectivity, Table 1.1 summarizes the main forms of each.

Underpinning selectivity is a decision that groups with certain characteristics deserve help, rather than others. The most common schemes provide payments only to women with young children or to those from scheduled castes and tribes, provide men and women over a certain age with a pension, or provide people with disabilities with a payment.

Many cash transfer schemes are both selective and targeted, so that, for instance, only women with children and with low incomes receive the payments. But with each decision on selective entitlement there are procedures that are hard to apply in local communities. Many of the reasons for failure of targeting are similar in the case of selectivity.

Universalism

In principle, a universal policy is preferable to one that targets on the poor, in that it does not suffer from large exclusion errors, while it also creates solidarity within communities. But critics of universalism say it would be too costly or result in under-funding, which would erode its legitimacy.

Advocates of universalism believe that net spending could be reduced by clawing back from the wealthier and that boosting incomes would have a positive macro-economic effect while reducing other social costs, notably by improving health and thus lowering healthcare costs. We acknowledge this is an open debate on which there is no consensus. In the end, the politics of priorities will be a decisive factor.

The problems with targeting raised a dilemma for the pilots. Either the cash could be given only to 'the poor' or it could be paid universally. In practice, the term 'universal' is slightly ambiguous. For example, should short-term immigrants in the pilot villages be included? However, a universal approach was taken. Within the villages every person received a cash transfer, which was individual and unconditional. We will not flag conclusions at this point, but merely state that the arguments for and against targeting, selectivity and universalism are likely to continue for some while.

Conditionality

The team designing the basic income pilots had extensive discussions on whether conditions should be applied, with a strong consensus against applying any. The main reason was moral. It was presumptuous to think people need to be steered to make decisions in their own interest. As adults they could make decisions for themselves. This was backed by SEWA's experience showing that people, especially poor people, used cash in the interest of their families and communities, often better than those who had more.

Across the world, governments, under international human rights law, have made binding commitments to do what they can to ensure all their populations attain basic material needs. Yet in recent years, many governments have introduced so-called conditional cash transfer schemes (CCTs) based on the imposition of forms of 'behavioural conditionality'.

What this means is that they offer to overcome people's poverty or vulnerability only if they meet certain conditions, acting in ways that policymakers regard as desirable. Implicit in that judgement are several presumptions.

It presumes people can be divided into a deserving group (defined by behaviour stipulated in the condition) and an undeserving one (defined as those not behaving in the desired way). It presumes that the condition is the relevant one in determining a person's poverty or vulnerability. It presumes that conditions are easy to comply with. And it presumes that if the recipient so desires he/she could easily access the resources required to fulfil the conditions.

CCTs have become hugely popular, with the World Bank pouring billions of dollars into loans to start and scale up CCT schemes in developing countries. The Bank has defined them as follows:

> Conditional cash transfers are programs that transfer cash, generally to poor households, on the condition that those households make prespecified investments in the human capital of their children.
>
> (Fiszbein and Schady et al., 2009, p. 1)

In reality, sometimes the motives have had little to do with human capital. But there are several types of condition – (i) those that must be satisfied prior to receipt of a benefit, (ii) those that must be satisfied during receipt, and (iii) those that must be satisfied afterwards.

The most common are behavioural conditions imposed on families during receipt of the cash transfers. In Brazil, entitlement is conditional on a child's attending school for at least 85 per cent of the time and/or taking an infant to a health clinic. In India, CCTs range from schemes to encourage schooling to schemes for reducing vulnerabilities of the girl child, encouraging institutional delivery and raising the age of marriage.

As can be gleaned from that last example, in practice, conditionality blends into selectivity (selecting particular types of people for benefit) and targeting (based on determining who is poor and who is not).

The main claims made by proponents of CCTs are that (i) they break the inter-generational transfer of poverty, (ii) they help to legitimize redistributive social transfers among middle-class voters, and (iii) they make use of scarce public (or donor) funds most efficiently.

In spite of frequent re-statements of these claims, all evaluations have focused on short-term impacts (Fiszbein and Schady et al., 2009; Cecchini and Madariaga, 2011), and most have focused largely if not exclusively on the impact on indicators of the applicable condition (e.g., school attendance). No evaluation has shown that CCTs break the inter-generational transfer of poverty, because they are based on short-term experiments and impact data over several years, rather than inter-generational data.

Conditionality is spreading in social policy in industrialized countries as well. Behind it is an influential school of thinking that emanates from the USA, 'behavioural economics', which has fed into a perspective known as 'libertarian paternalism' (Thaler and Sunstein, 2009).

Everywhere, the conditions have led to extensive exclusion, as people entitled to the cash withdraw when they cannot comply or find it hard to comply with some condition. In Mexico, those excluded were mainly the poorest, as the burden of compliance was too great (Alvarez et al., 2006). In Indonesia, a proxy means-test combined with conditions incorrectly excluded 52 per cent from the beneficiaries (Alatas et al., 2012). In Malawi, girls denied cash benefits because they dropped out of school ended up having a higher probability of becoming pregnant earlier than those who received cash unconditionally.

In India, conditionality is a major cause of exclusion and corruption, adding to the clogged pipes of delivery systems. Much money meant for poverty alleviation or for benefiting the more vulnerable is siphoned off by powerful people. When there is a condition, the recipient must prove she has fulfilled it. The proof is usually to be given by a person in authority who can certify that she has fulfilled the condition. Very often it is hard to obtain the certificate from the official. Often, the person authorized to certify that the condition is fulfilled is not available, and the recipient must spend days away from work seeking the official, who often demands a cut from the benefit, or a pre-payment.

To illustrate what happens, reflect on the Indira Gandhi *Matritva Sahyog Yojana*, a government scheme launched in 2009 intended to compensate women for loss of earnings during pregnancy and delivery, entitling a woman to Rs.4,000. According to the Department of Women and Children (2011), the conditions she is supposed to fulfil are:

> She must have 1 or 2 children, must be registered at the health centre in the first trimester of pregnancy, must have made at least three ante-natal care visits, must have delivered the child in a medical institution, must have breastfed in the first hour of birth, and must have had the child fully immunized.

To satisfy these conditions, she must have the following certificates:

- A letter from a local official stating she only has two children;
- A certified copy of her registration at the *anganwadi* or health centre;
- A certificate from an *anganwadi* worker (AWW) or auxiliary nurse midwife (ANM), or other proof that she made three ante-natal visits;
- A certificate from the hospital that she delivered the child there;
- A certificate from the hospital that she breast-fed in the first hour;
- A certificate from the AWW, ANM, doctor or health centre for each immunization;
- A certificate from the health or *anganwadi* centre that she attended counselling classes in each trimester.

It is scarcely surprising that many fail to gain any benefit (Dhar, 2012). The scheme omits women with more than two children. Others could not access the scheme because they could not fulfil the conditions, or could fulfil most conditions but could not afford to pay the bribe for the certificates. Those women who finally received it did so six months or more after the delivery, and many had to pay a fee to the postman to celebrate their benefit.

This example demonstrates other problems with conditionality. Conditions place a burden on women, intensifying the 'feminization of obligations'. They require women to spend time, money and energy when they are most vulnerable, and contribute to feelings of powerlessness. Conditions erode gender empowerment, since they affirm traditional divisions of labour and responsibility (Molyneux, 2006).

Another constraint is the dependence of conditions on the supply side. A woman can fulfil the conditions attached to maternity benefits only if health centres are available, if institutional delivery is accessible, if immunization facilities are available, and so on. In many areas there are no functioning health centres, often not even *anganwadi* centres. The ANMs rarely visit villages even where health centres exist and the facilities can be so minimal, and so unclean, that institutional delivery is not feasible or desirable.

Similarly, CCTs dependent on children's schooling are denied to families if there are no schools nearby. Many schools suffer from high teacher absenteeism. Obliging children to go to schools that have no teachers would scarcely be rational. There is no legitimate point in imposing conditions if the services are defective or absent.

Proponents of CCTs have reacted by saying that this has led to a language of 'co-responsibilities', suggesting that when recipients are obliged to comply with conditions the public authorities are pressurized by them to supply or improve public amenities. But this is asymmetrical. The costs of compliance and of non-compliance are huge for low-income families; the costs for the bureaucracies not performing are minimal.

Another objection to CCT schemes stems from the lack of information. If they are minimally fair, they should require policymakers to ensure those covered are fully informed of the conditions and the rationale for them.

The cost of informing potential recipients how the conditions are to be met is only one type of cost that arises. That is followed by the cost of monitoring behaviour, then the cost of regular re-certification of beneficiary records, then the cost of determining whether the condition has been met, then the cost of enforcing the behaviour, then the cost of taking remedial action, and then the cost of suspending entitlement if it is determined that a condition has not been met.

At every stage, bureaucratic or rules-based decisions have to be made. At each point there is an arbitrary element. For instance, did the person make enough effort to meet the condition? Was the person's excuse adequate to justify not meeting the condition? Was the obstacle cited really an obstacle and sufficient to be a reasonable barrier? Is ignorance of the implications justifiable?

Another problem with conditions is that evaluations tend to focus on the impact of the issue that is the objective of the condition, and give little or no priority to other outcomes. For example, an oft-cited evaluation of an experimental scheme for teenage girls in Malawi found that the conditional part of the scheme resulted in a greater increase in school attendance whereas those who received the cash unconditionally had a lower probability of becoming pregnant and were more likely to marry later (Baird et al., 2013).

Sometimes, the side-effects of CCTs can be pernicious. The *Ladli* (Delhi), *Ladli Laxmi* (Madhya Pradesh, Goa) and *Dhanlaxmi* (central government) schemes are intended to discourage female foeticide, and encourage girls' schooling, by providing a deposit in the girl's name which will mature when she is 18 years old and if she has been in school until then. Studies show this is encouraging the practice of dowry, a social evil prohibited by law (Nanda, 2012).

Nevertheless, in India as elsewhere, there is political pressure in favour of CCTs (Prabhu, 2009). Many policymakers reason that if one condition does not work, or does not work well enough, tougher conditions are needed. Conditions beget conditions, as they lurch towards social engineering, in which transfers are used as 'carrots and sticks', to be given or taken away depending on whether entitlement criteria accord with state-determined norms (Standing, 2011). Ethical principles are easily forgotten.

Choice of recipient

A question the study team debated was who should be the recipient of the cash and whether it should be paid on a household or family basis or on an individual basis.

In India, most benefits intended to alleviate poverty are given to the family, which means they go to the 'household head', generally the oldest male. This exacerbates intra-family inequality, with women taking second place in allocation of resources and in family decision-making. SEWA has been arguing that to reduce inequity, if a benefit is provided to the household, the main beneficiary should be the oldest female. This view has support, as many believe women make decisions on spending more responsibly than men (Kapur and Subramanian, 2009). But generalizations are always questionable.

The alternative is for each individual to be provided with an equal amount. The team had considerable discussion on this, as administratively it is harder to manage. The matter was settled when it was discussed with village women who said they would prefer individualized benefits. They said that if the household benefit was to accrue solely to the woman, it would create tensions within the household. However, they preferred the money for the children to come to them.

Individual benefits do not mean intra-household or family pressures will disappear. But they do provide scope for gender-based and age-based bargaining within households. We will come to this issue in Chapter 2, in discussing the methodology and design of the pilots.

As for linking cash transfers to family size or structure, note that a household is not exogenous. It may change in response to policy changes. For instance, if the amount to be paid is determined by how many are staying in a dwelling, people will have an incentive to have temporary migrants classified as usual residents. There are other moral hazards one could imagine. As households are endogenous, payments should not be provided on a household or family basis. The household is not a fixed unit, and will be less so in the future.

Cash transfers: Claims and counter-claims

This study is about a specific type of cash transfer, a basic income that is both unconditional and universal, with lower amounts paid to children. There may be differing views on the desirability or feasibility of universalizing. However, we are convinced that conditionalities are expensive, paternalistic, chronically inefficient and inequitable. Before turning to the design of the pilots, it may be useful to review the claims and counter-claims made about cash transfers in general.

Arguments against cash transfers

There are six objections that have been made against cash transfers in India. They are as follows:

'Cash transfers hide an ulterior ideological motivation'

The vehemence of opposition to cash transfers in India has been largely ideological and a standard resort to any new idea (Hirschmann, 1991). Much of the opposition stems from a belief that they are a 'smokescreen' for a policy of dismantling the public welfare system. But there is no necessary connection; many advocates are committed to strengthening public social services and anti-poverty measures.

The strident denigration of cash transfers is neither fair nor helpful (Shah, 2008). And to describe proponents as singing a 'siren song' is hyperbole. We all know that sirens lured sailors onto the rocks to destruction. The idea that giving people cash would destroy them is scaremongering (Ghosh, 2011a, 2011b). It is also unfair to say proponents suffer from an 'illusion' that cash can replace public services, which is 'remarkably dangerous' (Dreze, 2011; for a response, see Standing, 2011c). Not only are many proponents in favour of public social services, but arguments for public services and for cash transfers should stand on their own.

'Cash transfers are unjustifiable hand-outs'

Another criticism is that they are 'hand-outs', something for nothing. This could be claimed about many forms of support except for those that apply conditions to entitlement. It was used to justify conditionality in Latin America, when it was thought middle-class opposition would block cash transfers.

There are philosophical responses to the criticism. Wealthy people obtain numerous benefits without being required to give something in return, and their children receive hand-outs that village children could not dream about. A basic income would be a minor correction for brute ill-luck. Economic liberalization has benefited the elite and salariat much more than those in villages and slums.

There is also what might be called the Painian Principle, after reasoning developed by Thomas Paine in 1795. Any person's wealth owes less to their endeavours and skills than to those of past generations. We do not know if those who contributed the most were our ancestors or those of others around us. So, as a matter of social justice, a modest basic income would represent a 'social dividend' on the investment made by those generations. One could extend this by saying that the natural resources belong to everybody in the country and so a dividend should go to everybody.

However, it is probably the instrumental response that is most telling for policymakers. Cash transfers are social investments, rather than hand-outs. If they improve, directly or indirectly, health, education and productive activity, they reduce other social costs and boost economic development. It may be hard to demonstrate this, but the economic logic is surely telling.

'Cash transfers induce dependency and laziness'

A related claim is that cash transfers would promote dependency and laziness, reducing labour supply, because a guaranteed income, paid regardless of work status, age, marital status or need, would allow people to labour less. This criticism, if valid, would apply to any benefit, unless conditions were applied. But is it valid?

There is no evidence in India or elsewhere that people are inherently indolent. The normal human condition is to want to develop one's capabilities and improve one's family living standards. And if an impoverished person is suffering the effects of poverty – malnutrition, listlessness, lack of energy and confidence, a proneness to illness and so on – a modest basic income could make it possible for people to concentrate, learn, apply themselves and work more.

Another claim is that people would 'waste' the money if it were given without conditions, spending it on private 'bads', such as tobacco and alcohol. This is a patronizing presumption implying that people cannot learn to make rational choices. On that basis, one could say the rich should have money taken away because many waste it on whisky. The argument is disingenuous.

'Cash transfers have leakages'

One claim is that the leakages found with other benefits will remain with cash transfers. However, direct cash transfers would reduce the number of steps required for the benefit to reach the recipient. Given the technology of money transfer today, it would be possible for a cash transfer to go directly from a central fund into the account of a recipient, cutting out the many layers of bureaucracy and middlemen that are required for other schemes. This would considerably reduce the possibility of siphoning off funds into illegitimate hands.

Removing conditions would also reduce the possibility for leakage as it would reduce discretionary activity and the opportunity for corruption. And the less the income is targeted or selective and the more universal the basic income, the less the scope for leakages. Cash is more transparent than subsidies, offering fewer avenues for siphoning by officials.

'Cash transfers would be useless, as the supply side does not exist'

Another criticism is that even if cash transfers could be justified on the grounds that people could use the cash to buy services and goods, they would be 'useless' because there are insufficient schools and health services for the money to be used properly. This, it has been said (Ghosh, 2011a), is unlike the situation in Brazil where the CCT *Bolsa Família* has been successful.

What this argument overlooks is that in Brazil, when the scheme was being rolled out, there was also a dearth of decent social services, including schools and medical clinics. The money helped create a public demand for them and public pressure to provide better facilities.

A graphic example can be seen in the pilot basic income scheme in Namibia. Beforehand, the local clinic was a run-down place, with few medicines, demoralized nurses and dirty surroundings. Most HIV/AIDS sufferers did not go to it, as they could not afford to buy adequate food essential for the treatment, even though it was free. The basic income transformed the situation. Villagers were charged a small amount for each visit; the nurses used the money to buy medicines and improve the clinic; HIV/AIDS sufferers bought better food and so were nutritionally able to take the treatment. The basic income created a virtuous circle. The complementarity resulted in an improvement in the public service.

In India, the markets do work, and as far as food, clothing and other basic necessities are concerned a demand will surely produce a supply. The cash may lead to enhanced local production and a virtuous circle of local demand and supply. Health and education services too are supplied by the private sector. While in some states public services work well, in others they need to be strengthened considerably.

'Cash transfers would be inflationary'

Some critics contend that cash transfers would be inflationary. Narendar Pani (2011), for example, said this is the biggest danger of cash replacing subsidized commodities, because it would lead to an increase in demand. This is one-sided economics, for it neglects the supply side. If the supply of goods is price inelastic, it might be inflationary, but there is no reason to believe this would be true, given that the money would be spent mostly on basic goods and services. And to lessen the likelihood of initial inflation, it could be arranged that stocks of food and other basic goods could be released until there was time for supply to increase through the market.

Again, evidence from other countries suggests that the influx of money into local economies via transfers induces a rapid increase in the supply of basic goods and services, partly by inducing people to grow more food crops, make more clothes and so on, and partly by inducing merchants to direct more goods and services into these economies.

Arguments for cash transfers

Let us now turn to the claimed advantages, as identified internationally. We focus on the behavioural claims since most research has done so. But there are also macro-economic effects, in which the influx of money into local economies stimulates spending and investment, thus raising economic growth, through Keynesian multiplier effects (Davies and Davey, 2008). We will give more attention to the potential transformative effects in the course of the book. But let us start by reviewing the basic claims.

'Cash transfers would strengthen economic citizenship'

Humanitarian relief organizations have come to appreciate that the advantages of cash include speed, transparency and the fact that it allows those in need to make choices about how they spend, which enables them to retain dignity in times of crisis (Creti and Jaspars, 2006).

Basic incomes also offer a transparent means of reducing the growing inequalities systemic to an open economy. The inequality is neither socially healthy nor economically necessary. Research shows that high and rising inequality reduces economic growth, threatens social stability and worsens the welfare of all.

At present, India is the world's biggest subsidy state. All the subsidies are selective, intended to benefit certain groups and not others. Most are regressive, since they go to the salariat and elite as much as to the income poor. A fuel subsidy, for example, goes to those who can afford vehicles. Their annual cost, at over 2 per cent of GDP, could fund a universal basic income.

So a claim is that a basic income would give recipients a modicum of economic security and economic freedom. People assured of income to cover their basic needs would be better placed to make rational choices about consumption, work and personal relationships.

As far as economic citizenship is concerned, there is international evidence that individualized payments strengthen financial self-reliance and the dignity of family and community members. They would also strengthen the position of the elderly and women, by giving them their own income.

'Cash transfers would limit bureaucrats' discretionary power'

Defenders of the subsidy system cannot deny that it gives administrators and bureaucrats licence to be lax, discretionary and arbitrary in how they conduct themselves. Though most attention is given to blatant corruption, the basic problem is that the policies give too many bureaucrats the opportunity to make judgements on whom to help and whom not to help. It ill behoves progressive critics to ignore this inherent feature of policies that rely on subjective judgements by bureaucrats, from the top all the way to the bottom of the edifice of the subsidy state.

Would universal basic incomes overcome the discretionary tendency? Perhaps not entirely, but the transparency and simplicity would minimize the opportunity for it.

'Cash transfers would increase social policy efficiency'

As transfers are in money form, they involve lower administration and transaction costs than other forms of benefit. They have been criticized for being difficult to operate in the absence of individualized bank accounts. But think how much more difficult it is to operate a national system of distributing subsidized goods, with all the complexity of purchasing, collecting, storing, pricing, measuring and distributing items across thousands of villages.

International evidence is encouraging for those who believe cash transfers would reduce administrative costs of social policy. In Mexico, once initial take-up costs were covered, annual administrative costs fell to 5 US cents for each dollar's worth of transfer.

'Cash transfers would reduce poverty'

There is extensive evidence that cash transfers can reduce poverty substantially. In Mexico, *Oportunidades* cut the poverty headcount ratio by 10 per cent, the poverty gap by 30 per cent, and the poverty severity index by 45 per cent (Skoufias and Parker, 2001). In the Namibian pilot scheme, a small basic income dramatically reduced the number with insufficient income for food, housing needs and access to schooling and health facilities. The villagers used the additional money to improve living standards.

A social protection system anchored on cash transfers could make the difference between failure and success in achieving the Milliennium Development Goal of halving poverty by 2015 (Ortiz and Yablonski, 2010). Critics might say other policies could do even better. But they have not shown it.

'Cash transfers would strengthen social solidarity and reduce inequality'

People guaranteed a modest monthly cash transfer gain basic security. Psychologists have shown this leads to more altruism and social solidarity, intangibles with considerable social value. People who feel secure themselves are more inclined to be tolerant towards others, particularly towards those with different characteristics (ILO, 2005).

In India, this is important, given the caste system and religious tensions that have marred its history. If people know that everybody is receiving cash equally, they will surely feel less resentful towards others. There is also evidence that universalistic schemes strengthen solidarity, whereas those that are only for the poor invariably become poor programmes, a point made by Richard Titmuss long ago and reiterated by Amartya Sen (1995).

Cash transfers can also reduce inequality by lessening the debt and credit restraints on lower-income groups. In the Namibian pilot, in the year following the introduction of the basic income, the earnings of the poorest rose more than for those who had been higher earners. The poorest were able to buy seeds and small-scale equipment, such as sewing machines, and pay off debts.

Latin American experience also shows that transfers reduce inequality (Soares, 2007). At macro-economic level, Brazil is one of the few countries to have reduced inequality in the twenty-first century, an achievement linked to the introduction of extensive cash transfers. Meanwhile, with all its subsidies, inequality grew in India.

'Cash transfers would boost human development – education'

There are three aspects analysed more than any other: education, health and nutrition, and economic activity. First, there are links between cash transfers and 'human capital' formation, measured mainly by enrolment, attendance and performance in school. Here the arguments and evidence, although positive, are difficult to unravel, as the predominant form has been conditional cash transfers (CCTs) in which the main condition is regular attendance in school.

We may list the principal education-related hypotheses associated with cash transfers as follows:

1 They raise school enrolment;
2 They raise school attendance;
3 They improve school performance;
4 They reduce school drop-out rates;
5 They lead to prolonged schooling, mainly through the effects of (1) to (4);
6 They reduce child labour that disrupts schooling, through an income effect and through the increased propensity to attend and continue schooling;
7 They reduce inequalities in school attendance and attainment associated with family background, wealth and household income;
8 They reduce gender inequalities in all the above respects.

The primary difficulty of interpreting evaluations of CCTs is separating the effect of the cash from the effect of the conditions. The Latin American evidence is strong that CCTs boost school attendance; there is less strong evidence with respect to performance, although most has been positive (Fiszbein and Shady et al., 2009; Slavin, 2010). In Mexico, for instance, since *Oportunidades* was introduced (initially as *Progresa*), secondary school enrolment has risen by a third, school drop-out rates have fallen by 20 per cent, and attendance rates have risen.

In India, in the Odisha Girls' Incentive Programme (OGIP) covering the school year 2012–13, all girls from scheduled caste and scheduled tribe families joining grade 9 were provided with an annual incentive of Rs.2,000, paid into a bank or post-office account, which they received on condition that they had a monthly attendance record of 75 per cent or more (Shivakumar and Das, 2013). The project claimed the school drop-out rate fell by 50 per cent. But it was not clear whether this reflected the concerted campaign by the project designers, IPE Global, or whether the conditionality was relevant or applied.

A question is whether unconditional transfers would have the same effect, or whether conditionality is necessary or even positive. There is evidence that conditions are unnecessary. For instance, in the pilot unconditional scheme in Namibia school attendance went up sharply, although there was no pressure on parents to send their children to school.

The dynamics were revealing. The primary school was a state school, but parents were required to pay a fee equivalent to about Rs.50 per term for each child. Before the pilot, registration and attendance were low, and the school had too little income from fees to pay for basics, which made the school unattractive and lowered the teachers' morale. With the cash transfers, parents suddenly had enough money to pay school fees, and teachers had money to buy paper, pens, books, posters, paints and brushes. The school became more attractive, giving parents and children an incentive, while raising the morale and, probably, the capacity of the teachers.

An evaluation of another African scheme also suggested it was the cash rather than the conditions that had the positive effect. The finding was accidental, in that the scheme was meant to be conditional, but in one area the designers forgot to inform recipients about the conditions and forgot to implement them. So the evidence that emerged was by chance.

The pilot was in Malawi, a low-income country with poor infrastructure and long distances for children to travel to school. An econometric evaluation concluded that 'a $5/month transfer to a household made unconditionally had roughly the same impact on schooling outcomes as a $15/month transfer made conditional on school attendance' (Baird et al., 2009, p. 22).

Both unconditional and conditional schemes have been associated with a rise in school enrolment in Latin America and in African countries. In South Africa, the effect was particularly large for young children (Case et al., 2005; Samson et al., 2004). Similarly, in Malawi, cash transfers raised enrolment and reduced the school drop-out rate (Miller et al., 2006). There is also evidence that the impact varies by age. In low-income areas they seem to have a strong impact on early school attendance, whereas in higher-income areas the effect is stronger for teenagers.

The international evidence suggests that the effect on enrolment is particularly strong for young girls, as found in Bangladesh and Cambodia as well as in Latin America (Khandker et al., 2003; Filmer and Shady, 2006). This is surely of great significance for India today, where lack of attention to girls' schooling is notorious.

Finally, there is the impact on child labour, particularly in hazardous forms and in forms that interfere with schooling. The evidence is mostly positive. In Brazil, the Inter-American Development Bank estimated that the CCT reduced child labour substantially. Although some studies have been less sure, on balance, if cash transfers have positive effects on schooling, they also have a modest negative effect on the extent of child labour.

'Cash transfers would improve health and nutrition'

Then there is the effect on health. Some claim cash transfers do not have much effect (e.g. Narayanan, 2011). But many studies suggest strong positive effects on child nutrition, child and adult health, the incidence and severity of illness, and use and effectiveness of medical services. We may list the main health-related effects of cash transfers as follows:

1 They improve maternal health, thereby reducing female morbidity, health problems related to childbirth, and maternal mortality;
2 They improve child nutrition, resulting in less stunting and improved weight-for-age and height-for-age;
3 They raise the incidence of timely vaccinations of children, against diseases such as polio, diphtheria and tetanus;
4 They lead to more use of health services, including preventative services and services involving user fees.

Some studies have been sceptical about the impact on child nutrition and health (Hoddinott and Barrett, 2008). But most have been positive. For instance, in Colombia the CCT resulted in improvement in the average height-for-age among children (Ottanasio et al., 2005). In Mexico, the CCT reduced stunting among babies by 39 per cent for girls and 19 per cent for boys. The trouble with many studies is that it is unclear how much of the effect is due to the conditionality and how much to the cash. Fortunately, there is also evidence that unconditional transfers have similar positive effects (Aguero et al., 2007).

The Namibian pilot is worth highlighting. Using the WHO's z-score method-ology, within six months of the start of the unconditional transfers, the weight-for-age figures for infants aged 0–5 years dramatically improved, with underweight children moving towards the norm and overweight children also doing so due to improved diets. There was no pressure put on families to spend the cash in any particular way. They acted in the way most would, looking after the interests of their children.

Unconditional transfers have been shown to lead to dietary diversity, a devel-opment associated with enhanced child nutritional status (Adato and Bassett, 2009). However, as more conditional schemes have been launched, there is more evidence on their effects. Thus, Sri Lanka's *Samruddhi* cash scheme led to improved child nutrition. And in many places, including India, such schemes have been associated with a reduction in neonatal and perinatal deaths (Himaz, 2008).

There is also evidence, mainly from Latin America, that CCTs boost use of preventative health services, being associated with more health check-ups (Bastagli, 2009). This has also been found in India (Lim et al., 2010). But the same effect was also shown in the unconditional scheme in Namibia.

This is unsurprising; being rational, people soon work out that it is beneficial to have health check-ups if they can afford it and have the time, and if the facilities are available. Thus, in those Namibian villages, the basic income meant that visits to the local clinic became affordable, while the clinic could improve the premises and raise the morale and status of the nurses. With cash transfers, small user fees become more affordable. This does not mean that fee waivers should not be used for individuals or groups who are chronically poor or prone to illness and medical expenses (Bitran and Giedion, 2003).

Finally, there is evidence that having cash with which to pay for medical services leads to pressure on public and private services to improve what they provide.

'Cash transfers would enhance women's economic activity and labour supply'

Beyond better education and health, there are also arguments that cash transfers to low-income people and communities boost local economic activity and labour supply. There is much evidence to support this, ignored by critics of cash transfers. The evidence comes from large-scale statistical evaluations, from small-scale pilots and from anecdotal research.

In Brazil, the *Bolsa Família* has been associated with an increase in female labour force participation, because women were enabled to spend on transport and obtain childcare (ILO, 2005). In Mexico, evaluations of *Progresa-Oportunidades* concluded that the transfers had no net effect on labour force participation (Skoufias and di Maro, 2005). But there and elsewhere, they have been linked to reduction in child labour, compensated by a shift to adult labour.

In Namibia, the basic income led to an *increase* in work and labour by women and to more job-search activity by both men and women. In South Africa, the labour force participation rate of those receiving transfers increased by 13–17 per cent compared with those in similar households who did not receive them, with the greatest increase coming for women (Economic Policy Research Institute, 2004).

In sum, the claims in favour of cash rest on its potential for having multiple effects. Unlike the labour line, it does not impose onerous labour on disadvantaged people; unlike subsidized commodities, it enhances the freedom and agency of people who need and want more of both.

Concluding thoughts

We started this chapter by asserting ethical principles that should underlie the evaluation of a social policy. We will return to them at the end of this book, but the basic income does seem to conform to them. The Security Difference Principle and the related principle of reaching the weakest is satisfied as everybody benefits, even the most disadvantaged. As the weakest have the least resources, the basic income would mean more to them than to those who are better off.

Swaraj or self-reliance is strengthened through basic income since a small amount of money reduces the insecurity and uncertainty faced, and allows for more self-confidence. Basic income may also strengthen the *Swadeshi* Principle since the cash is likely to be spent locally. Studies have shown (Hirway et al., 2010) that cash infusion into villages, and especially to poor families, tends to strengthen the local economy by strengthening social reliance.

Finally, with regard to the principle of harmony and non-violence, an equal amount of cash to all should reduce inter-household jealousies and tensions. In that regard, earlier experiments have shown that basic income does strengthen collective action.

Notes

1 http://www.basicincome.org/bien/aboutbasicincome.html
2 Speech of Manmohan Singh, at the inauguration of the golden jubilee year of the Institute of Economic Growth, 15 December 2007, available at http://pmindia.nic.in/lseech.asp?id=629
3 Reported in *The Economist*, 10 September 2010, p. 30.

2

Launching Basic Income in Madhya Pradesh

In social science, there is no perfect methodology for evaluating social policies. Some methods are better for analysing direct effects, others for considering the wider implications, and some are valuable for gaining insights that could not be anticipated adequately beforehand. The optimum is a combination of approaches. But whatever approach is adopted, the most important features are transparency and bias.

In practice, most approaches contain biases, and it is rare for even the designers to be aware of all of them or indeed to be able to describe them. All one can do is present what has been done and leave it to a process of replication and refinement by others in the wake of each project.

The pilots on which the following analysis is based began with preparatory work in 2009–10. In the end, in Madhya Pradesh, one of India's most backward regions, two pilots were implemented. The bigger pilot involved payment of a monthly basic income to every man, woman and child in eight villages, whose subsequent experience was compared with what happened in 12 similar villages, called 'control' villages. The smaller pilot involved a basic income paid to everybody in one tribal village for 12 months, with evaluation done by comparing what happened in another similar tribal village where nobody was paid the basic income.

In recent years, the idea of pilots has become globally popular. In India, some commentators or planners use the term to describe the first phase of a roll-out of a policy that has been already decided, and the term 'trial' to describe what we call a pilot.

Ideally, pilot schemes have practical advantages. They enable local governments and donor agencies to test a policy without an alarming or dispiriting cost. They can help educate observers in the potential of new ideas, and help identify administrative and design conditions that should be satisfied if the policy were to be scaled up to state or national level (Standing, 2013).

The two pilots were partially inspired by two previous pilots. They were:

The Namibian Basic Income Grant Pilot: This was a small-scale experiment. An unconditional monthly basic income was given to everybody in a rural area where over 20 per cent were infected with HIV/AIDS and 25 per cent with TB. The experiment showed improved nutrition, school attendance and performance, better health and increased economic activity. That women were motivated to capitalize on the positive impacts of the intervention was evident in their picketing liquor shops to prevent men from spending their basic income on alcohol.

The Delhi 'Choice' Pilot: This was a small pilot in an urban slum in West Delhi, conducted by SEWA in partnership with the United Nations Development Programme (UNDP). Respondents were given the choice of continuing to receive the subsidized ration shop produce or a monthly cash payment of equivalent value. The pilot showed that those who opted for cash tended to have better nutrition, and they increased spending on healthcare. During several rounds of evaluation, many of those who initially took the rations expressed a desire to switch to the basic income.

Building in agency

Unconditional cash transfers are usually piloted where other social policies and schemes are already running and where various forms of 'Voice' or agency are already operational. A pilot social policy should take account of agency effects. These vary. Always the group provided with a 'treatment' has some agency, which may vary in different communities. The agency may exist before the experiment or emerge during or as a result of it. In other words, agency may be exogenous or endogenous or both.

In the Namibian pilot, agency was endogenous, in that within months of starting, the villagers formed an advisory committee to advise villagers how to use their money rationally and to defend themselves against anybody inclined to take advantage of them. To what extent did that affect the outcomes? The research team believed the effects were positive, but could not tell how important they were.

Other cash transfer schemes have picked up a positive effect of agency, as in Nicaragua, where in areas with a high number of 'community leaders' the effects were stronger (Macours and Vakis, 2008). That is only one type of agency that could be tested in a pilot.

When pilots are scaled up it must be recognized that the most vulnerable may be excluded or exploited. Combating vulnerability requires the capacity to exercise effective 'Voice' in their defence. This leads to thinking that a basic income would work optimally if those receiving it had individual agency and some form of collective Voice to represent and defend their interests.

In the Indian pilots, the research team adopted a rare methodology. It first identified a Voice mechanism, namely SEWA, and reasoned that the basic income would have more impact on behaviour and attitudes in areas where it was operative, other things being equal.

This allowed the team to test the hypothesis that basic income with Voice works 'better' than basic income alone. To pre-empt a concern, note that the questionnaires in the baseline and subsequent evaluation surveys allowed identification of other forms of agency that might have existed before the pilot or that emerged during it. Although SEWA was the Voice organization, and the project's coordinating body, the design of the main pilot was shaped by independent experts.

Determining entitlement to the basic income

One of the hardest tasks in designing the pilot was determining who should, and who should not, receive the basic income. Some pragmatic rules had to be applied. The main rule adopted was that all men, women and children listed in households as usually resident at the outset were entitled to it. But that was insufficient, as decisions had to be made on entitlement by anybody entering the household or establishing a household after the start of the pilot.

Any member of a recipient household who subsequently moved within the village or who set up an independent household in it continued to be entitled to the basic income. Any baby born after the pilot began was entitled, as were newly married women who came into recipient households.

However, migrants entering the villages independently were not entitled to the basic income, which meant that in a few cases households and individuals were excluded, although they were recorded as residents.

Calculating the amount

On the amount to be paid as a basic income, there is no golden rule. Some proponents would argue that it should be set to equal basic subsistence, equivalent to the official 'poverty line' income. But it was decided to set the level as enough to make a difference to living standards but not enough to improve them considerably. As such, it was set at about 30 per cent of the income of lower-income families.

The calculation was made in 2009 when the project proposal was submitted. According to figures available then, the poverty line (PL) was Rs.327 per capita, or Rs.1,635 a month for a family of five. Vulnerable families, as defined in the National Commission for Enterprises in the Unorganized Sector (NCEUS) report, were those whose per capita expenditure was less than twice the PL, that is, below Rs.3,270. The share of families below the poverty line in Madhya Pradesh was 31 per cent; the share consisting of vulnerable families was over 50 per cent. The PL figures, however, were based on the 2004–5 round of the National Sample Surveys (NSS). We estimated a 30 per cent increase due to inflation from 2009 to the start of the project. So, the estimated expenditure for vulnerable families was below Rs.4,350 per month.

The amount of the basic income was calculated to be Rs.700–800 per family (depending on the number of children and adults). For those at Rs.4,350 – that is, the maximum income in the vulnerable group – the basic income was less than 20 per cent of expenditure. But for those at the poverty line, it was about 30 per cent. So, an amount of Rs.200 per adult and Rs.100 per child was paid each month from June 2011 to May 2012. Then the monthly amount was increased by 50 per cent to adjust for inflation. The revised amount of Rs.300 per adult and Rs.150 per child was paid up to November 2012.

The modified randomized control trial

The pilot's design was intended to allow comparisons between what happened in villages and households where residents received the basic income and similar villages and households where nobody received it. Both types of village were to be selected randomly from a set of villages with similar characteristics.

It was decided not to select randomly *within* villages. If the objective is to test a medical treatment, it is feasible to randomly select individuals, who might be living next door to one another or be in neighbouring beds. And to overcome the risk of psychosomatic effects in such experiments a placebo can be administered to a third of the sample. Then one can compare outcomes by matching pairs of otherwise similar individuals from the three groups.

However, for a social policy pilot, when moral and behavioural adaptation considerations come into play, one cannot proceed in that way. For instance, if the pilot gave cash to one household and not to its neighbour, resentment would be probable; either sharing would take place or some form of retributive justice would be exacted. This is why the pilot restricted randomization to the village level.[1]

Independence of research

To respect the integrity of research, all instruments used for evaluation were designed by an independent economist, and all enumerators were recruited from colleges near Indore, without prior knowledge of the project.

The sample of villages was selected randomly from a list of similar villages and the sample was drawn by an independent body. The methodology was reviewed in workshops beforehand, at which independent specialists participated.

Finally, it was stipulated that no SEWA activity should be initiated in non-SEWA villages during the project. In SEWA villages no information was to be given to anybody about expected or desired outcomes. Apart from that, it was regarded as a part of the test of Voice to allow SEWA's normal activities to continue. After all, that was the idea behind the project.

Selecting the villages

The general village pilot and the tribal village pilot were undertaken in Indore District in Madhya Pradesh (for details, see Jhabvala et al., 2014). Eight villages were selected for receipt of the basic income, 12 others as control villages. All had to be roughly similar in size, the intention being to choose randomly from a universe of villages with similar socio-economic structures, roughly equidistant from an urban centre, Indore. All had to have close proximity to a public primary school.

It was decided to draw a sample of villages of about 100 households each, and to try to ensure that the basic income and control villages should be about the same size on average. The pragmatic reasons for selecting villages of that size were budgetary restrictions and a view that 100 households was roughly the average for small Indian villages. The villages were designated as non-tribal, since tribal villages are more homogeneous in terms of demographics, economic activities and social hierarchy. So, villages from which the 20 were drawn were selected from those having a non-tribal share of the population of over 50 per cent.

The filtering produced a sample of 50 villages (20 SEWA, 30 non-SEWA), which were identified by an independent group.[2] There had to be at least ten villages for each stratum (SEWA and non-SEWA). This resulted in a cluster of 12 similar SEWA villages and a cluster of 15 similar non-SEWA villages. Ten villages were randomly selected from each cluster. The final step was to select randomly four villages from each set of ten for entitlement to basic income, leading to eight in the basic income group, 12 in the control group.

Some village differences were bound to show up. However, the 20 villages did have fairly similar structures in terms of access to amenities and services, such as schools, medical facilities and shops. The mean average distance to the nearest ration shop was 3.1 kilometres for the basic income villages, 3.0 for the control group. The mean average distance to a *pucca* road was 1.5 and 1.0 kilometres respectively.

Household identification

The concept of a 'household' is not as obvious as many commentators presume. It can be defined by usual residence or by actual residence at the time of enumeration. Neither definition is ideal. It was decided to adopt a conventional approach, defining a household as consisting of those sharing a common, independent kitchen. Membership was defined as those *usually* residing in the household, i.e. usually sleeping there for at least four nights a week.

In any project lasting a considerable time, one must allow for changes in household formation and dissolution. Again, pragmatic rules must be applied. New households were allowed after the pilot began only if members had been members of enumerated households at the outset. So, if in basic income villages, they were entitled to continue to receive the basic income. In addition, babies and newly married women entering the village were not just added to the household roster but were entitled to the basic income.

Sample size

Determining the sample size was a tricky issue, as the number living in a village typically fluctuates, so the number receiving the basic income will vary as well. Pragmatic decisions had to be made on what criteria should be used to identify who should be included in any household. In the general villages, at the outset, there were 4,874 individuals eligible for the basic income, according to the baseline survey. But others came forward at the launch, or just afterwards, saying they had been excluded. They were added, and their basic income backdated. There were 673 of those, which increased the number to 5,547 eligible to receive the basic income.

In June 2011, 3,670 people received the basic income. Of those, 2,740 received cash by hand, and 930 had the money paid into their bank accounts. That left 1,877 who were eligible but not receiving basic income in the first month, for a variety of reasons. About 220 refused to accept the basic income. The remainder received the payments for that month retrospectively. Some of the 220 who initially refused came back and asked to be included in the list. Counting recipients and control villagers, 11,231 individuals in 2,034 households were covered by the evaluation surveys, 938 households receiving the basic income.

The Awareness Day

At the outset, a baseline survey was conducted in all villages. People were not informed of its purpose. Afterwards, eight villages were randomly selected to receive the basic income, and 12 others selected as control villages. The process of informing villagers was through what we called an Awareness Day.

On the day, at a public assembly in each village, residents were informed of the purpose, with UNICEF and SEWA being named. The pilot was described as an experiment designed to understand the impact of cash transfers. The villagers were told that the payments were unconditional, and that they could be spent on anything they wished. The basic income would be transferred to bank or cooperative accounts without middlemen. In SEWA villages, the SEWA Thrift and Credit Cooperative Society team would come to open accounts for women. For others, SEWA would assist in opening accounts in the nearest bank.

The reaction of some people was disbelief. There were questions about motives, and incomprehension on the part of some about why there were no conditions. Being careful to avoid any promises, the team explained that results would be presented to the government, and might evolve into a policy.

Financial facilitation

A feature of the larger pilot was that cash would be transferred into a bank account. The biggest challenge was to prepare conditions needed for this, which meant liaising with banks. As most households did not have accounts, this was a major exercise. It was also part of the pilot design that for women in SEWA villages, accounts had to be opened in the SEWA Cooperative. For others, including women in non-SEWA villages, accounts had to be opened in banks. It was decided that until all recipients had a reasonable chance to open an account, the basic income would be paid by hand. Three months was allowed for this. From June 2011, cash was distributed to those eligible who did not have a bank account and for others money was transferred into their accounts.

The cash transfer team faced difficulties that would dog any such effort. The first was the problem of establishing the identity of residents and gathering documentary proof that the money was going to the right person. Establishing identity proof was the main obstacle to opening bank accounts, as most villagers, certainly the poorest, rarely had documentary proof of who they were. The team overcame this by distributing the cash in the presence of a government official or *sarpanch*, who signed affidavits certifying that the cash went to the right beneficiary.

Shortly after the physical transfer of the cash began, the monsoons arrived. As cars could not reach four of the villages, the team went on foot. By August, three villages were cut off; the rest were hard to reach. One village, surrounded by a river, is particularly hard to reach in monsoons as there is no bridge; villagers cross the river on a small ferry pulled by a rope. When the water was shallow, the team carried the cash boxes on their heads and walked through the river. When the water was rough, they risked losing their cash boxes. After crossing, the ordeal was not over because the road to the village was a *kutcha* (mud-based) one.

The process of opening accounts began in May 2011, ending in August 2011. In SEWA villages, the task was undertaken by SEWA organizers; in non-SEWA villages it was done by a team appointed and supervised by an outside body.

The result was that within a few months, 98 per cent of households were receiving basic income. Though identification of household members was based on their status as usual residents, some households felt this excluded some members. While 66 per cent of households reported that all in their households had received basic income for 12 months, 33 per cent said that some but not all members had received it.

The most common reason for not receiving the cash was that the person's name was not on the list of the entitled; 42 per cent who did not receive it gave this reason. Possibly some whose name was reported to be missing were actually ineligible, due to the definition of a household. The second most common reason was not having a bank account; over 22 per cent of those who did not receive the cash cited that reason, while over 17 per cent had banking difficulties, such as a wrong account number.

In sum, about 7 per cent of the total village population did not receive the basic income due to being unable to open a bank account and 5 per cent did not receive it due to banking difficulties.

'Door-step banking' may be the most promising mode of banking for rural dwellers. A recipient of a basic income would not need to travel a long way, or depend on efficient service, or require bank staff to be cooperative. This is the most desirable way to extend access to financial services. In that regard, SEWA's Cooperative could reach people more easily than the banks, whose much-publicized 'business correspondents' were non-existent.

Having gone through the difficulties with the banking system, in the tribal pilot, which started six months later, a different strategy was adopted. To ensure that money reached recipients' hands every month, the stipulation that money should be transferred only through a bank account was relaxed. All were given the money by hand.

Getting off the ground

Pilots that involve social change often flounder soon after they begin. Experiments rushed into effect can lead to backlashes due to misunderstandings and suspicion about motives. After all, they are not done in the controlled atmosphere of a laboratory. A new idea risks facing resistance that may be ideological or born from suspicion and fear. SEWA's Delhi 'choice' pilot faced such ideological opposition and had to deal with attempts to derail it. Other pilots, such as the government's in Kotkasim, received adverse publicity because the initial process was mishandled, and similar experiments in Bihar by private research agencies stalled due to local opposition.

The Madhya Pradesh pilot faced suspicion from some villagers who believed that nobody would hand out cash without a motive, wondering if the pilot was an attempt to dupe them and take their land. Some well-off farmers were worried that cash coming into the village would change behaviour and reduce labour supply at harvest time. The tension was more acute in non-SEWA villages, as SEWA could not intervene for the sake of the experiment.

As noted earlier, some people refused to take the basic income and needed to be individually convinced. They were mainly rich farming families, who typically said they did not need the money, did not want to open bank accounts, or that taking 'free money' was against their religion (Brahmins being unable to accept cash). However, most were persuaded to change their minds and to regard the experiment as useful. The change of mind among women is considered in a later chapter.

The evaluation process

The main way by which the impact of the basic income was assessed was through a baseline survey or census conducted before the pilot started, followed by an Interim Evaluation Survey (IES), set to be done half-way through the pilot, and a Final Evaluation Survey (FES) done at the end of the pilot. To complete the statistical approach, a Community Survey was done at the beginning and end of the pilot, and a Post-Final Evaluation Survey (PFES) was done in several villages some months after the end of the pilot. In addition, detailed information was collected for one hundred case studies of families, and specialist information was collected from designated key informants.

The baseline survey was a census of all households, in which information was gathered on household characteristics and on the behaviour and status of household members. Much of the implementation was contracted out to a research institute, which proved unfortunate. It was important to ensure that as many women as men were interviewed. Because those conducting the baseline survey focused on interviewing household heads, no less than 86 per cent of primary respondents were men. This failing was largely rectified in the evaluation surveys.

The questionnaire used for the baseline rested on three pillars – a household roster, a set of modules on key subjects and a questionnaire addressed to mothers of young children. The roster contained standard demographic and social characteristics of all household members, with a question to ensure that all household members, including anybody temporarily away, were included. The modules covered living conditions, health, healthcare, nutrition, schooling, consumption, production, assets, and access to and use of government schemes. The questions addressed to mothers related to their children's nutrition and schooling.

In a project of this type, questions on behaviour and attitudes necessarily rely on asking respondents for actions in the past. So, a decision must be made in each case on what period to cover and what length of reference period should be chosen.

On some issues, a long reference period would raise reliability issues. For other matters, the event would be sufficiently rare or memorable that one could expect memory recall problems to be slight. Thus, one could not expect somebody to remember what he or she was doing a year ago, except vaguely. But one could be more confident that they would know when a relative died or was hospitalized.

For work activity, a one-month reference period is much better than a full-year period, since main and secondary activities vary over 12 months. In all cases, some reference period must be applied, and be presented in the resultant tables and figures.

An important preliminary in a project such as this is 'pre-piloting' the instrument to be used for collecting the information. This is sometimes overlooked. Members of the research team conducted field interviews with drafts of the questionnaire for the baseline survey, doing so in villages that were not those selected for the basic income or control villages. Pre-testing was done in stages, by the questionnaire designers, then by others to determine whether the questions worked and could be understood by enumerators.

It was regarded as important to select and train competent enumerators and supervisors. For this, a training manual was prepared in English and Hindi. For all the surveys, after the initial training, enumerators conducted one round of interviews, after which there was a review of any difficulties encountered. Initially, pairs of enumerators conducted single interviews, to ensure they understood their task and could gain confidence in undertaking it.

For the baseline and evaluation surveys, teams of enumerators were recruited from colleges around Indore. Enrolment in an undergraduate course, preferably in the humanities, was the minimum requirement. Five members of the research team conducted the training, which included fieldwork etiquette, conceptual clarification on the meaning of key terms, definitions of government schemes and related matters. Crucially, the enumerators were not informed of the objectives of the survey, to prevent them telling respondents and to limit the tendency to be side-tracked in conducting what were lengthy interviews.

The Interim Evaluation Survey

The first evaluation was conducted via an Interim Evaluation Survey (IES), initially called the Midline Evaluation Survey, except that it had to be delayed, largely due to weather and a local health epidemic. It was conducted eight months after the start of the pilot.

Due to the logistical problems, the IES was made into a sample survey. It was also decided to add more focus on issues of implementation and financial inclusion, including challenges of take-up. The questionnaire also covered substantive issues, with modules on health, use of healthcare services, schooling, consumption and economic activity.

The IES was conducted in four basic income villages – two SEWA, two not – and in four control villages – again with two SEWA, two not. In each village, a random sample of 50 per cent of households was surveyed. Two respondents were selected randomly from each household, one man and one woman. In sample surveys, this is still a rare procedure, and it is one we recommend whenever attitudinal information is sought.

The Final Evaluation Survey

Because of concerns over the quality and comprehensiveness of the baseline, it was decided to make the Final Evaluation Survey (FES) more detailed. Built into the questionnaire was a series of *retrospective* questions. Recall dependability inevitably arises in such data. That in itself necessitates making questions more impressionistic than purists would wish. But this objection can be over-emphasized, since precise questions do not necessarily elicit better data than slightly vaguer questions.

Be that as it may, the FES became the primary evaluation instrument. It covered all subjects and questions included in the baseline, although changes were made in the formatting and in the sequencing.

After a four-day training of supervisors and enumerators and a two-day refresher course, the team went into the field. Most modules were addressed to the main respondent, but the consumption one was addressed to the main female respondent. The survey took a little over six weeks to complete.

The Post-Final Evaluation Survey

At the end of the pilot, it was decided to re-visit several villages where the basic income had been paid, to find out the recipients' reflective views. The questionnaire for this took account of findings from the IES and FES. The Post-Final Evaluation Survey (PFES) was conducted in two basic income villages, in which all adults were interviewed, 732 in total. This was carried out in December 2012 and took two weeks of fieldwork.

Besides a household roster, the PFES questionnaire had modules of questions on perceptions of basic income transfers, debt and spending, income, work and economic activity, and access to and use of government schemes, with a special section addressed to those with disabilities or chronic illnesses.

Community Surveys

To complement the household surveys, a Community Survey was conducted in all 20 villages, at the outset and at the end. The main intended uses of community-level data were to determine whether there were structural differences between villages, which should not arise if the sampling methodology was perfect, and to create macro-level measures for use as control variables in multivariate analysis.

The Community Survey questionnaires were designed to show the socio-economic structures of the villages and changes as perceived by key informants, designated as people of authority, such as *sarpanchs*, *panchayat* secretaries, *anganwadis*, doctors and school teachers. Besides covering infrastructural matters, such as access to roads and social amenities, the questionnaires covered demographic issues, including infant and maternal mortality, women's social and economic position, and interactions between castes.

In brief, while there was some variation in population size of the villages, the average was similar. Most had primary schools nearby, with longer distances to a secondary school.

The research team also collected additional data from community figures, notably *anganwadis*, shopkeepers, *sarpanchs*, doctors, SEWA village leaders and school teachers. These data turned out to be more useful than anticipated, particularly statistical data gathered from their records, including records of children's performance in schools.

Perhaps most importantly, data were collected from *anganwadis* on the weight and age of children in the villages. Such data are supposed to be kept by all *anganwadis*. We had to bear in mind that they might exaggerate the nutritional status of children in their charge. However, we were careful not to stipulate why we wished to collect the data and made it clear that we had collected our own data on the same subject.

Case studies

Although primary emphasis is placed on data from household and individual surveys, a supplementary part of the project consisted of case studies of families. Over a period of a year, precisely one hundred were conducted. Many families were visited several times in order to collect all the desired information.

Case studies are useful supplements to statistical evaluation, but are also valid tools for probing issues of causality and the difficulty of fungibility of money. The project undertook structured interviews of basic income recipients – a majority being women – with seven modules of discussion followed by a section on the basic income. The seven were sources of income and patterns of expenditure, food and nutrition, illness and health, education, savings and debt, and work, employment and farming. Case studies were done in 12 of the villages – including eight basic income villages.

Interviews were conducted by a team of eight enumerators hired for the purpose but not employed by SEWA. The main fieldwork was conducted in March–April 2012, nine months after the start of the larger pilot. Follow-up interviews were conducted three months after the end of the pilot, in July 2012. These showed a positive interruption effect, in that many villagers expressed appreciation for what they had gained and for what they had lost through the ending of the payments.

The tribal village pilot

After the larger pilot was launched, it was decided to conduct a pilot of one tribal village, recognizing that tribal villages are more homogeneous in terms of social profile. This pilot was partly due to a proposal by a senior official of the Madhya Pradesh government, made in a meeting in which he expressed frustration at their inability to reach tribal areas effectively.

Accordingly, one Bhil (scheduled tribe) village was selected for receipt of the basic income, drawn randomly from a list where SEWA had been operating. Another Bhil village with similar structural features was selected as the control village. Both were in the Mhow *taluk* of Indore District. Although the resultant number of households was modest – 127 with 756 individuals in the basic income village, 97 with 817 individuals in the control village – it was felt that this could provide valuable additional analysis.

In the basic income village, almost every household owned between two and four bigha of land. The village is perched on hilly terrain near Choral dam, about 23 kilometres from Mhow and 70 kilometres from Indore city. The control village was six kilometres away.

As mentioned earlier, in order to restrict the experiment to the impact of basic income alone, the research team gave cash to individuals each month, avoiding the problems of setting up accounts. Whereas the SEWA Cooperative opened accounts for women, men were given cash in hand. This ensured that money reached every household every month.

The basic income was Rs.300 a month for each adult and Rs.150 for each child. The children's money was transferred to the mother's account. The basic incomes started in February 2012 and ended in January 2013. The number of recipients was 756, and the total transferred to the village was Rs.19.45 lakhs (nearly Rs.2 million). The average amount received by each family was Rs.15,315 annually, or Rs.1,276 monthly.

During the pilot, three surveys were done in the two villages. The baseline survey was conducted in January 2012, the Interim Evaluation Survey in July 2012 and the Final Evaluation Survey in January 2013. In addition, 20 case studies were conducted in the villages. A short Community Survey was also conducted at the beginning and end.

Concluding remarks

In sum, over the three years covered by these pilots, including the Delhi pilot, 5,850 men, women and children received monthly basic income payments for a year or more. The methodologies to evaluate the effects were exploratory in themselves. What readers must judge for themselves are (i) whether or not the combination of methods chosen provides a convincing analysis and a convincing narrative, and (ii) that as little bias as possible is involved. One objective has been to make the analysis as transparent as possible, backed up by findings from more than one methodology, recognizing that no project such as this can ever avoid mistakes of omission or commission.

Notes

1 The main reason for randomization is to deal with what is called selection bias. The technique should enable researchers to control for independent effects of environmental factors common to the 'treatment' and 'non-treatment' samples. But, to reiterate, randomized control trials (RCTs) are only one of a range of acceptable methodologies, some of which are better for evaluating processes. RCTs are best for evaluating 'low-hanging fruit', i.e. direct treatment effects. For an excellent critique of randomization, see Deaton, 2008.

2 A clustering procedure used a binary similarity coefficient measure for locating matches. Taking village-level variables from secondary sources, clustering was done by using five variables – proximity of a secondary (middle-level) school, registered doctor, distance and access to a *pucca* road, bus connectivity and a PDS ration shop. A similarity coefficient gives the proportion of matches between two observations. Therefore, for each village, similarity coefficients for every other village could be obtained from the dataset. For operational purposes, a cut-off of 70 per cent on the similarity coefficient was kept, so that two villages were judged similar (hence included in the same cluster) if the value of the coefficient for them was greater than or equal to the cut-off. For further details, see the SEWA-UNICEF report (Jhabvala et al., 2014).

3

Basic Income's Emancipatory Value

Introduction

Let us imagine what happens to villagers when they start to receive their modest basic income. The money might go straight into consumption expenditure, or part might go into savings and investment in some form, or part might go to pay off debt or at least reduce its extent. In other countries, experience with cash transfers has suggested that recipients often give high priority to paying off debt, if they can (Kabede, 2005). This makes good sense, in that it represents a modest assertion of control over life.

So, on debt, our primary hypotheses are that the basic income enables some households to reduce their debt, that it enables some to avoid going into debt (notably by improving health and thus reducing the need to borrow), and that for some households the money enables them to borrow more in order to invest or improve living conditions or production.

Above all, because debt is a mode of exploitation in the village economy, the basic income has an *emancipatory value* that is greater than the *monetary value*, a thesis elaborated in this chapter. This is an argument that has not been made in the protracted debates on cash transfers.

On savings, the key hypotheses are, first, that the basic income boosts savings modestly, and second, that part of the money is used to provide a modicum of financial liquidity, thereby lessening the probability that a financial shock or hazard will precipitate a financial crisis, leading to more indebtedness. We suggest that, while the basic income cannot prevent a shock or hazard from occurring, it can reduce the detrimental impact, a point to which we will return. But first we need to clarify the normal situation of indebtedness.

The Lauderdale Paradox and the 'scarcity mindset'

There is a famous image popularized by the monetarist economist Milton Friedman. He presented a model in which a helicopter scattered bank notes over an economy. Suppose that doubled the amount of money. In a fully monetized market economy in which all resources are fully employed, all prices would double, leaving relative prices unchanged.

In the real world, none of Friedman's assumptions apply. In fact, in most Indian villages money itself is a scarce commodity. Worse, its scarcity is contrived, with implications for relative prices of other commodities and for the reproduction of power relations.

This relates to what is known as the Lauderdale Paradox, first formulated by the Earl of Lauderdale in 1804. The paradox states, essentially, that the value of a commodity is increased by making it scarce. In Indian villages, power relations over many generations have solidified conditions of contrived scarcity, generating a rent-based distribution system in which the weaker sections cannot escape. Being a comparatively efficient medium of exchange, money is the most important scarce commodity. It thus has a high price, and those who possess it can exploit those who do not. We will see the significance of this shortly. But essentially our claim is that the emancipatory value of a basic income is much greater than the monetary value simply because money is a scarce commodity. The scarcity has driven up the cost of loans, debt and the prospective costs of shocks and hazards.

The emancipatory value arises not just because a recipient of basic income has the freedom to spend how he or she chooses. The money also reduces the scarcity of the commodity and thus lowers the price of monetary transactions.

Given the growing significance of money in the Indian economy, its scarcity value must rise. But we need to reflect on a separate set of effects linked to scarcity, which psychologists have recently explored. Those who lack a key commodity apparently react differently from those who do not experience a sense of scarcity. Anybody who experiences a scarcity of money – or even time or food – is prone to suffer from a 'scarcity mindset' (Mullainathan and Shafir, 2013).

This has a host of effects that determine behaviour and attitudes, mostly in a debilitating way. It shortens a person's planning horizons and narrows their perspective, effectively blocking out consideration of options. The scarcity produces a deep anxiety that becomes so ingrained that it is hardly noticed or recognized. The term that has been used is 'mental bandwidth'. Thus, it has been found that Indian farmers score worse on intelligence tests before a harvest when money is scarce (Mullainathan and Shafir, 2013).

The effects do not stop there. Scarcity colonizes the mind. While it lasts, it generates a mindset that helps to perpetuate the scarcity, for people cannot psychologically prepare themselves for launching initiatives or taking entrepreneurial risks. This may help to explain why so many well-intentioned schemes to assist the income poor fail, because the intended recipients cannot sustain the effort to take advantage of them.

Conversely, we may suggest that if insecurity and lack of a key commodity make people more anxious and less ready to take risks and undertake new initiatives, then having income security and monetary liquidity should have the opposite effect. This has profound implications. If money is a vital scarce commodity, its absence will induce many of those without it to make inappropriate choices. If it becomes less scarce, better or more entrepreneurial decision-making should follow.

The scourge of debt

Most families in rural India struggle along from one debt to many debts, and few are out of debt for any length of time. Indebtedness is simply a structural feature of village life, and is a complex mechanism for intensifying class-based and caste-based inequalities while preserving a very hierarchical social structure. But, as we shall see, the basic income transfers had some effect on the extent of debt and on the related use of credit and loans.

Before considering these issues, let us reflect on the sheer scale of debt and the mechanisms by which villagers are mired in chronic debt, that is, a level that could be expected to last for as long as could be anticipated, even for generations. This differs from entrepreneurial debt that arises from rich farmers borrowing to expand production. We are talking about the debt that threatens family survival. Such exploitative debt in Madhya Pradesh villages seems to arise in five ways:

- Landlords and moneylenders provide loans to earn themselves a high rental income, usually lending at 3 per cent, 5 per cent, and up to 10 per cent per month, rarely less. They can do so because most families do not have liquidity or other sources of credit.
- Large-scale farmers and business operators advance loans or provide low-income families with food or agricultural inputs at a time of acute

need, in order to put an individual or family in debt bondage, with the obligation to provide part or even all of their crop at the end of the harvest.

- They lend in order to oblige the family to provide labour when and as required, for a wage that is less than a market wage.
- Landowners or moneylenders lend for medical emergencies or for hazards such as marriages, with land or jewellery as security, leading families to lose their only assets when they cannot repay the loan, which then forces them to have to borrow at even higher interest rates at the time of the next crisis.
- Shopkeepers sell food or other goods on credit, charging high interest after a month or so of non-payment. Some credit providers demand that the purchasers provide labour or crops in return.

These mechanisms have different implications in village life. The practice of tying labour through debt bondage reflects the fact that the labour process in Madhya Pradesh villages is essentially semi-feudal; landlords or powerful interests lock many peasants into labour relations well in advance of their need for the labour. By doing so, they underpay the villagers, by paying them less than the labour market price, the money wage, that would otherwise apply at the time of the need for the labour. Some economists would call this super-exploitation. We consider the implications of the payment of basic income later.

However it arises, debt is a life-defining burden in Indian villages. Consider a few more examples from the case studies. Most illustrate the critical point, that money itself is a scarce commodity. This gives possession of it a considerable value, its absence a considerable cost.

The case studies conducted during the pilots give a perspective on this. Take the example of Kalabai, aged 52, and her husband, from a scheduled caste, with a modest 1.5 bighas of land:

> My husband met with an accident ten years ago, and his right leg was seriously damaged. We spent 80,000 Rupees for his treatment. I borrowed from a money-lender at 3 per cent a month. I finally repaid it two years ago.

This debt stemmed from what we may call an economic *shock*. Over those eight years, that loan almost certainly cost more than 100 per cent to repay. In those circumstances, incidentally, it is surely remarkable that the family only had an APL card. But their life of indebtedness went on. As she told the enumeration team:

> I have an outstanding loan of 50,000 Rupees, which I had to borrow from a moneylender for my son's marriage one year ago, at 3 per cent a month. In

addition, I often borrow for groceries or other necessities. I don't have to pay interest for that because I repay as soon as possible. In this manner, I borrow about 700 Rupees a month. We repay debt by working for the moneylender or saving from our wage. Our labour is mostly for the repayment of loans, for which we work in the households of landlords because I have nothing to mortgage.

This situation stemmed from what we may call an economic *hazard*. In a cash-scarce economy, paying just the 3 per cent a month would be financially crippling. It is scarcely surprising that once in serious debt such households remain in those circumstances for many years, if not permanently.

Now consider the situation of Rajaram Sain, a 60-year-old man who combined being a barber with animal husbandry. He told the team:

Each year the income is going down. It is mainly when there are deaths or other ceremonies in the village that my services are sought, for shaving heads. And for these services, the villagers pay me in kind, in wheat. The grain I get through this is hardly sufficient for the whole year.

I have an APL [Above Poverty Line] ration card, which was given to me six years ago after a survey. It is torn completely now. I have applied for a new one. But nobody listens to us in this village. Because of this I am able to get only a small quantity of wheat from the village and this makes it difficult for me to run my yearly household expenses.

In the morning, after completing my barbering tasks, if any, I go to the field to get fodder and water for my buffaloes. I bought these buffaloes two years ago with a loan from the milk contractor from Indore. When I bought them, they were not giving milk. After they gave birth to calves four months ago, they started giving milk. Since then, I have been repaying the debt through milk. Every day, the contractor sends cans for collection of milk.

I owe the milk contractor money that I borrowed from him to purchase the buffaloes. I have another outstanding loan of 35,000 Rupees which I took for my daughter's wedding from my neighbour at 3 per cent interest rate, monthly. In addition to that we buy food items from the grocery shop on credit at 2.5 per cent interest rate, monthly, and repay it by working on his farm. Brother, I have too many debts, and I can only repay them gradually, by selling milk and doing wage labour.

This could be described, generously, as *entrepreneurial risk-taking*. But his main transactions were non-monetary, which was likely to mean they were inefficient and to his disadvantage, making the value of the actions less remunerative. The barber's customers were hardly likely to give him their good-quality wheat, and were less likely to take care of all their wheat, since they were using it for such informal purposes, rather than for their family needs or for sale in an open market where the quality would be examined. The person paid in wheat was not in a position to stipulate quality. He was in a lender's market.

Moreover, given the barber's weak bargaining position over his milk contract, the contractor was, for many reasons, likely to demand more milk from him than was justified by the original loan. Now consider the barber's indebtedness and the exorbitant rental interest he would have to pay, stretching into the distant future, in a system of income extraction. A monthly interest of 3 per cent amounts to well over 40 per cent a year.

Another example is illustrative of another widespread means by which moneylenders gain rental income from possession of the scarce commodity of money. A respondent, Manju Behen, told the case study team:

> We take money from the milk contractor from Mhow in order to buy buffaloes and then we sell the milk to him only. We don't get any money from selling the milk because we first have to pay off the money that we took for buying the buffalo. If for some reason the buffalo does not give enough milk, then the *seth* deducts the entire month's money. How much milk the buffalo will give is never certain. A buffalo costs 40,000 Rupees. After that the fodder costs 35,000 Rupees.
>
> If we consume the milk at our homes or if we add too much water in the milk, then there is the risk of mounting debt. The basic income that we were getting helped us in our household expenses and because of that we didn't have to take loans from the milk contractor. If we don't give the milk to the same *seth* from whom we take money to buy the buffalo, then he takes the buffalo.

This is what could be called *dependency*, or *downside*, *risk*, since the acquisition of buffaloes was probably a survival strategy, not an entrepreneurial one. Such actions lead to a structural characteristic of these communities, which should be called monopsony debt, in that the moneylender retains sole right to the milk and thus can pay the supplier below the market price, while imposing all the risks or costs on the debtor family, so gaining extra income.

In economics, a monopolist is a sole seller of a commodity; a monopsonist is a sole buyer. In policy circles, attention is given to the social and economic costs of monopoly. More should be given to the evils of monopsony.

Anyhow, such rental income is a pervasive form of exploitation. Then consider Premabai, a 60-year-old scheduled tribe woman who mixed farming with agricultural wage labour over the course of the year:

> I have about 1 lakh Rupees as an outstanding loan to be repaid at 3 per cent interest per month. I borrowed this amount for the treatment of my husband and

grand-daughter from neighbours. I also often borrow from our village grocery shop because he doesn't take interest. Sometimes I buy ration on credit. I work at the moneylender's houses or fields to repay the loan. All members of my family work to repay the loan. I have nothing mortgaged, but I have not been able to save anything.

Here was someone just living in debt. Another example was the situation described by Devkanyabai, a 45-year-old woman from the Chamar scheduled sub-caste, who described herself as a labourer:

> If we have money, then we buy our groceries in cash; otherwise we buy on credit. There are two shops in the village … from where we buy things on credit. We pay them back whenever we have money. They sell stuff at a hiked price – 9 Rupees if we pay cash, 13 if we buy on credit – because we have no other option but to buy from them.
>
> When we are in need of money, we have to take a loan from the big farmers in the village. They charge an interest rate of 3 per cent. We remove these debts by doing labour work for them every crop season.

This is *monopsony credit*, taking advantage of villagers' dire need to live by credit. As well as indicating the scale of debt through high interest rates, it shows how costly it is to operate via credit rather than be able to pay in cash. Often the families cannot begin to repay the credit until the next harvest, meaning that the cost accumulates month after month.

We have given these examples – and numerous others could be added – to highlight the potential impact of an influx of money to such families and to their neighbours and kin in the vicinity. Other case studies indicate an advantage of formal financial inclusion as well, in that the nationalized banks and the SEWA Cooperative usually charge a lower interest rate than moneylenders.

This means the pressure to open bank or cooperative accounts would have helped reduce debt, although it could not prevent it. The crucial point is that the chronic indebtedness defines the ingrained structural problems of rural India and is a reason why an injection of cash in the form of monthly basic incomes could be transformative.

How basic income affects debt

The pervasiveness of indebtedness was brought out in all the evaluation surveys. Well over 70 per cent of all households reported being in financial debt. But the inflow of basic income payments seems to have made a difference, quite quickly.

In all the 20 non-tribal villages, by the time of the Interim Evaluation Survey, whereas over half of all households reported that debt had increased over the past 12 months and only 8 per cent had reduced it, the basic income households were significantly less likely to have increased their debt and were significantly more likely to have reduced it.

Whereas two-thirds of the control village households had increased debt, only 46 per cent of the basic income households had done so. And about 14 per cent of basic income households had reduced debt compared with just 3 per cent of the control village households.

These results were sustained by the FES. While over three-quarters of all households said they owed a substantial amount to outsiders, this was significantly less common in basic income households (just over 71 per cent compared to 79 per cent in control villages). And as one might expect, the probability of having reduced debt in the period covered by the pilot was considerably greater in the basic income villages.

Whereas 12.5 per cent of basic income village households had reduced their debt, only 5 per cent of control village households had done so. And whereas 5 per cent of the former had increased debt, over 58 per cent of control households had done so. The end result was that the average amount owed was also lower in basic income households. And nearly two-thirds of those reducing debt attributed that to the basic income.

Households containing somebody with a disability were more likely to be indebted. And among both the low-educated and higher-educated households, the basic income was associated with a lower probability of being in debt. To make better sense of these correlations, we estimated a logit function, in which the dependent variable was the probability of having reduced debt (expressed as a binary, 1 for reducing debt, 0 otherwise). The function included control variables (described in the Appendix) for caste, household size, land ownership, SEWA presence, female headship, education of household head, disability and child-to-adult ratio.

The results showed that basic income households were significantly more likely to have reduced debt, the only other significant factor being the child ratio. Although a more refined model might bring out the significance of other influences, this gives strong support for a direct positive link between basic income and debt reduction.

To recap, the basic income reduced indebtedness in at least five ways:

- By being used to reduce previously incurred debt;

- By enabling households to avoid incurring new debt or to reduce the amount of new debt;
- By enabling households to avoid taking food or other items on credit;
- By inducing moneylenders or shops to advance credit or loans at a lower interest rate or even without charging interest;
- By enabling the poorest households to borrow softer loans from relatives or friends, rather than resorting to exploitative forms of distress borrowing.

Those last two ways are easily overlooked. In a local economy characterized by scarce money, one way by which a universal basic income could reduce the cost of living is by increasing the confidence of those making loans that they will be repaid. That could make them more inclined to charge a lower rate of interest, since the risk of non-reimbursement would be reduced. This was brought out by one case study respondent, interviewed after the pilot had ended:

> When the transfers were coming, the moneylending farmers were also sure that their money would be paid on time. They would lend us money without too much interest. Now that the money has stopped, the farmers are charging 5 per cent or 10 per cent. If you start giving the money again, then give it like before. Don't give it via the village *sarpanch* (headman) or ministers.

This is another aspect of the emancipatory value of the basic income, indicating why it exceeds the direct money value.

Other respondents described how they used the basic income to reduce their debt. Thus Sunita, a 28-year-old woman who combined housework as her main activity with casual wage labour, said:

> We have no debts of any kind on us anymore. We had a little bit of debt to pay; I don't know how much it was; my brother-in-law knows. Whatever it was, we have paid it back this year; and this has happened with the help of the cash transfers.

Another, Pratap, a 35-year-old *chowkidaar* (village headman), told the enumeration team:

> The cash transfers have helped us immensely. We have put more and good quality seed, fertilizer and pesticide in the fields due to this money. This will yield us a better crop. Apart from that, we bought two goats to add to our income. The most important benefit from this money was that we didn't have to borrow money from anyone, and neither did we have to buy things on credit. Earlier we had to do both.

We have paid back whatever petty debts were there; 500 to someone and 1,000 to someone else. And due to this money, our monthly grocery and foodstuffs were bought in an organized manner; otherwise we had to buy lesser stuff.

Another respondent told the team:

This money has been of great help ever since the time we started getting it. Because of this money we don't have to take any debt for either rations or medicines. Even if someone gets sick or distressed, we don't have to go around begging people for money. Earlier we would take things on credit from the Kirana store for which the shopkeeper would charge us interest as well. Since we have been receiving this money, this is not the case.

Another was almost poetic in his assessment:

Some time ago, I took 2,000 Rupees on credit from the Kirana shop and bought things for the household from there, little by little. Within a year, the shop-owner brought my credit amount to 24,700 Rupees after adding the interest. In order to pay this debt I had to mortgage the one bigha given to me by the government. Now I am left with no land. Our monthly expenses are being covered by this cash transfer we are getting. This money is to us like a stick is to a blind man.

Turning to the tribal villages, debt was also just a regrettable way of life for most families, with over two-thirds being in serious debt at the outset of the pilot. Since labour opportunities are meagre and incomes low, almost every aspect of their lives is governed by debt. They borrow for seeds and farming inputs, and usually must repay those debts at 100 per cent interest after the following harvest. They also often have to borrow to pay for their daily or weekly food purchases.

But the basic incomes certainly made a difference, and were the means of liberating some of them from the debt burden. In the basic income village, by comparison with the control village, within six months many had reduced debt and many fewer had gone into more debt. By the end of the pilot, as recorded in the FES, an extraordinary 73 per cent of households in the basic income village had reduced their debt and none had increased it. By contrast, 18 per cent of the control village households had reduced debt, 50 per cent had increased it.

In sum, in both the general villages and in the tribal village the basic income led to a reduction in indebtedness. In doing so, it must have lessened the pressure on daily living, and enabled some households to gain more freedom to pursue their own economic activities.

Combating debt bondage

In Madhya Pradesh villages, indebtedness plays a central role in the social relations of production and distribution through a form of debt bondage known as the *naukar* (servant), by which men 'voluntarily' enter an annual contract with a landlord to supply labour as and when required in return for an initial loan. If a boy enters such a contract, it is known as a *gwala* (cowherd) relationship, because the main labour of boys is grazing and caring for cattle.

In many cases, as probably intended by the landlord, the *naukar* or *gwala* cannot pay off the debt and this is rolled over and built up over years and even generations. A *naukar* can change landlord only after the debt has been repaid, but otherwise must do all labour assigned to him by the landlord; the type, extent and timing of labour is at the landlord's discretion.

These two phenomena are so systemic in Madhya Pradesh villages that any policy that could break the social system that embodies them should be welcomed as transformative. They may be disrupted by the basic income, which would mean that this policy would have an unheralded advantage over subsidy or direct labour schemes of the sort reviewed in Chapter 1.

Reflect on several of the case studies and what they tell us about the debt bondage that the *naukar* system represents. Gumaan Singh, a 55-year-old landless member of a scheduled tribe, told the enumerators:

We require about 7 quintals of wheat each year for home consumption. We collect this wheat by doing labour during the wheat harvest. All adult members in the family do labour. I used to work as a bonded labourer until last year, for which I received 18,000 Rupees annually. I have been a *naukar* with the landlords in our village for nearly 35 years. I have stopped doing that now. I had to work as a bonded labourer because there wasn't any work available in the village. But now we are getting the basic income money, with which we try to meet our monthly household expenses. Now I'm working only on the season's crop, irrigating the fields, harvesting, etc. For irrigating and harvesting a one bigha field, we get 60 kilograms [12 dhari] of wheat.

Only last November, after my daughter married, I discontinued my *naukar* work. From morning till night, I used to work on the landlord's farm and also looked after his buffaloes. Except cooking, I did everything for him. He did not provide food. I had to come home to have my *roti*, and go back to work. From time to time, I would borrow money from him for my daily needs, or when I would go to the weekly market, which he used to deduct from the wage. Last year, at the time of my daughter's marriage, I asked him for money, but he gave me only 10,000 Rupees. I was very disappointed, and when I completed half a year in November, I quit. After that I started doing daily wage work wherever and whenever I could. At least I don't have to be at his beck and call. There is of course this big support from the cash transfer. A small part of income comes from rearing goats and hens. Now, I have only four hens and one rooster. I had two goats which I gave to Harli [his daughter] at the time of her marriage ...

... We were greatly helped by the basic income money. If we didn't get any labour, then we didn't have to think about where to get food from. We could go to the doctor for treatment whenever required. Earlier it wasn't like this. If it weren't for this money, then perhaps I'd still be working as a bonded labourer. After all one needs money to run a household and there is almost no labour available in our village. Until now, it was fine as we were getting the money. Now that it has stopped, let us see what happens.

Remarkably, Gumaan Singh and his family only had an APL card. They were deeply impoverished and should have qualified for a BPL card. But the emancipation from the bonded labour was a major development in the family's life.

Now consider Paramanand, a 19-year-old Bhil, who was also a *naukar*. He said he was supposed to be paid an annual wage, from which he received an advance as a loan. The trouble was that over the year he had been obliged to take a series of small loans from the landlord, enmeshing him in a web, so that he had to be at the beck and call of the landlord. He had ended up constantly having to labour to pay back a stream of loans, meaning that he never saw any cash.

Another case was described by the mother, whose two elder sons were in debt bondage:

My husband and both of my sons go out to earn a living, and I take care of the household work. My elder son [Vinod, aged 17] is a *naukar* at 15,000 Rupees per year and the younger son [Lakshman] at 10,000 Rupees a year. My husband does casual labour. The children go to their *malik* [master] early in the morning and return in the evening. Vinod takes care of the cattle along with doing farming work; Lakshman only does the job of herding cattle at their *malik's* residence. They don't let these children come home for lunch and feed them there so that they can save time to extract more work from them.

Typically, the landlord benefits doubly from having a *naukar*, because not only can he pay little or nothing, rather than a market wage, but he can also demand labour as and when he requires it. In return, the *naukar* receives from the landlord or *malik* (master) some sort of 'food security', but at best receives only a minimal amount of money, probably as a loan. Some villagers reported that such loans spanned more than 12 years.

In assessing the impact of the basic income on the *naukar* phenomenon, the data from the evaluation surveys do not reveal the full extent of debt bondage. The reason is that questions on main and second main economic activity focused on the activity itself rather than on the motivation for doing it.

However, the FES questionnaire asked whether any person in the household did labour to pay off debt. By the end of the pilot, a significantly smaller percentage of basic income households had someone doing that than control village households. And among families that had been in a *naukar* relationship significantly more basic income households had managed to end it.

An unappreciated aspect of the *naukar* system is that it also indirectly lowers the income of the person placed in that position. The obligation to labour during the harvest season, for instance, limits the time and effort that could otherwise be devoted to their own production.

The loss of freedom has two negative effects on income, one in that way, the other because someone locked into a labour relation in advance will almost invariably gain a lower wage than if they could bargain with a landlord employer when they are required. These are further reasons for saying the basic income's emancipatory value exceeds the monetary value.

Borrowing and basic income

Obviously, borrowing and 'being in debt' are not the same. Many people have to borrow, or try to do so, to deal with emergencies. This is when the 'sharks' lie in wait to take advantage of their vulnerability, charging high interest rates and imposing arduous conditions, often demanding the mortgage of something they can ill afford to lose. They may then fall into chronic debt that weighs down their capacity to survive or escape income poverty.

However, some households also borrow to try to increase their income or production, doing so more strategically than in distress situations. Borrowing by the rich is primarily to expand; borrowing by the poor is to survive. The first stems from a desire to risk rationally; the second stems from dire necessity.

Sadly, the money poor are likely to have to pay a much higher interest rate on any credit or loan. Then any money they borrow is likely to have a lower rate of return, if any, than is gained by the wealthy who borrow strategically. As such, the institution of borrowing is a mechanism for increasing inequality. By deduction, anything that reduces the need for the poor to borrow should have a multiple beneficial effect in terms of equity.

Consider what seems to have happened in this respect. The FES data suggest that overall there were no major differences in borrowing habits between basic income and control households. However, the former were significantly less likely to have borrowed for food, which corresponded to evidence from case studies. Borrowing for housing was more common among basic income households, which also corresponded to case studies showing families using their basic income to make house improvements.

Scheduled tribe households were the least likely to borrow for whatever purpose. For them, debt was very likely to arise from simply trying to meet their daily needs. And they were the least likely to be able to borrow from institutional sources.

In the tribal villages, the evaluation surveys asked for the main reason for borrowing in order to detect any shifts linked to the basic income. Comparing the borrowing by the difference-in-difference method, there was a significant reduction in borrowing for both normal living expenses and medical expenses among basic income recipients. In the control village, the proportion borrowing for regular living expenses increased from 20 per cent to 36 per cent, whereas in the basic income village it remained at 23 per cent. What declined for basic income recipients was classic distress borrowing. In the basic income village, borrowing was less likely for most reasons.

In the tribal villages, the most common reason for borrowing was to cover medical expenses. For small items, families generally borrowed from relatives or neighbours; for larger sums they resorted to moneylenders. But during the pilot, basic income households shifted from borrowing to relying on savings. Thus, whereas 44 per cent reported that borrowing was the main means of financing medical treatment at the outset, by the end only 19 per cent reported that. At the outset, 33 per cent said they relied mainly on savings; at the end 74 per cent did so. Meanwhile, in the control village, the share relying on savings rose modestly from 47 per cent to 54 per cent; the share relying on borrowing remained roughly the same, as did reliance on assistance from relatives.

However one interprets the shifts, the key point is that the basic income allowed families to reduce their need to borrow, in circumstances where borrowing is a route into chronic debt.

The impact on saving

As India has no comprehensive social security system, savings in some form are the main means by which families try to protect themselves against the vagaries of life, in the form of cash saved at home, gold or silver, money kept in a post office, bank or other financial institution, or investment in land or other property.

In villages covered by the pilots, even though debt was pervasive, some households did manage to save money, and the basic income increased that significantly. Even by the time of the IES, those who had received it were much more likely to be saving.

And there appeared to have been a positive influence of both the basic income and SEWA. Over 51 per cent of households in the SEWA basic income villages had savings by then, compared with 38 per cent of non-SEWA basic income households. By contrast, just 16 per cent of SEWA and 11 per cent of non-SEWA control villages had any savings. Both the SEWA and basic income differences were statistically highly significant.

Although the latter remained significant at the time of the FES, the SEWA correlation only persisted within the basic income villages (23 per cent vs. 18 per cent saving). By the time of the FES, the difference between the basic income and control villages was even greater. In the former, 20.5 per cent were making savings compared with just 9 per cent in the control villages.

Of course, many factors influence savings behaviour. Accordingly, a set of logit functions was estimated in which the dependent variable was the probability of saving, expressed as a binary (1 if saved; 0 if not), with the same control variables as for the functions for debt reduction.

The function estimated for all households for which all data were available, which came to 2,000 cases, showed that the basic income had a strong positive effect. Also statistically significant as influencing the propensity to save were the schooling of the head, landholding, caste and household size.

Separate functions were tested for, first, scheduled caste and tribe households and, second, for general and other households. The strong positive effect of basic income showed up for both social groups, as did schooling of head and landholding.

In terms of the amount of saving specifically from the basic income, the FES indicated that the amount was higher in non-SEWA (Rs.694) than in SEWA households (Rs.586). This may have been because it was easier for women to withdraw money from the SEWA Cooperative than from a bank outside the village, so that SEWA women were more inclined to use the basic income money for daily needs.

The pattern emerging from the tribal villages was similar, although there were slight differences. Tribal families tend to have lower incomes and living standards, most living a hand-to-mouth existence, having to borrow even for their everyday needs.

Nevertheless, the basic income induced more to save. The share of households that saved money in the control village actually declined from 9 per cent at the time of the baseline survey to 3 per cent in the FES. In contrast, in the basic income village, the share rose from 7 per cent initially to 25 per cent a year later. Clearly, the saving propensity was much higher in the basic income village.

In sum, the basic income enabled families to save, obtaining vital financial liquidity needed to gain a modicum of control over their lives.

Forms of saving

As is well known, the most common forms of savings in India are maintaining a stock of cash in 'the home' and purchasing gold or jewellery. One might anticipate that the basic income would induce households to shift from the former to saving in a bank or cooperative, particularly as it was linked to banking.

After a few months, according to the IES, not surprisingly – given the requirement to open bank or cooperative accounts – basic income recipients were more likely to be saving in a bank than at home, only about 9 per cent doing the latter compared with over 41 per cent of those not receiving the basic income.

In effect, it contributed to a securitization of saving, a significant benefit if one accepts that savings in banks are more secure and so more valuable. So, basic income boosted savings directly, through providing more money, and indirectly, through inducing more financial inclusion.

The FES also asked about the form of saving from the basic income and what institutions were used for saving from any source. Just over half (52 per cent) of those who saved from the basic income did so mainly in bank accounts, while 40 per cent did so mainly in their homes. According to the broader question, among basic income households who saved, 53 per cent saved mainly in a bank, compared to just 30 per cent of control village households.

These results are not contradictory. The second question asked if households saved in any of the possible institutions, whereas the question on saving from the basic income asked for the main place of saving. So, for instance, 15 per cent of basic income recipients said they saved some money in their homes, compared with 39 per cent of those who saved among control households. This also shows how the basic income encouraged financial securitization.

Now consider what happened in the tribal villages. An objective of the drive for financial inclusion is to bring individuals into the financial system in which they can save and borrow more effectively. As the tribal villagers were not required to open bank accounts in order to receive the basic income very few saved in a bank. However, as the SEWA Cooperative was active in the village, most institutional saving was in it, with 75 per cent of households saving in the Cooperative and 22 per cent at home.

During the course of the pilot, the savings behaviour changed in the basic income village. In the baseline survey, 38 per cent of households that were saving were doing so mainly in a bank, the remainder at home. By the FES, 30 per cent were saving in the bank, 20 per cent were saving in the Cooperative and only 50 per cent at home. This shift towards institutional saving was probably due in part to the active role taken by the SEWA Cooperative.

As there are good reasons for believing that financial securitization is a desirable development in the struggle against poverty and economic insecurity, these results for the combination of basic income and SEWA could be said to add evidence of the emancipatory value of the basic income.

Intended uses of savings

In the FES, households that were saving were asked about their reasons for doing so. The main response was 'keep for security' (60 per cent), followed by 'nothing in particular' (30 per cent). With 5 per cent saying 'don't know', we can see that overwhelmingly the primary rationale was to give themselves liquidity in case of need. The most common reason given for saving was for illnesses and medical treatment. A typical situation was that of Radhabai, a Bhil caste member, aged 30, who was mainly a wage labourer. She put it as follows:

> Having spent the first few cash transfers on clothes and an ox, the family started to save from them in order to cover for possible illnesses, after several bouts of sickness.

Having financial liquidity is essential in circumstances characterized by uncertainty, where at any time unforeseen needs could arise. Without ready money, households easily fall into the hands of unscrupulous moneylenders, which is perhaps why several were reported to have been unhappy about the basic income. That should be regarded as good news.

It is possible that rural households see different sources of income in different ways. Some forms may be regarded as for daily, weekly and monthly needs, whereas something like a basic income may be regarded more as a potential source of security. This could apply even though all money is fungible. But again the key point is that any enhancement of financial liquidity represents enhancement of security.

Households in the tribal villages were also asked about the reasons for saving. Most saved for security and for investing in income-generating activities. Some said they had no specific reason, which can also be interpreted as for security. Medical emergencies are what people usually fear and part of what they called 'security' probably meant this.

However, in the course of the pilot, there was a subtle shift in thinking about the purpose of saving, as more were planning to use it for investment in livestock, fertilizers and other agricultural inputs. In the IES, 62 per cent reported they were saving for security, 3 per cent for purchasing animals, and 28 per cent for 'no specific reason'. By the FES, 47 per cent reported they kept savings mainly for security. Those who were saving to buy animals or fertilizers rose to 13 per cent. This may reflect the upward swing in the economy due to the basic income itself. Confidence breeds entrepreneurial instincts of the better kind.

The odd couple: Debt and saving

One puzzle remains. It might be presumed that if a household had substantial debt it would use any cash to reduce it. But having financial liquidity is actually a basic need. Families want liquidity, especially for unanticipated demands, such as an illness when they need to pay for a visit to the doctor or to buy medicine. Liquidity is vital. However, there are strong incentives to reduce debt as well, since most pay high rates of interest.

The result is that families try to do both. Thus, in the general villages, according to the FES, 69 per cent of households that had made savings in the past 12 months also had substantial unpaid debt. And of those with debt, 13 per cent reported making savings, compared with 18 per cent of those households with no debt. That difference was statistically significant, indicating how debts and savings coincided.

Among households that had debt, those with the basic income had a significantly higher propensity to save (19 per cent compared with 11 per cent of control households). The result was similar in the IES and FES, which further testifies to the positive effect of basic income on savings.

Hazards and shocks: Does basic income help?

A feature of the globalization era is that more people are exposed to shocks and hazards that are more damaging and cause greater difficulties in coping and recovering from them. Everywhere, this is posing a challenge to *resilience*, the ability to withstand, cope with and recover from such shocks and hazards. It seems that more people are fragile and less resilient (Taleb, 2012). As fragility is associated with income insecurity, a basic income can surely help strengthen personal, family and community resilience.

Most households in rural India experience socio-economic shocks – sudden events that threaten them financially and materially – and hazards – events, perhaps desirable in themselves, such as weddings and births, which arise from time to time and cause financial stress. As a general point, more should be done to reduce the obligatory costs imposed on low-income households by hazards. Finding ways of limiting the cost of such life-cycle events has preoccupied the Madhya Pradesh government, which has given financial support for group weddings under the *Mukhyamantri Kanyadan Yojana*. There is no reason for doubting that hazards impoverish too many people.

As a benchmark, we have done a rough division of shocks and life-cycle hazards in Table 3.1. A key point is that often a hazard is something that is welcomed, whereas a shock is an event that is not, however much it might be anticipated.

The FES contained a module of questions on shocks, hazards and financial crises experienced by households. Shocks and hazards may have been random, or be due to events that had nothing to do with the basic income. But the hypothesis is that the probability of such events leading to a financial crisis would have been lessened by the basic income, giving households the assurance of funds to deal with them.

A first question was whether there had been a financial crisis in the past 12 months. In the general villages, 48 per cent of all households reported having experienced at least one financial crisis. There was no apparent difference by whether or not they had received the basic income, as shown in a multivariate

Table 3.1   Causes of financial crises: Shocks and life-cycle hazards

Shocks	Life-cycle hazard
Death of child	Birth of child
Medical costs	Marriage costs
Crop failure	Cost of weddings, funerals, other
Rising price of goods needed for trade, business or farming	ceremonies and feasts
	Repayment of loans/debt
Loss of job	Children's schooling
Death of income earner	
Lost income due to insufficient demand for products	
Loss of work due to illness or injury	
Natural disaster (flood, drought, etc.)	
Eviction or threatened eviction from house	
Child stopping work for family	

logit function in which household characteristics and assets were taken into account. Although a crisis was more likely in households containing someone with a disability and if there were more children, in most respects the probability of a crisis was random. It is how people coped with crises and recovered from them that matters.

Before considering this, it is worth noting that case studies revealed how most families experienced financial crises. Take the situation of Ramkanya, a 40-year-old woman from a scheduled caste, with a small plot of land, having to support a mentally disabled husband and their three adolescent children:

> From my cash transfer account, I took out 1,000 Rupees in bulk when in one week there were two weddings in my husband's family... Also, when the ration shop suddenly provided rations for six months, I had to purchase 1 quintal and 16 kilos of wheat, 5 litres of kerosene and 7 kilos of rice at one go. I had to pay 560 Rupees. I used the cash transfer money for that.

These are instances where, without the basic income money, the options would have been to incur a debt or to do without. Now consider Ramesh, a 45-year-old who described his main activities as farm labour and own-account farming. He experienced a classic shock, induced by a government subsidy scheme and the uncertainties of agricultural prices:

> I had sowed a garden of papaya in one bigha of my land during the Holi season [March]. The government had provided these plants, fertilizers and pesticides for the cultivation. Other than that, we were given 2,000–3,000 Rupees for the

labour on the papaya field through 'job card'. We suffered a loss of two crops by sowing papaya, wheat and soya. We get two sacks of soybean from this land, which sell for 6,000 Rupees, and five sacks of wheat, which means we lost 11,000–12,000 Rupees. Other than this, I had planted chilli among the papaya plants. But it didn't grow because of shade from the papaya plants. So, 2,000 Rupees were spent in its removal, which came from my own pocket. The chilli had completely spoilt …

… One *seth* came from outside to buy our papaya, paying a price of 3–4 Rupees per kilogram. He has not returned, because the market price for papaya is low this year. We did a lot of hard work for this crop, but have suffered a huge loss due to the low market price. I will never grow papaya again … The bank people came some time back and were asking for the money. They told us that if we didn't pay back the money, they would have our land auctioned.

Here we have somebody struggling to overcome setbacks caused by a well-intentioned subsidy scheme that had produced a negative shock. The designers of the scheme were inadvertently responsible for the financial crisis. To compound the crisis, Ramesh had to deal with a typical hazard:

This year, as well as suffering a lot of damage due to the papaya crop, I also have had to marry off my three children, one daughter and two sons. For the sons we shall have to give 30,000 Rupees to the bride's side and we'll have to put aside some money for our daughter. There will be other expenses which may go up to 1 lakh Rupees. I will have to borrow money on interest from some moneylender. This year the crop is also not flourishing because of the pond water being cold. There is also a tradition in our community of giving seven kitchen utensils for the daughter's wedding.

Since the distribution of this money [basic income], the villagers have started to give 100 Rupees from each house to the family in which there is a marriage. A total of 10,000 Rupees is collected from the whole village. This money is enough to pay at least the food expenses in the marriage. This is support from the villagers.

Here we hear of a collective response to individualized hazards, made possible by the basic income. It is about asserting a degree of control of sources of economic insecurity.

Now reflect on a classic shock that so often has devastating consequences for rural families. Chandaben from Jagmalpipliya, of the Balai caste, a 45-year-old woman whose main occupation was labouring, told our team:

My husband was sick for nearly two years. He passed away recently. He had acquired this disease where his whole body had swollen up. We got him admitted to the private hospital in Indore. He was there for 15 days but we were not able to afford further treatment. Finally, we managed to borrow 40,000–50,000 Rupees from relatives. After spending that on treatment we had to admit him to the government hospital in Indore. He stayed there for a month but no improvement was shown. We had no money to get him admitted to a private hospital. His condition kept deteriorating and within a month he expired.

After that all responsibility of the household came to me. He used to earn about 24,000 Rupees a year by working as a domestic in some household. After his demise, I and my son Narendra increased our hours of labour but one of my sons is mentally challenged so is unable to do much labour. He is easily exploited by employers. Three of my boys are studying and we have to bear the expenditure for their education.

… We borrowed money for my husband's treatment. And my husband had also borrowed money for our daughter's wedding. After that we have also borrowed small amounts, and today I have a debt of 1 lakh Rupees. I do not know about the rate of interest. Right now our financial situation is very bad. I do not know how I am going to repay my debt.

… The basic income money is spent on food items only. The intake of food has increased a little ever since we started receiving it. We have been able to buy provisions on time. We get basic income money for five members in my family. Since my son is mentally challenged, his money is also credited to my account. This money has helped us a lot. If it were not for it, we would have had to send our children for labour work. But because of this money we were able to send them to school. We are happy with the money we receive. But it would be good if it increased a little as we are in a very difficult situation.

Clearly, the basic income did not enable the family to overcome their loss, but it did help them cope by providing the means of obtaining food during the crisis. Regardless of whether a crisis arises from a shock or a hazard, it is how people can cope with it and recover from it that is crucial.

Economists have shown that if a shock causes a crisis, people tend to become more cautious and less entrepreneurial, often to their longer-term disadvantage. If fewer people in a community have a crisis from which they cannot recover, the community benefits by becoming more adventurous, even among those who had experienced the crisis (Knupfer et al., 2013).

So, if a basic income increases the capacity to cope and to recover, that could have wider positive ramifications. In that regard, respondents who had experienced a crisis were asked what had been their main and second main source of financial support during their most serious crisis.

In almost all cases, they did borrow to some extent, whether or not they had been receiving the basic income. However, there was a shift in type of lender in basic income households. More were able to keep moneylenders at bay. Only 41 per cent of basic income households hit by a crisis resorted to them, whereas 54.5 per cent of control households hit by one did so. The universal nature of the basic income meant that in a crisis, families or individuals could turn to informal sources of support.

The standard multivariate logit function was run to see if the basic income lowered the probability of a household hit by a financial crisis going to a money-lender. It was associated with a significantly lower probability of resorting to one, further supporting the hypothesis that its full value exceeds the monetary value. Implicit in this finding is the claim that basic income lowers the cost of crises, presumably because families can draw on the support of kin and neighbours, whether formally pooling money or providing it as and when needed.

A related issue is whether households hit by a financial crisis had to sell or mortgage assets, which is potentially the most serious implication. Some 10.5 per cent of all those hit by a crisis resorted to this, again with no observable difference by whether or not they received the basic income. In a logit function, the coefficient on basic income was not significant, although it was negative as hypothesized.

Concluding reflections

The key point made in this chapter is that the basic income's emancipatory value exceeds the monetary value, and as such could be expected to have a bigger impact on other issues than might be imagined from just considering the modest amount that was paid out.

Crucially, the basic income deprives rent-seeking exploiters of opportunities. By contrast, a subsidized commodity has an emancipatory value that is less than the monetary value of the subsidy. There are at least three dimensions to this.

First, the amount spent on any subsidy vastly exceeds the actual monetary value received by the recipient, as has been widely documented. Second, even if the quality of the subsidized commodity is as good as the equivalent in the market, there is a value in having a choice of when, where and how much one buys. Third, the person may not want that commodity and may want something else.

By contrast, the basic income represents money pouring into the villages. Its effects include cheapening the cost of borrowing and credit. In its absence, borrowing may cost as much as 50 per cent a year, or much more than that. With a basic income, the cost of money or its near substitute drops, raising the emancipatory value, through

- saving from reduced loans and debt,
- saving from reduced interest on outstanding loans,
- saving from a lower tendency to buy food or other goods on credit,
- saving from buying productive inputs such as seeds and fertilizers on credit,
- saving from gaining interest-free loans or transfers from family or neighbours to meet needs arising from shocks and hazards. Without the availability of pooled money, people would be at the mercy of market-oriented moneylenders who could raise interest rates because of the borrowers' urgency of need.

We do not know the full effects of these induced changes, but if, say, three-quarters of villagers customarily borrow each year, and if we knew how much on average they borrowed and how much the average rate of interest was before the start of the basic income and after some months, we could estimate the emancipatory value of the basic income.

4

The Impact on Living Conditions

Introduction

The early phase of the basic income pilot must have struck many villagers as puzzling, prompting discussions in and around the houses as they came to terms with this unfamiliar unconditional source of monetary liquidity. Gradually, families and individual members of households would have seen the cash as a potential means of improving their lives in little but significant ways.

In some cases, it may have just made the difference between endlessly postponed acquisition of something and a decision to go ahead. In others, it may have led to agreements to pool part of the money so as to save for some more substantial improvement. In closely-knit village communities, one family's big decision could have set up demonstration effects, exciting others to plan to do likewise, or even better. This particularly affects little improvements to housing.

Evidence of change came quite early, shown by the results from the IES and from accounts given in case studies. By the end of the pilot, in the FES, some of the changes were quite impressive. People's living conditions are the most basic aspect of life, determining or influencing almost everything else. Provided with extra cash, families could be expected to make modest improvements to their housing, unless the critics are correct in thinking that recipients would dissipate the money in idleness and waste.

Latrines

Although other changes may have been the first to be made by many households, it is appropriate to start by considering the impact on the most basic of human needs. A scourge of Indian village life is that most people's dwellings lack any kind of toilet.

This has a serious adverse effect on health, particularly of young children, as well as those who are frail, disabled or ill. Poor public hygiene is known to be the cause of many deaths from diarrhoea and encephalitis. Indeed, many economists and other social observers (e.g. Virmani, 2013) claim quite plausibly that the primary cause of malnutrition in India is the abysmal state of public health, in terms of sanitation, clean drinking water and public knowledge about the importance of cleanliness.

According to the Indian Population Census of 2011, only 47 per cent of all households in the whole country had access to any type of toilet, and the extent of rural access lagged well behind the urban level, with less than one-third of rural households having a toilet of some kind (Kapoor and Mamgin, 2013).

Villages in Madhya Pradesh had done even less well; only one in every six had access to a toilet in 2011, the second lowest in the country, although the incidence seems to have been a little higher in the areas covered by the pilots. But the trend unleashed by the basic income was encouraging.

During the first year of the pilot, nearly one in every six households (16 per cent) made improvements of some kind, compared with one in ten in the control villages. Another indicator is that, by comparison with the control villages, nearly twice as many households that did not have a latrine in their dwelling at the outset did have one by the end of the pilot. Almost certainly for no other reason than their low incomes and lack of space in non-permanent dwellings, the least likely to have made any change were scheduled tribe and caste households. However, a very few did so.

This might not seem a great deal, but significantly more basic income families made improvements. The case studies also revealed an increasing consciousness that installing a latrine was feasible and that the basic incomes could be pooled within families or even across households, so as to take advantage of the *Nirmal Bharat Abhiyan* (Total Sanitation Campaign), under which a subsidy was provided to those who wished to build a latrine. In the SEWA villages local organizers have tried to advise households to consider this option, but have had limited success. As it was, there did not seem to be much difference between basic income and control villages in this respect.

While lacking a toilet is an indicator of impoverishment, in cruel ways the lack of access to one helps to perpetuate poverty, simply because it increases the probability of ill-health, which costs more in treatment. And the ill-health limits the chances of children going to school regularly and lowers the productivity of adults in their work and labour.

It is a well-known debilitative cycle. A breakthrough in sanitation could have a corresponding set of beneficial effects. If the basic income could break the cycle of impoverishment at any point, the positive effects would be multiple.

A significant aspect of private sanitation was the widely different beliefs about the cost of installing a latrine, which ranged from about Rs.10,000 to Rs.25,000. One Jaat caste family, headed by a 45-year-old man, Sitabai, who mainly worked as a wage labourer, reported that they pooled all their individual basic incomes and by combining them with some savings managed to build a toilet for Rs.25,000.

One is inclined to surmise that this family would not have made the effort to install it without the basic income, partly because the assurance of the flow of money in coming months would have made them more willing to risk their savings.

To complete the picture, family members worked on the construction of the toilet, guided by the *mistri* (mason) who supervised as well as did the construction. Sitabai told our team that without their own work, the total cost would have been Rs.5,000 more. In short, it was a classic case of a little more, how much it was. The basic incomes made the difference between doing nothing and making a change to living conditions that could have a transformative effect on family life and well-being.

This is an interesting case because it shows the social dynamics that can be released by an individualized basic income. And psychologically, a facility built with the family's own money and collectively is likely to induce a greater sense of care to maintain it in good condition. The initiative stemmed not from pure charity but from what must have been a debated decision for their common good.

There are several reasons why more families do not construct or improve toilets. Their reticence is surely partly due to a legacy of generations not having them and using open spaces. It also reflects not having enough space on which to construct one. This is a major social problem. Women have a particularly strong need for toilets, since they cannot defecate in the open during the day, and suffer many diseases as a result. The trouble is that women have been unable to determine spending priorities or make decisions. So, when a household decides on what items to buy, it is more likely to be a motorcycle than a toilet.

On a societal level too, sanitation has been considered less important than many other needs, which is one reason why Indian towns and villages are so unclean. Religion has not helped, regrettably. Thus, it was not surprising that in the tribal village where the basic income was paid, when asked whether any collective village-level decisions had been made on spending money from the basic incomes, the main actions had been to upgrade the temple or to upgrade the road.

Policymakers are beginning to alter the public consciousness. Across party lines, prominent politicians have called for 'toilets instead of temples'. Thus, Jairam Ramesh, then Union Minister for Rural Development, in April 2013 made a much-publicized statement saying that toilets were more important than temples (*Indian Express*, 2013). And in October 2013, Narendra Modi, then Chief Minister of Gujarat, urged people to 'build toilets first and temples later' (*Times of India*, 2013).

Mindsets are changing, especially as more families show that better amenities can be installed. Shortly after the pilot was completed, a young Dalit woman became famous for walking out on her husband, taking her children back to her parents' house, saying she would not return until the husband had built a toilet (Singh, 2014).

Among the reasons for families not constructing toilets must be inertia. But, of course, so is simple affordability. The Total Sanitation Campaign, now called the *Nirmal Bharat Abhiyan* (NBA), was intended to overcome this constraint. It evidently has failed to do so. Bureaucratic inefficiencies play a big role, as does corruption.

During the UPA government, the Secretary of the Union Ministry of Drinking Water and Sanitation set up a high-level committee to investigate the huge discrepancy between the reported number of toilets built under its sanitation programme and the reality. The discrepancy had come to light when the 2011 Population Census showed that the number of rural households without a toilet was much larger than the ministry's data had reported (Down to Earth, 2013). The census showed that just 31 per cent had toilets, whereas the ministry's figures indicated that 53 per cent of rural households had been covered by its sanitation drive by December 2010.

The situation is dire, and the basic income could only have been expected to lead to a few changes. It was clear during the course of the pilot that many families overestimated the cost of installing a latrine, although the data suggest that many others were induced to spend more than should have been necessary.

In villages across India, government has promoted the construction of 'pit latrines', based on technical designs by Indian agencies such as Safai Vidyalaya and Sulabh and international agencies such as UNICEF. These cost less than Rs.12,000, and are widespread in western and southern India. However, in

Madhya Pradesh and much of northern India, villages have not adopted pit latrines, and have tended to opt for septic tanks, which are much more expensive.

Informed discussion in the area covered by the pilot suggested that the cost of installing a *pucca* latrine should have been between about Rs.10,000 and Rs.12,000, including the cost of labour. In the PFES, respondents were asked how much they had paid if they had installed a latrine, and surprisingly the average was Rs.26,000. Those who had not installed one were asked how much they thought it would cost. The average was Rs.13,700. And when asked how much they would be prepared to pay, the mean average was nearly Rs.4,700.

Finally, many households seemed to expect installation to be paid through a government scheme, and were waiting until some government official organized the construction for them. On that basis, the NBA should be more successful in extending latrines to such villages. The impasse is surely solvable, and the basic income might have set valuable precedents, albeit with only a minority of households.

Water sources

Many Madhya Pradesh villages lack a reliable water supply, with most households forced to rely on a public tap or hand-pump. Indicative of the difficulties that such a situation imposes, on average households had to spend over an hour every day collecting water.

But in the course of the pilots, something happened. Many households installed a tube well. The most striking change in this regard happened in the tribal village.

All households in the basic income and control villages were asked about their main source of general water and main source of drinking water. Before the pilot was launched, most used a public tap or hand-pump or a government/municipal or *panchayat* tanker. But during the pilot, shifts took place in both the basic income and control villages.

The main improvement was either gaining a tube well or having a private tap or pump in the house. Although the increase was also substantial in the control villages (12 per cent), in basic income villages, between the baseline and the FES, there was a shift from where there were almost no pumps to one where over 14 per cent of households had one.

However, the really dramatic change occurred in the tribal village where the basic income was paid. In the course of the pilot, one in every five households installed a pump and another one in five invested in a shared one with a neighbouring household, in both cases doing so instead of relying on a public hand-pump as they had done. In the meantime, there was hardly any change in the pattern in the control village, where about 60 per cent still relied on a public hand-pump.

What happened was that in the basic income village there was a pond. Near the pond was a recharged well. Although no villagers reported using the pond as a direct source of drinking water, many used part of their basic income money to buy motors and lay underground plastic pipes, in some cases, to pump water onto their farm. They bought the materials in the nearby town of Mhow, paying in monthly instalments from their basic income.

A main justification for what was a significant cost was that the pumps were needed for irrigation, the lack of which has been a major impediment to production and higher productivity. The effect of basic income on work and production is considered later. But clearly the basic income induced improved access to drinking water and to productive investment.

Energy

Although electrification was widespread in the villages at over 85 per cent, between the baseline and the FES, the proportion of households that had electricity rose by 12 per cent in the basic income villages, whereas the proportion rose by half that in the control villages. This was a statistically significant difference.

The evaluation surveys probed changes in sources of energy for cooking and for lighting. In the non-tribal villages, nearly one in every five households that were receiving the basic income reported that they had made some change in one or the other or both. By contrast, only one in every ten did so in the control villages. Again, this was statistically significant, indicating that the basic income had made a difference.

In recent years, households in these villages had been moving towards using electricity for lighting, since there was a local supply and the monthly costs were moderate. Most had been able to use electricity for part of the time, if not all of the time every day. The basic income seems to have made a significant difference to the extent of electricity use, through encouraging some to invest in more sockets and more wiring. For some reason, this was more common in the SEWA villages, perhaps because the women in households had a greater say in the decisions on domestic spending.

With lighting there were only modest changes. But there was a much greater shift in fuel for cooking, with four times as many reporting a change among the basic income households.

The most common change was from charcoal and dung to wood. The switch from charcoal could be explained in part by the ban on use of local charcoal. But the basic income villages seem to have been able to switch to wood, whereas more in the control villages switched to cheaper fuels. In the former, between the baseline and the final point, the share using wood rose from 30 per cent to 42.5 per cent, whereas in the control villages it rose from 24.5 per cent to 32 per cent. It is worth noting that dung cakes were used both as organic fertilizer and as fuel, so that those who shifted to dung for fuel would have less for fertilizing their land, potentially lowering production.

Across all these villages, the main fuel is either wood or dung cakes, some of which come from free collection on the commons. But there is also a market in wood, which seems to have been used by those receiving the basic income. Those favouring the PDS subsidy on kerosene should ponder on the fact that hardly any household was using it as a main source of energy, under 2 per cent among basic income households and 3 per cent in the control villages.

Very similar patterns were observed in the tribal villages, except that the relationships were stronger. In the basic income village, 16 times as many households reported making an improvement to their cooking fuel than in the control village, and 14 times as many reported making an improvement to their lighting arrangements. In sum, in these respects, the basic income had made a difference.

Housing

Most households in most villages are in a gradual transition from traditional *kutcha* houses to relatively modern *pucca* buildings. The terms defy easy explanation. Roughly speaking, a *pucca* house is one having walls and a roof made of burnt bricks, stone, cement or timber, whereas a *kutcha* dwelling would have walls and a roof of unburnt bricks, bamboo, mud, grass, reeds and loosely packed stones.

In reality, most had walls, floors and roofs made of mud and bamboo, rarely being fully *pucca*, constructed mainly or wholly with brick and mortar. Often, roofs are leaky, walls are made of *kutcha* materials and floors are muddy in the rainy season.

Conversations during the course of case studies suggested that most villagers had an ambition to make their dwellings more *pucca*, especially because *kutcha* structures leaked during monsoons, could not withstand strong winds and were invaded by insects, rats and other pests. *Kutcha* dwellings require regular upkeep, whereas a *pucca* dwelling was seen as needing repair or repainting only every few years.

The research team, visiting the villages from time to time during the 18 months covered by the pilots, was able to see improvements being made to houses, some quite remarkable in themselves. What was unclear at the time was whether or not apparent changes would show up in the statistical evaluation surveys, and whether or not they were any different from what was happening in the control villages.

The case studies certainly threw up some encouraging anecdotal evidence. An example was Kalabai, a woman in a scheduled caste household with a small landholding of 1.5 bighas, who reported that the family pooled their basic income money:

> Last month [June 2012], before the start of the monsoon, with the last cash transfer of 600 Rupees and adding 200 Rupees, we put a *kutcha* roof on the verandah. The previous year it was so bad, because we had no roof on it, and so all the rainwater came inside the house. This year we thought we should do something. Thankfully, at the right time we had this money. On a bamboo frame, we put a plastic sheet and on top of it stones to protect it from the wind. The bamboo frame cost us 300 Rupees and the plastic sheets cost 500 Rupees, and since we did all the work, there was no spending on labour.

There were other such cases, systematically suggesting that the liquidity was operating to release a constraint that may have been as much in the mind as in reality. But the statistical data from the FES backed up this trend, for significantly more households in basic income villages reported making some improvement than in the control villages.

Somewhat surprisingly, the most widely reported change was construction of a new dwelling, although the biggest difference was that more basic income households made improvements to their house walls. This also applied to a tendency to increase their dwelling size by adding a room.

Improving or repairing roofs was also quite common. Again a case study can illustrate the sort of changes that occurred. Gokul, a 40-year-old wage labourer, described his family's actions as follows:

> The roof of my house was made of dry grass and straw, which used to create a difficulty in the rainy season. After I started to receive this money [basic

income], I bought metal sheets to cover the roof and this has given us some comfort ... We used the cash transfer money for house repairs. In the rainy season, water used to collect in the house, which is why we put mooram for 3,000 Rupees and one iron angle and sheet to cover the roof. We used some of the cash transfer money and some of our savings from our wages for this purpose; altogether we spent about 5,000 Rupees for the house repairs.

Not all those who made changes attributed them to the basic income, but in most cases they said it was at least partly due to it and, as Figure 4.1 indicates, that was obviously more the case with repairs than with major construction.

In the tribal villages, the research team devoted more attention to studying changes in housing, drawing on lessons learned from watching what seemed to be happening in the larger pilot that had begun earlier. But again it was a few case studies that revealed the full extent of what happened. The case of Draupadibai was outstanding:

I have four girls and one boy. My mother-in-law lives with us. Each month we received 1,350 Rupees, which includes my husband's money. My mother-in-law kept her money for herself. Last year, three months after the basic incomes began, my husband and I decided to build a new house on our farm near the pond. Before that we were living in a hut far away from the village in the forest.

Figure 4.1   General villages: Percentage judging whether change in dwelling was due to the basic income

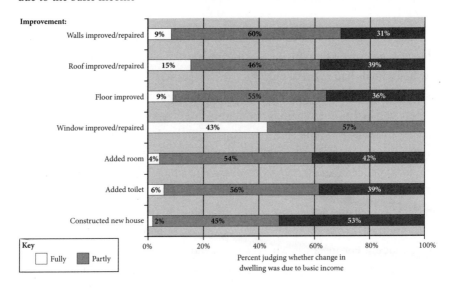

In total we spent about 15,000 Rupees. We had four masons who stayed in our house for two weeks. We had to pay them 200 Rupees per day. They were my husband's relatives. We had saved 3,000 Rupees from the basic incomes and started the work. Gradually, we paid the masons the rest of the money. After they had done the basic structure and the roof, my husband and I did all the other work. So, the cash grant money gave me a new house. After that, my husband went away to work in a brick kiln. While he was away, I did almost the entire plastering of the outside.

We make no claim that this was typical; indeed, it was exceptional. But where one woman set an example, was it not likely that others would wish to follow?

In fact, no less than one in ten families in the tribal village where the basic income was paid constructed a new dwelling or part of one, and 43 per cent of all the households did some upgrading during the course of the pilot, compared with 28 per cent in the control village. This was a statistically significant difference.

Household assets

Besides making improvements to their dwellings, basic income households were more likely to buy items that made their living conditions more pleasant. Thus, nearly one in every five (19.4 per cent) households in the non-tribal villages purchased furniture during the pilot period, compared with one in seven in the control villages. More also bought items of transport, such as bicycles, scooters or motorbikes.

However, again it was in the tribal village where the impact was greater. This was not surprising, given that incomes were generally much lower and few households had many assets. But the changes were dramatic. Among them, many households in the basic income village bought beds, so the share having at least one bed rose from 35.5 per cent before the pilot began to over 83 per cent by the end of it. The share owning a mobile phone rose from 9 per cent to 61 per cent. The proportion owning a scooter or motorcycle rose from 3 per cent to 30 per cent, and the proportion owning a bicycle rose from 7 per cent to 17.5 per cent. There was also an increase in the number of households having an electrical fan and a television, with some sharing one or both.

By contrast, in the control village, acquisition of household assets was much more modest. For instance, whereas many more there had a scooter or motor-cycle at the outset of the pilot, the change was merely one percentage point in the period. For some reason, more households had a bed at the outset, and fewer purchased one in the pilot period.

In sum, whereas the basic income had a modest positive effect on the acquisition of household assets in the general non-tribal villages, it seemed to have had a major impact in the tribal village.

Mosquito protection

Some modifications to living conditions are very small in themselves but have wider, even transformative implications. Protecting against mosquitoes at night is one such small change that has potentially major effects, particularly with regard to children's health and development.

So it is intriguing that during the course of the pilot some basic income households shifted from not doing anything to protect themselves, and others shifted from just using traditional methods to do so, to using what might be called modern methods of protection, through use of chemical repellents or mosquito nets.

That was significantly more likely to have occurred in the basic income villages than in the control villages. Of course, many believe traditional methods are as effective as chemical repellents. But the change itself was indicative of a desire to improve their protection.

Concluding reflections

The story that comes across from the evaluation survey data and from case studies is that families that received the basic income were more likely to make small but cumulatively significant changes to their housing and living conditions, improving household amenities and practices in the process.

As we proceed through the analysis of the impact of the basic incomes, we should keep in the back of our minds how these small changes can have a series of positive effects on other aspects of life, from health to child development and economic activity. They may appear to be matters of welfare, but one should recognize them as both emancipatory, in freeing up time and energies for living better, and developmental, in enabling people to work and learn more effectively.

5

The Impact on Nutrition

Introduction

In one village covered by this study, two young women sat cross-legged outside their newly painted little house, in the midday heat. In front of them were two large mats, one with wheat spread across it, the other with *padi* (rice). Three young children were running around, occasionally tugging on the saris of the women, demanding attention and reassurance as strangers asked their mothers questions. The women were sifting the wheat and *padi* meticulously. They said that doing this chore normally took about four hours.

The wheat and *padi* had come from the ration shop. The women said both sacks had been adulterated by the addition of small stones and bits of grit that had been added to bring the weight of the sacks of grain and rice to the required level in the ration shop. To compound their problem, the women said that the wheat and *padi* were of low quality and made their children sick.

We tell this story as a means of highlighting a likely failing of any scheme that makes the recipient a *supplicant*, that is, someone without the capacity to make choices sensibly or to demand that the supplier treats them fairly and with respect. The villagers have had to take the food that they are offered, and if they were to object they would risk losing their entitlement to even that. Either way, it is their children who suffer most.

To understand and evaluate the impact of the basic incomes on nutrition, we need to appreciate the institutional realities in Madhya Pradesh villages. In some respects they were much like most of the rest of India, suffering from pervasive 'food poverty'. The general situation is dire. In 2012, across India, 42 per cent of all children were officially categorized as underweight, and the Prime Minister, Manmohan Singh, called the country's malnutrition levels 'a national shame'.

The main effort made by the UPA government to redress this was through a Food Security Act, intended to provide more subsidized food for a much larger share of the Indian population. Although that obviously had no impact on the pilots, the main features would have been unchanged, since the Act was mainly intended to extend the number of people covered by the Public Distribution System (PDS).

The PDS has been designed to provide subsidized wheat grain, rice and sugar depending on possession of one of three types of card, AAY (*Antyodaya Anna Yojana*), BPL (Below Poverty Line) or APL (Above Poverty Line).

The Government of India launched the *Antyodaya Anna Yojana* (AAY) scheme in 2009 to ensure food security for the poorest of the poor in rural and urban areas of the country. The scheme targeted households that, it was estimated, could not afford two meals a day, which apparently came to about 5 per cent of India's total population. State governments had launched efforts to identify households eligible for the scheme, mainly by selecting from among the number of BPL families previously identified within the state.

It should be borne in mind that in 2013–14, the national government and various state governments were planning to introduce conditional and targeted cash transfer schemes based on targeting through use of these various cards or the principles underlying them.

At the very least, the planned extension of food subsidies through the Food Security Act and the planned use of similar criteria for cash transfer schemes would be justifiable only if the card system was working efficiently and equitably, in identifying households that should be beneficiaries. This means not excluding those that should be covered, not including those who should be excluded, and doing this in a way that is not administratively very costly. We are entitled to ask whether or not these principles or conditions will be met.

It is hard to be optimistic. The food subsidy system is extremely complex. The three items chosen for the subsidies assume and perpetuate a very limited diet – wheat grain, rice and sugar. The amounts seem arbitrary – 30 kg of wheat grain, 5 kg of rice and 2.1 kg of sugar a month for those with BPL or AAY cards.

The market rate is calculated on the basis of what PDS-quality goods cost in the market. The quality of the PDS items is lower because the wheat is two or three years old, sugar is smaller grain and rice is mostly broken (*choorivalachaval*). In the market, Basmati rice costs at least Rs.60 a kilo, and medium-quality rice costs Rs.40–45 a kilo. But the broken rice supplied by the PDS is sold in the market at Rs.26–28.

And the amount is stipulated as per family, taking no account of the great variation in size or age composition, implying that a family of two adults and one child would be entitled to the same as another with two parents, two grand parents and five children. A family-based system for communities in which families and households vary so widely makes no sense in terms of equity.

The arbitrary amounts create problems and costs of administration, what with the need to weigh the grain and control its quality. But then there are also the myriad problems with determining eligibility to the type of card, with difficulties in obtaining cards, retaining cards, replacing lost or damaged cards and changing status. Each layer of complexity adds Type 1 errors – excluding those who should be included under the poverty criteria – and Type 2 errors – including those who should be excluded on those criteria, in principle.

The arbitrary nature of the scheme is shown further by considering the variation in the subsidy. Bearing in mind that the pilots were conducted in wheat-growing areas, the subsidy on wheat grain worked out to be 79 per cent for BPL cardholders, 86 per cent for AAY cardholders and 36 per cent for APL cardholders, based on estimates of the differences between the subsidized price and the local market price.

Meanwhile, the subsidy on rice worked out to be 79.5 per cent for BPL cardholders and 86 per cent for AAY cardholders. And the subsidy on sugar worked out to be 64.5 per cent for both BPL and AAY card-holders. The subsidy rate for kerosene worked out as 67 per cent for all groups, but it varied by distance of the household's village from the depot. The ration shop that was furthest away from the depot charged Rs.17 a litre, while the nearest charged Rs.15.

When examined closely, the difference in the value of the subsidized items for BPL and AAY cardholders came to just Rs.400 a year, if they received all the rations to which they were supposedly entitled.

Perhaps the worst structural feature of the subsidy scheme in the pilot villages is that for the BPL 77.5 per cent, for the AAY 77.7 per cent and for the APL all of the subsidy went on wheat and kerosene combined. Wheat is the local staple crop. So, subsidized wheat from Punjab was undercutting local wheat, when it was not really needed. And kerosene is not used as a domestic fuel. So the subsidy was thoroughly misplaced.

Another failing is that the disbursement of subsidized grain by the ration ('control') shop is uncertain, depending on the vagaries of supply and logistical problems. Beneficiaries are expected to be ready with cash for purchase at very short notice. For instance, in the rainy season of 2011 when the basic income pilot had just started, the state government decided to disburse three months of rations in the month of August. Again, in the rainy season of 2012, the state government asked those with funds to pick up rations for six months. Often when a situation like this arises, poor people must borrow money to make the purchases.

When the government decided to disburse rations for six months in one go, a BPL family had to have in hand Rs.1,295 while an AAY family had to possess Rs.1,070. Unable to arrange cash at short notice, most poor families ended up borrowing at very high interest rates.

The crucial implication of these situations is that the PDS as it operated in reality depended on supplicants having liquidity or impoverishing themselves through having to resort to high-cost loans or credit. This adds to the argument made earlier that the emancipatory value of the basic income was greater than the monetary value.

There are several other points about the subsidy system as it was operating in the villages. Obliging low-income households to buy rations in bulk put considerable strain on storage capacities. Most households did not have reliable equipment, meaning that rot was likely to be common, along with a risk of losing the grain to insects and pests.

To give an idea of how it worked, in the general villages only about 29 per cent of the households at the time of the FES had either a BPL or an *Antyodaya Anna Yojana* (AAY) card. The subsidy, however, seemed to be reaching rich households as well, with 39 per cent of households in the top 40 per cent of the wealth distribution having either a BPL or an AAY card, similar to the proportion of households in the poorest wealth quintile having the card.

Some revealing reports came in the case studies, as illustrated in Plate 5, showing the home of Santoshbai and family, a household covered in the pilot in one of the general villages. For some inexplicable reason, the family only qualified for an APL card. There was no way that this could have been justifiable. And in fact, all the family had received was less than 2 kilos of grain, because the ration shop had a shortage of stocks.

If the family really qualified for an APL card, the amount it received was less than one-tenth of its entitlement. If, as was much more likely, it should have been entitled to a BPL card, the amount was less than one-fiftieth (7 per cent) of what it should have received.

Consider some others who came into the case studies. Genabai, aged 52, a Bhil wage labourer, told the enumeration team:

> We don't have a ration card. So neither do we go to the control [PDS]. Nor do we buy anything from there. So I have no idea of the quality of the ration. We

had a ration card five years back, which was taken by the *sachiv* [secretary of the *panchayat*] to make a new one. We haven't received a new ration card so far … Our neighbours also don't get anything from the control because they do not have a ration card.

This is a typical case of somebody losing entitlement due to a local bureaucratic decision, without any justification. Perhaps they had offended someone. Others pay a heavy price just in the process of obtaining one. Ramesh, a 45-year-old Bhil smallhold farmer and labourer, told the case study team:

I have a BPL card, which was recently renewed. They took 300 Rupees for the renewal, and gave us 1.7 kilos of sugar and 2 kilos of rice on it.

Here we have something that seems to have received little attention in the research on the BPL card system, which is that perversely it is a means of rent-seeking exploitation. Another widespread failing is illustrated by the case of Gabbulal, a 55-year-old disabled man from the Bhoi caste, who was chronically indebted. He told the team:

We get only kerosene from the control, with the help of an APL card, at the rate of 20 Rupees a litre. We should have a BPL card. Sometimes we borrow 200 Rupees from neighbours for grocery items.

He was actually paying more than an APL cardholder should have been paying. But he had no means of redress. And he should have been entitled to some wheat as well.

Then there was Santoshbai, aged 55, a landless labourer with three children, quite clearly very poor, who said:

We have no ration card, but we have to borrow for food which we pay back by labour.

He could not afford food for his family, but did not qualify as being poor. His plight has echoes of our discussion of the role of indebtedness. Recall the case of Gumaan Singh, aged 55, a landless member of a scheduled tribe, who had been a *naukar* for 35 years, now just surviving:

I have an APL card. I have debts of 30,000 Rupees. I am a casual wage labourer now. The ration card has become so old and worn out that it is in shreds. I have asked them to change it and give me a new card. But they haven't.

A bonded labourer who apparently only qualified for an Above Poverty Line card! But even those who have such cards have rather prosaic and practical problems, as in the case of Rajaram, a 60-year-old landless labourer and barber from Jalodkeu village:

> I have an APL ration card, which was given to me six years ago after a survey. It is completely torn now. I have applied for a new one. But nobody listens to us in this village.

Then there were the many reports in the case studies of how the poverty card system was not working well simply because obtaining decent quality food was denied. The Bhils seemed to suffer particularly badly. One couple, Tejubai and Nanuram, who had an AAY card and who had to go four kilometres to the nearest ration shop, reported that the food bought from it was often poor, and that it took a great deal of time to clean the grain.

Another Bhil, Seema, a young agricultural labourer, commented:

> We go to the ration shop once a month to bring wheat, rice, sugar and kerosene. The shopkeeper does not provide the items on time. And the quality of the wheat and rice we get is not good.

So, she was making multiple time-consuming and costly trips without a high probability that the cost would be justified. That is another underappreciated failing of the PDS. It imposes financial and time costs on those least able to afford them.

A further failing, highlighted by the case studies, is that the ration shops were providing just three subsidized food items, if anything, and many eligible families just happened to grow wheat, one of those items.

Many critical reports came through the case studies. However, for the statistically minded, a more convincing indicator of the failure of the PDS to deliver subsidized food is that in the evaluation surveys conducted during the course of the pilots only a minority had a BPL card and only 3 per cent of all households had an AAY card.

Measuring household wealth by an index based on ownership of assets, only just over a third of the bottom 40 per cent had a BPL or AAY card. And only 47 per cent of scheduled tribe households and 43 per cent of scheduled caste households had either of these cards. Landless households were the most likely to have no card at all.

All these figures and case studies should be considered in a context where prominent observers have been defending the reach and effectiveness of the PDS in reducing malnutrition and poverty (e.g. Khera, 2011b). At least in these Madhya Pradesh villages, it was failing in two respects – not providing poverty cards to those who should have been receiving them and not providing the quantity and quality of food to which they should have been entitled. That is the context in which the basic income pilot began to operate in 2011.

Income sufficiency for food

With what was happening with the 'control' system in mind, the first relevant question in the evaluation surveys asked whether or not the household usually had enough income to cover its food needs. In the general villages, by the time of the FES, while most households said their income was sufficient, the probability of having enough was significantly higher for those that had been receiving the basic income.

The differences were strikingly large in the case of scheduled caste and scheduled tribe households. This suggested that households were using the basic income to improve their nutrition.

However, the impact was much more visible in the tribal village, especially as a substantial number of families had insufficient income at the start to cover their food needs, in both the basic income and control villages. From the baseline, through the interim and into the final evaluation survey period, there was a steady and fairly dramatic improvement in the basic income village, whereas there was no change in the control village. By the end, the difference was highly significant statistically.

Whereas at the outset, 45 per cent of all households in the basic income village said their income was insufficient for their food needs, by the end only 19 per cent were saying this. By contrast, the respective figures in the control village were 41 per cent and 42 per cent.

Diet and eating habits

Having enough money for food is one matter; spending it and developing a different pattern of eating are not necessarily what follows. But having liquidity at least gives people greater capacity to make choices. We believed that there would be several beneficial effects.

The normal diet in the villages covered by the pilots has been wheat-based. The children receive, or are supposed to receive, supplementary meals at the *anganwadis*, consisting of cereals mainly. But in households in the villages there was overwhelming dependence on *rotis* (flat bread). When the project started, very few were able to afford fish or meat, and few were able to buy fresh vegetables or fruit.

Cash transfers in other countries have been found to lead to improved nutrition among children, as in Brazil, where the *Bolsa Família* was found to have improved nutrition among babies aged between six and eleven months, but not between a year and three years (Soares, 2010).

We will consider the impact on children later. But first let us highlight what happened to the diets and food consumption practices. Again, we will focus on what happened in the tribal villages, since the nutritional crisis at the beginning was greater there. What happened was nothing less than heart-warming.

Although there were some changes in the consumption of different food items in the control village, they were modest compared with what happened in the basic income village, where there was huge relative and absolute expansion in the consumption of more nutritious items, most notably pulses and lentils (up by over 1,000 per cent, or from 0.3 kilos per family to 3.3 kilos) and fresh vegetables (up 888 per cent, or from 0.6 kilos to 5.5 kilos). These figures were far greater than what occurred in the control village.

The increase in consumption of fish and meat, expressed in Rupee cost, was over 500 per cent, or from Rs.20.6 to Rs.135. We will also come back to that later. There was also an increase of over 460 per cent in the consumption of eggs, and a 213 per cent increase in the consumption of wheat.

These substantial shifts could be the outcome of one or more of three changes – more purchased from the ration shop, more purchased from local markets or more produced on village farms. Clearly, the increased purchases were unlikely to come from the ration shops. But the first key point is that the basic income was associated with an improvement in the diet of most people.

One scheduled caste woman, Bhavarsingh, who described herself as mainly a wage labourer, summed up what a number of others also said:

> There has been a vast change in the food habits over the last year. We used to eat *roti* with chutney in the past. But since receiving this money, we have been buying vegetables. Now we eat *roti* with *sabji* [vegetable dish]. Our food tastes better because we eat *masalas* [spiced dishes].

Anecdotes such as this may not be definitive evidence, but they capture the typical behavioural dynamics of a simple transparent scheme of assistance.

Ration shops and food markets

Let us consider what happens to the sources of food. Two changes occurred. First, by having more cash, families in the basic income villages were at least more able to purchase the subsidized items in the control shops, if they wished and if the food was available.

In fact, about 4 per cent of households in the basic income villages reported an increase in food purchased from the ration shops, which was not much different from what was happening in the control villages. But for all villages combined, there was a net reduction in such purchases, and about three-quarters reported that they did not alter their level of purchases from the ration shops, presumably because they bought just what was made available; 13 per cent did not buy anything from them.

The general picture is that what was happening around the ration shops was not part of the dynamics. The other two factors explained the change. According to the FES, there was a net shift to the use of food markets and non-ration shops in all types of village, but the shift was significantly greater in the basic income villages; 46.5 per cent of households reported that they purchased more of their food in the market compared to 35 per cent in the control villages, with just 2 per cent and 4 per cent respectively reporting that they had reduced their use of the market.

In the Post-Final Evaluation Survey, conducted in two basic income villages, questions were asked about the regularity of buying various food items. It was clear that many had increased the number of times they bought fresh vegetables (53 per cent saying they had increased the regularity with which they purchased them), milk (64 per cent) and pulses (54 per cent). In all three cases, the vast majority attributed the change to the basic income.

Something else was happening; along with increased regularity of purchase, families were using their basic income to buy food with cash instead of doing so on credit, and thus saving on a potentially high rate of interest, either monetary or, more likely, in food. For instance, when buying on credit, the household would purchase, say, one quintal of wheat and have to pay back later with two quintals, as noted in Chapter 3.

This tendency effectively reproduced 'food poverty' even in post-harvest periods. The basic income thus indirectly reduced such food poverty or 'food debt'. In effect, the basic income helped households to retain more of the food that they produced and enabled them to smooth the pattern of food consumption.

A traditional pattern was for households to borrow to buy, say, a kilo of soybean and agree to pay back 1.5 kilos of soybean when their harvest came due. This not only deprived some households of soybean in the slack season but also meant that they were effectively 'mortgaging' their own food production. To some extent at least, the basic income enabled them to break out of this debt cycle.

An example was a family in Ghodakhurd. Dasrath, a landowning farmer from a scheduled tribe, told the fieldwork team:

> The cash transfer money has helped us a lot ... We saved every family member's money and we went to buy the groceries once for an entire month. Because of this, we saved on transport costs and the trouble of going to market again and again. Earlier, we had to go to the market three or four times a month and buy less each time, due to lack of cash ... Earlier, we had to buy soybean and wheat seed on credit as well ... We had to buy the soybean and wheat seed from the *seth* and had to pay back double the amount of soybean seed and 1.5 times that of wheat.

To break out of such a situation is an important improvement in family welfare. Another case shows how the little more made a big difference. It was the story told by Ramda, another member of a scheduled tribe in the tribal basic income village of Ghodakhurd:

> We buy ration for the whole month because going to the market again and again was too expensive. And if the ration ran out by the middle of the month, then we bought a little bit from the village shop, and if there were no oil and spices, we made do with salt and chilli. But we did not face that problem this year because of the cash transfers.

Another aspect, brought out by this example among others, is that it was with regard to food that pooling the money was so common, with those from scheduled castes and tribes being particularly likely to do so.

Child nutrition and weight-for-age

Among the major hypotheses underpinning the pilot was that basic income would result in an improvement in the nutrition, and thus health and eventual development, of babies and young children. To test this hypothesis, relevant data were collected in several ways. Mothers were asked for their opinions, information was collected from the *anganwadis* serving the villages and all children up to the age of five years were weighed.

The main method was the third, which was an object lesson in the pitfalls of what is usually called 'fieldwork'. The underlying objective was to determine whether or not a child was 'underweight', or conceivably 'overweight' (obese), for his or her age, according to a methodology developed over the years by the World Health Organization (WHO).[1]

Before coming to the results of this exercise, we should acknowledge that obtaining reliable measures of weight-for-age was doubly complicated. Obtaining a child's exact age in months was not easy because in some cases the mother herself was uncertain. It often took several visits and checks with relatives to ascertain the exact month of birth. Some were unfamiliar with calendar months. So, they were asked for the Hindi month, such as Saawan and Bhadon. If they were unable to recall that, questions were asked about the birth being before or after major festivals, such as Diwali, Dussehra, Rakhi or Holi. Gradually, the date was narrowed down to a reasonable estimate.

Then there was the practical problem of finding all the children and being able to weigh them properly, which required multiple visits with the equipment. The original team delegated to deal with this challenge proved less than competent. Fortunately, we were able to organize another and obtain training from UNICEF staff in the state.

However, because of the initial difficulties, we had to rely on *anganwadi* records from around the time of the outset of the pilot. These data are not ideal, since it turned out that some *anganwadis* kept incomplete or inaccurate data, possibly due to lack of training or proper equipment, perhaps because they thought it was unimportant or perhaps because they wished to give a better impression of the condition of the children in their charge than was the case.

In any case, the *anganwadis* are supposed to keep monthly records of the weight of the children and, if they are deemed to be underweight, their arm circumference, as well as keep a record of any remedial treatment.

In light of the institutional deficiencies in the *anganwadi* system, enumeration team members were delegated to weigh all the children themselves, aided by training from the UNICEF office in Madhya Pradesh and their provision of weighing machines.

As a result of all this, there is reason for more confidence in the quality of the data collected for the FES, although we had to use data from the *anganwadis* for the baseline period. There is reason to think that the data from the *anganwadis* are biased. But there is no reason to think this bias would vary by type of village. So for analytical purposes the bias can be regarded as random.

With these considerations in mind, the data showed that in basic income villages the share of children with normal weight increased from 39 per cent in April 2011 (as recorded by the *anganwadis*) to 59 per cent in September 2012, an improvement of nearly 20 percentage points. That was twice as great as in the control villages,

But what was even more notable is that, while the nutritional status of boys improved, the absolute and relative improvements for girls were much greater. In the basic income villages, the share of girls with normal weight increased by over 25 percentage points, more than double that in the control villages. The share of boys attaining normal weight-for-age rose by 14 percentage points in the basic income villages, compared with only 9 percentage points in the control villages.

So, the basic income was associated with a stronger positive effect on the nutritional status of girls. This is consistent with findings in countries such as Mexico, where a CCT was found to have reduced stunting among girls by 39 per cent and among boys by 19 per cent (Aguero et al., 2007).

Probing further, the effects on age groups varied considerably. The weakest positive effect was among the youngest, babies up to the age of six months. The impact was substantial in the case of infants aged seven to 36 months, with a drop in severe malnourishment being twice that found in the control villages. The reduction in the moderately malnourished was even more pronounced and different, being 10.5 percentage points in the basic income villages compared with a small increase in the control villages.

Figure 5.1   General villages: Weight-for-age distribution for basic income villages, by gender

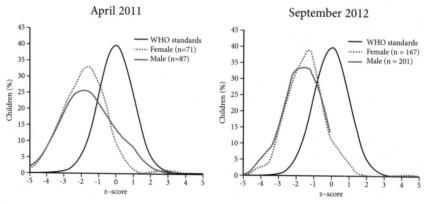

Source: *Anganwadi* records for April 2011 and MPUCT FES data for September 2012

So, the overall effect was that the share of infants in that age group who moved into the normal bracket rose by nearly six times as much in the basic income villages. These are highly significant figures. And again it was among girls that a significantly bigger improvement took place (a 24 percentage point increase compared with a 15 percentage point increase for boys).

While children in all social groups benefited, the main improvement in nutritional status took place among tribal family children and the least among the upper caste, or general, family children. Most striking of all, whereas none of the tribal children in the basic income villages had normal weight for their age at the outset of the pilot, by the end nearly a quarter had attained that weight. And the share of tribal children severely underweight for their age fell from 32 per cent to 15 per cent.

One other tantalizing finding was that within basic income villages, the improvement in normal weight-for-age was 27 percentage points in SEWA villages and under 20 percentage points in non-SEWA villages, suggesting that SEWA's activities were making an additional difference.

The age factor here is relevant. By the time they reach seven months of age most children have shifted to solid food and by the age of two years most should have begun to receive food from the *anganwadi*. This continues until they are five years old, at which point they begin school. In many of the SEWA villages, complaints about the running of the *anganwadi* would be brought to the SEWA village leader who would talk to the *anganwadi* worker and the Integrated Child Development Scheme (ICDS) supervisor. In cases where she was unable to resolve the issue, she would contact the SEWA office in Indore. One SEWA organizer, Lakhina, summed up a particularly fraught situation as follows:

> In our village there is a lot of casteism. The *anganwadi* teacher is a Brahmin and she did not allow scheduled caste children in the *anganwadi*. So children who needed it most were deprived. I went to the teacher and tried to talk to her. But instead of listening to me she started threatening the families in the scheduled caste locality and told them not to complain, as she had connections with the higher-ups, she was not afraid of the SEWA workers. So at our next meeting of SEWA in Indore, I brought this up and a written complaint went to the local supervisor of ICDS.
>
> Later, along with the SEWA organizer and some women from the village, I met the supervisor and we said that she should resolve the issue; otherwise a written complaint would be sent to the Principal Secretary of the department and the concerned minister. Hearing this, the supervisor became scared and immediately went to Jagmalpipliya and convinced the *anganwadi* teacher. The next day we sent scheduled caste children to the *anganwadi* and monitored

the issue after that. The midday meal was also not cooked daily, an insufficient amount of food was being cooked and the food was not properly cooked either. With the help of the supervisor, this issue was also resolved and I was asked to supervise the cooking daily. I ensured that the children were having enough food every day.

So there is reason to think Voice also played a part. In sum, the data show that the basic incomes were linked to an overall improvement in child nutrition, in a bigger improvement for girls than for boys and in a bigger improvement for children in the more vulnerable lower caste and tribal families. They thus point to an improvement in welfare and in equity, with the basic incomes helping to reduce one of the most pernicious forms of structural inequality.

We should add that the results in the tribal villages were mixed; improvements were observed but they were of a lower magnitude than in the larger sample of general villages, while there was a bigger improvement among boys than among girls.

The fishing cooperative

There was one particular development that affected nutrition in the tribal village where the basic incomes were paid, discussed in Chapter 8. The establishment of a fishing cooperative led to a transformation of the diet of the villagers, who suddenly had access to fresh fish on a fairly regular basis. By the end of the pilot, the fishing cooperative had become firmly established and a year later it had flourished into a regular provider of fish for the villagers over much of the year. Fish had become a normal feature of village eating, whereas it had been virtually absent before the pilot began.

The alcohol bogey

A common claim by critics of a basic income is that people will waste their money on 'private bads', most notably on alcohol and tobacco, or *bhang*, rather than on nutritious food. Therefore, it is highly relevant that, according to the FES, in the general villages a lower proportion of the basic income households increased spending on alcohol than control households, 3 per cent compared with 7.5 per cent. And more basic income households reduced their spending on it (4 per cent compared with 2.5 per cent).

The same pattern emerged in the tribal villages, where 12 per cent of basic income households reduced their spending on alcohol compared with just 1 per cent in the control village and where a lower proportion purchased more, 9 per cent compared with 12 per cent. In short, the common claim is a matter of prejudice. These results correspond to similar findings in African cash transfer schemes, most notably in Kenya (Kenya CT-OBC Evaluation Team, 2012).

One can only speculate on the reasons for a net reduction in spending on alcohol. One reason mentioned in one of the case studies may be a lead to the answer, although it is speculative. It is that more of the men were working in the fields and around the home rather than going to seek wage labour in the local town labour market.

Concluding reflections

Although the evidence on some aspects is limited, a broad narrative emerges from the evaluation data. Food deficiency fell, diets became more nutritious and balanced, and there was a relative shift from reliance on the control or ration shops to the market and own production of food. Child nutrition improved, probably quite dramatically, in that there was a substantial improvement in the weight-for-age measures and a reduction in severe malnourishment.

Improvements in nutrition affect capabilities, by tending to reduce the incidence of ill-health, particularly among infants, and by aiding concentration and school attendance. They also help in boosting economic growth and development, in that better-nourished adults tend to be more productive in their work. It is hard to measure these effects with any precision. But intuitively they make very good sense.

6

From Ill-Health to Regular Medicine

Introduction

Identifying the impact of basic income on health is complex, given that a person's health fluctuates and that it is often difficult to separate out the determinants of particular developments. Some claim that cash transfers do not have much effect on health (Narayanan, 2011). And the well-known economist Amartya Sen has commented, 'When you know that the health system is full of quacks and crooks, cash transfers will be a waste.'

This oversimplifies the situation, and implies that all doctors, nurses and clinics are corrupt or useless, which is surely not the case. It also implies that people cannot not put pressure on medical practitioners to deliver proper care.

Internationally, many studies have shown strong positive effects of cash transfers on child and adult health, incidence and severity of illness, and use and effectiveness of medical services. There is evidence from many Latin American CCT schemes that cash transfers boost use of preventative health services, and lead to people going for more health check-ups (Bastagli, 2009). This was also seen in the Namibian basic income pilot.

The health effects may be four-fold. First, basic income may improve resilience, enabling people to have more resistance to sickness, through better diets, more regular treatment, diminished stress due to economic insecurity, and so on.

Second, it may improve preparedness, the ability to respond in a timely manner to an illness or accident. This may involve hospitalizing the person or incurring needed medical expenses, or going in for preventative practices such as immunizing children and taking out health insurance.

Third, there may be a reduction of debt incurred to fund medical expenses. The basic income may give families the ability to save or pool resources for such expenditure, rather than rely on high-interest debt.

Fourth, and something that has received less attention, is that besides the effect of cash or income in itself there is a powerful positive effect of income security – the assurance of having money – through inducing people to have longer planning horizons, less stress and less anxiety (Marmot and Wilkinson, 1999). For example, in a universal income security scheme in Manitoba, Canada, the community effects improved individual states of mind and healthcare (Forget, 2011).

With those four considerations in mind, this chapter considers the impact basic income can have on health, drawing mainly on the evaluation surveys. But before doing so, it may be useful to review the institutional features of the medical system.

The medical system in rural Madhya Pradesh

India spends only 1.2 per cent of its GDP on health, compared with 2.7 per cent in China. Other Asian countries that spend proportionately more than India include Indonesia, Malaysia, Nepal, the Philippines and Sri Lanka (Kohler, 2014). Healthcare in India has been dominated by provision of public health services that are in theory universal and subsidized, delivered through a network of Primary Health Centres (PHCs), visiting Auxiliary Nurse Midwives (ANMs) and Accredited Social Health Activists (ASHAs).

This system has concentrated mostly on family planning and maternal and child health, especially child immunization and reducing maternal mortality through monetary incentives for women to opt for institutional delivery. In this regard, data from the project indicated that the public service has been effective and fairly comprehensive, particularly with regard to child immunization.

Alongside the public services, a private system of primary healthcare consists of private doctors, mostly local medical practitioners (LMPs), colloquially called Bengali doctors as many of them are non-locals from West Bengal. They have been living and working in the villages for many years and have been providing a service that seems appreciated by villagers. As one LMP told the research team, referring to one village covered by the pilot:

Many people from Sahavada come to me for treatment. If someone is seriously ill, they come to fetch me. During monsoon months, the only way to go to the village is by boat. I treat mainly seasonal illnesses. For more serious illnesses, I refer them to the hospital in Depalpur, which is 13 kilometres from here, or to Indore, which is 55 kilometres from here.

Private and government hospitals are mainly in small towns, and are used by villagers not only for serious cases requiring hospitalization, but also for diseases and ailments requiring out-patient treatment. Primary Health Centres are used more as health outposts for first aid and immunization. In general, distance to health outposts was a problem in the pilot villages, particularly in the tribal basic income village. Residents there had to go more than eight kilometres to reach the primary health sub-centre; the nearest government hospital was 23 kilometres away. In the non-tribal villages, the distance to the nearest government hospital was about 17 kilometres.

Basic income and health resilience

Across India, ill-health and disability associated with deprivation and lack of access to preventative and remedial healthcare are among the most serious social and economic challenges, leading to chronic poverty. The possible impact of basic income on ill-health was among the more sensitive subjects in the project. And perhaps the results were among the most encouraging.

Note that, in general, across all the villages covered by the pilots, there was a greater incidence of what could be called health poverty, in that many of those households who professed to have enough income for food were suffering from ill-health or disability, and lacked easy access to affordable medical attention.

Reducing incidence of illness

In all villages covered by the pilot, households were asked whether anybody had fallen ill in the previous three months, defined as having had an illness lasting for more than 24 hours and needing treatment, but not hospitalization.

By the time of the FES, after the basic income had been operating for a year, while 64 per cent of households in the control villages reported an episode of illness in the previous three months, only 52 per cent of households in the basic income villages reported an episode of illness (Figure 6.1). And fewer basic income households had more than one person ill. This pattern held for all social and demographic groups, including the elderly (those above the age of 60) and children below the age of 5, even though both these groups had a relatively higher propensity to fall ill in both types of village (Table 6.1).

Figure 6.1   General villages: Percentage of households having sick or injured members in past three months, by type of village

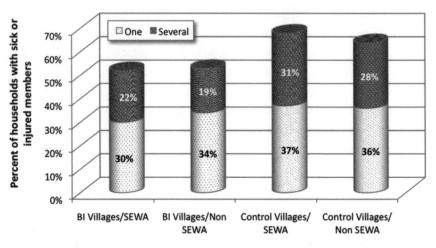

Source: MPUCT FES, 2012; n= 2034

Table 6.1   General villages: Percentage of individuals falling ill in past three months, by characteristics and type of village

	Men	Women	0–5 years	6–17 years	Working age (18–59 years)	Elderly	Disabled
BI villages	13.1	15.5	18.0	10.1	13.8	23.7	19.0
Control villages	18.5	20.0	25.1	15.3	18.5	27.9	29.0

Source: MPUCT FES, 2012; n=1988

In the tribal village, the basic income also had a salutary effect on health. Whereas 70 per cent of households in the control village reported that at least one person had been ill during the three months before the FES, only about 58 per cent of households in the basic income village had an illness in that period. The effects were even stronger for women, with women in the basic income village reporting a significantly lower likelihood of falling ill, a 15 percentage point difference. In the case of men, there was an 11 percentage point difference.

Improving health

Resilience to ill-health, or the ability to recover from illness, is influenced by various factors. Food insecurity, defined for practical purposes as having insufficient income for two meals a day, reduces the ability to fight off illness, particularly among the ultra-poor. Lack of money can induce people to curtail treatment when they start to feel better. Medical courses of treatment must be completed to be effective. In reducing these insecurities the basic income could be expected to have positive effects.

Even by the time of the Interim Evaluation Survey, the basic income was correlated with an improvement in health, the main reason cited being that households could afford medicines or treatment. This trend persisted to the end of the pilot, by which time a majority of basic income recipients (66 per cent) attributed improvement in health to the enhanced ability to afford medicines and/or treatment (Figure 6.2). Some households (about 27 per cent) also spoke of having food more regularly and how the cash had helped reduce anxiety (16 per cent), leading to the perceived improvement in health.

Similar changes took place in the tribal village. Nearly 22 per cent of households in the basic income village spoke of taking medicines more regularly, whereas only 4 per cent said this in the control village.

In the general villages, scheduled tribe respondents were relatively more inclined to cite more regular food intake as a reason for the improvement. Nearly 37 per cent of tribal basic income recipients spoke of having more food as the most important reason for an improvement in health compared to 27 per cent for all households.

Figure 6.2   General villages: Percentage of basic income households with health improvement, by perceived main reason

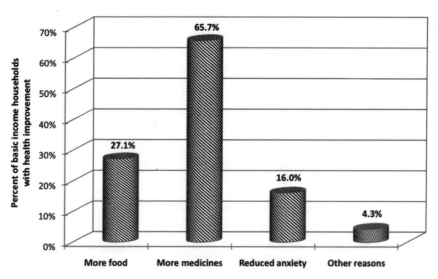

Source: MPUCT FES, 2012; n=705; multiple responses possible

Irrespective of the channel through which an improvement in health was obtained, over three-quarters of basic income households attributed the improvement partly or fully to the basic income payments. Also, for some reason, more households in SEWA villages spoke of an improvement in their health (81 per cent) compared with those in non-SEWA villages (69 per cent).

Higher food consumption could be a reason. When asked what had led to the improvement in health, 29 per cent of households in SEWA basic income villages said they had been able to afford more food, compared to 24 per cent who said this in non-SEWA villages. Similarly, 17 per cent of households in the SEWA basic income villages reported taking medicines more regularly, compared to 12 per cent in non-SEWA villages.

The combination of women receiving the cash and the presence of SEWA did seem to result in changes in healthcare behaviour. During the course of the pilot, women often expressed concern about their family's health and their own, and many reported that they did not know what to do. Here, SEWA's actions may have made a significant difference.

Women wanted to know how to take care of their health, particularly preventative actions. Many complained about not receiving healthcare to which they were entitled from the government. Some worried whether it was right to spend money on their own healthcare. On all these aspects, during regular visits to the villages, SEWA *agewans* helped women by providing information on healthcare facilities, guiding them on how to monitor the work of ANMs and ASHAs, and advising them on where to file complaints in case these workers were not performing their duties properly.

The major implication of these findings is that the basic income facilitates a more rational response to illness, largely through acquiring medicines and taking them regularly. A higher intake of food too can explain potential improvements in health status, particularly for tribal households. These are aspects of healthcare that are well known but underappreciated.

The impact on healthcare practices

When somebody shows signs of having an illness or disease, the first initiative undertaken by the family, if it has the means, is to seek treatment, perhaps taking the person to a hospital. It was hypothesized that the basic income would enable recipients to take such decisions by allowing them to make timely use of local health services.

Asked what was their initial reaction, the most common practice in the 20 general villages was to go to a private hospital (41 per cent), followed by private doctors or local medical practitioners (34 per cent) and then government hospitals (18 per cent). Most hospitals, private and public, have out-patient departments, which are widely used, meaning that about 60 per cent of people go to a hospital of some kind.

The fact is that relatively few went to government hospitals. One may presume that the first and second categories include some who resorted to the so-called Bengali doctors. Only just over 1 per cent said they went to a Primary Health Centre, ANM or ASHA organizer. This is remarkable, as it means that scarcely any households were using a public health facility other than a government hospital as a first point of contact.

Discussions in the villages revealed that public health facilities were used by residents primarily for preventative care, particularly immunization of children. When it came to illnesses that could be addressed through out-patient care, most respondents in both types of village reported using private hospitals, local doctors and government hospitals.

Over the period of the pilot, use of government hospitals as a first port of call declined slightly, from 20 per cent to 18 per cent. More private hospitals and primary doctors were being used at the time we did our final evaluation survey – private hospitals up from 40 per cent to 41 per cent, and primary doctors and local medical practitioners up from 33 per cent to over 34 per cent.

But was the shift from public to private healthcare greater in basic income villages? At the time of the FES, half the households in basic income villages said that their first point of contact was a private hospital, followed by a private doctor or local medical practitioner/chemist/medical shop (35 per cent). Only 12 per cent went to government hospitals.

However, it was not the basic income that had induced them to shift to private care. While there was a shift from government hospitals to private health services in basic income villages – slightly more went to private hospitals than they did a year previously (50 per cent compared to 48 per cent) – it was modest. More households in the basic income villages were already using private health services, and the basic income merely increased an already strong tendency to rely on private healthcare.

By comparison, in the control villages, 33 per cent of households opted for a private hospital as a first point of contact at the time of the FES (up only marginally from 32 per cent) while 41 per cent went to local doctors/chemists/

medical shops, the same as 12 months earlier. There was a modest decline in use of government hospitals, from 25 per cent to 23 per cent.

In sum, by the end of the pilot, about 85 per cent of patients were being taken to a private practitioner/doctor/hospital as a first point of contact in basic income villages, compared to 74 per cent in control villages.

The shift was also seen in the Post-Final Evaluation Survey (PFES), the short survey aimed at gathering reflections from respondents in two basic income villages regarding the impact of the benefits on various aspects of their lives. Respondents confirmed the shift to private hospitals, with 36 per cent reporting that they had used more private health services, 50 per cent saying they had made no change, another 12 per cent saying that they had used more of both public and private services, and only 3 per cent saying they had used more government medical services than 12 months before.

In the tribal villages, when people fell ill, their first contact tended to be the local medical practitioner or local chemist, while the second most common was the out-patient department of a hospital. This pattern could have been because there was no PHC in their vicinity. However, by the end of the pilot, while households in the basic income village had shifted their preferences to a private hospital, in the control village there was a shift to home remedies, even though LMPs remained the main first preference.

More significantly, the shift from government hospital was much more pronounced. At the time of the baseline, an almost identical 20 per cent were using a government hospital. By the end of the pilot, only 12.5 per cent were doing so in the basic income village, compared to 18 per cent in the control village.

Hospitalization

In the general villages, although the rate of hospitalization during the course of the pilot was similar in both types of village, with about 40 per cent of households having at least one person hospitalized, the survey data revealed several patterns.

Although the proportion of men and women in the population was similar, as was their propensity to fall ill, nevertheless by the end of the pilot more women were taken to hospital in the basic income villages (56 per cent) than in the control villages (53 per cent). So, it may have been the case that the individualized basic income improved the chances of women receiving proper treatment in hospital.

Private hospitals were the first choice for hospitalizing both men and women, a pattern observed in the baseline that had strengthened slightly by the time of the FES. At the time of the baseline, nearly 84 per cent in basic income villages and 81 per cent in control villages reported having used private hospitals when needed; the figures had increased to 86 per cent and 83 per cent respectively by the end of the pilot.

A higher proportion of men were taken to private hospitals in both types of village. Women were twice as likely as men to use government hospitals. No significant differences were observed between women in SEWA and non-SEWA villages. Although the basic income was associated with a higher probability of women being hospitalized, there remained a differentiation in kind of hospital. Women were still taken to government hospitals more often than men.

Nevertheless, here there was a notable change. The probability of women going to a private hospital or clinic was much higher in the basic income villages than in control villages – rising from 77 per cent to 83 per cent – whereas the impact for men was less – rising from 88 per cent to 91 per cent. So, if private care was better, the basic income effect was a relative improvement for women.

The evaluation data also indicated that the ill or injured were taken earlier to hospitals in the basic income villages. While 16 per cent of households in the control villages said that they took ill members to the hospital seven days or more after the onset of illness or injury, only 14 per cent delayed that long in the basic income villages.

The basic income, and the savings associated with it, may have enabled families to hospitalize an ill person as soon as a diagnosis was made, rather than delay, leading to someone becoming sicker. This is the sort of effect that can easily be overlooked or underestimated. Treatment delayed can sometimes be treatment too late. And this is another aspect of the emancipatory value of the basic income, since going for treatment earlier almost certainly reduces the eventual total cost.

Healthcare privatization

A feature of contemporary rural India is the powerful trend to private rather than government health services. This was shown vividly in the pilots. When households received cash, a majority opted for private healthcare, in private hospitals or through treatment by private doctors, LMPs, chemists or medical shops.

Was this treatment better than the treatment available at government hospitals or PHCs? The survey data available do not enable us to analyse the effectiveness of public services. But the reasons for resort to commercial medical services seemed numerous, including convenience. Many respondents in the case studies expressed broadly similar views. Thus, Kalabai, a 52-year-old agricultural worker and wife of a small-scale farmer and agricultural labourer, commented:

> We go to a private doctor regularly because we do not get government doctors on time and they do not cure illness.

Devi Singh, a small-scale Bhil caste farmer, was a typical case of somebody needing long-term medical care:

> I have been suffering from asthma for the past four years. I need treatment twice a month, for which I spend 700–800 Rupees. For any illness, we go to a private doctor. The government hospital is far away and does not provide good treatment. So we don't go to government hospitals, and rather visit private doctors. Actually, we spend the cash transfer money mostly on health.

Even Gumaan Singh, the former *naukar* and agricultural labourer described in Chapter 3, resorted to private care:

> There is a government doctor in Bavlia [four kilometres away]. But we generally go to a private one. The government doctor also takes fees, but he does not provide treatment properly.

Reshambai, a landless backward caste householder, was another who had multiple reasons for opting for private care, in spite of the cost:

> We go to private doctors because the government doctors are not available all the time, and the treatment is not good. Private doctors are always available. They take 200 Rupees as consultation fee. But the medicine they give works.

Kesar Singh, a 65-year-old Bhil wage labourer, summed up the widespread sense of frustration:

> We fall ill a lot during summer. We go to the nearby village for treatment. There is no doctor in our village. There is a private doctor at Jamburi who does not take a fee. He charges only the cost of the medicine. There is a government doctor eight kilometres away from our village but we always go to the private one because the private doctor cures quickly and properly. The government doctor does not listen to us.

In short, many villagers expressed a preference for private doctors, for diverse reasons ranging from quality to reliability and proximity, and even cost. Going private therefore was seen as less expensive, because of the cost of obtaining public services.

The evaluation data also suggested that whereas private healthcare was mainly a preserve of the rich before the pilot, it was mostly the poor who shifted. They had been dependent on 'failing public services' and, given the enhanced freedom to choose, decided to emulate, for better or worse, the norm in their community by moving to private doctors, LMPs and private hospitals.

We used four proxies for poverty to test the hypothesis that the shift was by the income poor – literacy of head of household, whether the household owned any land, whether it possessed a BPL or AAY card, and type of roof (*pucca* or *kutcha*). Low-income families were identified as those with illiterate heads, no land, a *kutcha* roof or a BPL/AAY card.

Using the first point of medical contact at the time of the FES and before the pilot started as the variable of interest, we found that the poor as defined by these proxies in basic income villages shifted more to private health services than the rich, who were mostly already relying on them before the start of the pilot.

There was a small percentage increase (49 per cent to 52 per cent) in the proportion of households with illiterate heads accessing private hospitals in basic income villages as compared to no increase in control villages. Similarly, the proportion of those using private hospitals increased from 42 per cent to 44 per cent for households with a *kutcha* roof, from 44 per cent to 46.5 per cent for landless households and from 33 per cent to 35 per cent for BPL households in basic income villages, whereas there was no change in the control villages.

Preventative practices – immunization

One justification for the basic income being unconditional is the view that there is no need to require recipients to undertake preventative measures because they can work out what is desirable for themselves, as long as facilities are available and people are informed of the advantages of particular practices. This view is supported by foreign evidence. In Brazil, with the mildly conditional *Bolsa Família*, it was found that the condition that families had to take designated actions if they wanted the cash had no impact on the frequency of health check-ups or child immunization (Soares et al., 2010).

This implies that people can be relied upon to act rationally. The presumption of rationality can be tested by reviewing the actual incidence of child immunization in the villages. Levels of child immunization were over 90 per cent in the

20 general villages and the two tribal villages covered for the pilot, except for the MMR (measles, mumps and rubella), where the rate was slightly below 90 per cent. Although the differences were not statistically significant, a slightly higher proportion of children received immunization in basic income villages, with more boys as compared to girls receiving immunization in those villages, whereas slightly more girls received immunization in the control villages. The overall rates were so high that none of those differences could be regarded as significant.

Health insurance

Although a health incident is a classic shock, as discussed in Chapter 3, and thus can lead to a financial crisis, the classic remedy of health insurance is rare in rural India. Nevertheless, all respondents were asked whether or not they had taken out any health insurance. Very few had; merely 5 per cent in the general villages said they had taken health cover in the six months prior to the FES, mostly from private providers.

However, there was a difference between basic income and control villages. While 8 per cent of basic income recipients said they had taken out health insurance in the period, only 2.5 per cent of control village households had done so. Among those who had done so in basic income villages, nearly three in every four reported that this was due partly or fully to the basic income.

Of course, a more common form of health insurance has been personal savings. As noted in Chapter 3, among those who were saving from their basic income, quite a few reported that they saved in case they suddenly needed money for medical expenses. It was a form of informal health insurance. The liquidity provided cover in case some other contingency became their priority.

Spending and borrowing for healthcare

The amount of basic income was very modest in comparison to healthcare costs faced by most villagers. Yet one of the most significant findings was that households receiving the basic income were more likely to have increased spending on all aspects of medical care.

Eight months into the pilot, at the time of the Interim Evaluation Survey, the differences were statistically significant for spending on medicine, doctor's treatment and hospital treatment, with households receiving the basic income more likely to have increased spending in each case (Table 6.2).

Table 6.2 General villages: Percentage of households with increased medical spending, by receipt of basic income

	Receiving basic income		
Sphere of spending	**Yes**	**No**	**Chi-square**
Medicines	77.3	63.1	21.971***
Doctor's fees	68.4	57.4	21.683***
Hospitalization	65.9	53.1	15.227***

Source: MPUCT IES, 2012; n=893

Among those in basic income villages who reported increased spending on doctors and medicines, nearly two-thirds attributed the increase partly or fully to the basic income, with a greater proportion of households in SEWA villages saying they were able to increase their medical spending on account of the basic income (72 per cent) than in non-SEWA villages (60 per cent).

Disaggregating by social groups, it seemed scheduled caste households, particularly in SEWA villages, were the main group benefiting in this respect, significantly increasing their spending, both on medicine and doctors, compared to counterparts in control villages.

However, medical expenses are a major source of debt for poor families, the one most likely to impoverish them. So, it was notable that borrowing for hospital expenses was significantly lower in basic income villages by the end of the pilot, 46 per cent doing so compared to 55 per cent in control villages (Figure 6.3).

More households in basic income villages reported using their own income/savings to pay for hospitalization. Reliance on own income and savings was slightly higher in SEWA villages receiving the basic income. The case of Jitmal, an elderly person from Jagmalpipliya, describes the shift.

> In case of any illness we go to the Kanadiya private hospital where 100 to 200 Rupees are spent on medicine in each visit. Some time back I got sick because of diarrhea. Some 2,000 Rupees were spent on the treatment. I was able to pay the money from the money I had been saving from the basic income. If this money had not been there, I would have had to borrow from people and would have fallen into debt with an interest rate of 3 per cent to 5 per cent.

What was also encouraging was that scheduled caste (SC) and scheduled tribe (ST) households in basic income villages tended to rely less on loans than counterparts in control villages. So while around 64 per cent of SC respondents and 68 per cent of ST respondents in control villages had used loans or had sold/

Figure 6.3   General villages: Source of funding for hospitalization, by type of village

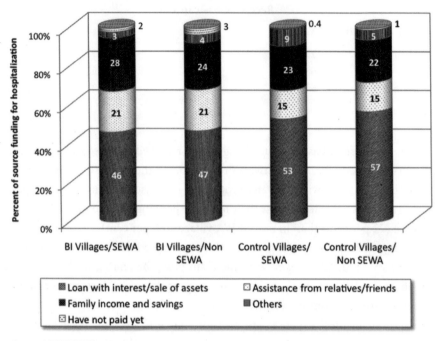

Source: MPUCT FES, 2012; n=954

mortgaged their assets to fund hospitalization expenses, in basic income villages only 52 per cent of SC respondents and 46 per cent of ST respondents did so.

They relied more on their income and savings to fund the expenses, and also spoke of pooling some of their basic income money to finance healthcare for one or more members needing treatment. The testimony of Rajmal, an SC farmer from the village of Gogakhedi, is illustrative of the manner in which such pooling was done:

> There are five members in our family who are getting the cash. The elder son's account is separate and his money is not yet withdrawn as he stays away from home. The other four of us get 800 Rupees collectively in a month. I have been saving the last 3–4 months' money. My daughter came home six months back for her first delivery. That took place at Mission Hospital and it cost 12,000 Rupees. We used some of the money to provide my daughter with good food, fruit and health drinks.

A similar pattern was revealed in the tribal village pilot. Only half resorted to loans with interest or asset sales to pay for hospital treatment, compared with 58 per cent in the control village. Correspondingly more in the basic income village relied on assistance from relatives and friends and their own income and saving.

Conclusions

The impact of basic income on two groups that have particular problems is considered in a later chapter. Thus far, we can see that it has several effects, some of which are easily overlooked. There seems to have been a generally positive effect on health, reducing the incidence of ill-health. No doubt, a virtuous circle of more and better food, less financial anxiety and more financial liquidity has helped.

The basic income seems also to have facilitated a more rational or considered response to illness, through more regular medication and, for some households, more intake of food.

The basic income gave families more choice in the type and in the timing of healthcare. Clearly, there is an institutional crisis in Indian healthcare, and there is no point in concealing the fact that public healthcare services are inadequate. They may or may not be worse than what people think is on offer by opting for private treatment.

What is clear is that when given the choice, more opt to pay for private services. Perhaps this is a switch from government to private services, perhaps a tendency to opt for treatment rather than forego any. All we can say is that the shift to private healthcare is a reality and that the basic income enabled more families to obtain treatment.

Finally, the basic income seems to have reduced the burden on households to fund their health expenses through a vicious cycle of debt. It seems to have given them an opportunity to pool money to fund health shocks and finance illnesses requiring hospitalization through their own (higher) income and savings. In all these respects, the basic income could be said to have been both emancipatory and developmental. It loosened constraints in one vital sphere of rural life.

Note

1 Allowance should be made for the possibility that there may be cases of obesity even in conditions of widespread malnourishment. One argument in favour of

straightforward cash benefits in developed countries is that they would reduce stress among parents and the high incidence of obesity due to improved diets for children. See: 'Low-income moms under stress may over-feed infants'. http://www. eurekalert.org/pub_releases/2012-04/aaop-lmu042312.php; 'Fear of not having enough food may lead to obesity'. http://www.eurekalert.org/pub_releases/2012-04/aaop-fon042312.php

7

Schooling: Loosening Constraints, Boosting Education?

Introduction

The most widespread condition stipulated in conditional cash transfer (CCT) schemes in Latin America has been that recipients should send their children to school. As pointed out in Chapter 1, the trouble is that the financial and administrative costs of enforcement of this condition are always high, while the likelihood of having much permanent effect on parental or even child behaviour is low.

Above all, the moral implications of penalizing parents and children if they do not meet the conditions are unpleasant at best. And why should parents desperate for financial help be forced to do something when others are not? If school enrolment is mandatory, then the same rules should apply to all groups, with the same penalties.

The reason for rejecting conditionality is moral or ethical, not practical. Even if conditions could be shown to increase schooling, one would still oppose them on grounds of freedom. Conditions in most cases should be rejected on principle.

While the pilots did not apply any condition, one question that deserves to be answered is whether it is even necessary to apply conditionality. Are parents merely constrained by lack of money, so that if that constraint is loosened they will behave rationally, without being obliged to do so? In considering this, we also consider what aspects of schooling are affected by the basic income.

There are several possible effects. It may enable some families to spend on essential or useful items that enable their children to go to school more easily or cheaply. It may facilitate better eating habits – having breakfasts, most notably – giving children more energy and health, and thus making it more likely they will go to school and be able to learn properly while there. It may induce families to shift their children from public to private schools, or from a low-quality local school to a better one further away. The basic income may also facilitate payment for private tuition outside the school. And it may lessen the pressure on families to put their children to work or to labour on farms or do other labour.

Of course, all these aspects are linked. What this chapter tries to do is identify the direct relationships and the contextual trends taking place in the villages.

Schooling in rural Madhya Pradesh

India spends 3.1 per cent of its GDP on schooling, which is in the middle range in Asia (UNDP, 2013, p. 162). Across the country, numerous national and state schemes have been designed to promote schooling. Few have had unqualified success.

Madhya Pradesh has traditionally had a poor record in schooling. But successive state governments have tried to tackle the problems through a series of interventions. The Madhya Pradesh government has focused on improving literacy and enrolment in schools for over a decade, most notably through establishing more primary schools under the District Primary Education Programme, the Education Guarantee Scheme for primary education in the tribal areas since 1997, and the *Sarva Shiksha Abhiyan* since the 11th Five Year Plan.

Besides those initiatives, there has also been a CCT scholarship scheme known as *Baliki Samriddhi Yojana*, which started in 1997. This aims to create an environment that supports the birth of a girl child and her schooling so that she can become an educated and healthy adult. The scheme begins with a post-delivery grant of Rs.500 given to the mother. This is followed by annual scholarships at various stages of the girl's schooling up to grade 12. The scholarship is available as long as the girl remains unmarried and attends school regularly.

Then there are initiatives such as the *Akshaya Patra* and the Mid Day Meal Scheme. They are intended to ensure high school attendance and low drop-out rates, by providing an incentive for parents to send their children to school in the form of meals. But the performance of many of these schemes is patchy, due to administrative failure, lack of infrastructure and constant wrangling between bureaucracies that reflects the unclear sharing of responsibility for education, which is both a state and national matter in India. Several studies have shown the extent of these problems (Government of India, 2011).

Plate 1 Villagers at Awareness Meeting

Plate 2 Researcher at work

Plate 3 Women receiving cash from the Cooperative

Plate 4   Bank manager brought to village by SEWA to open accounts

Plate 5   Agricultural worker leaning on her home roof

Plate 6 Naukar at brick kiln

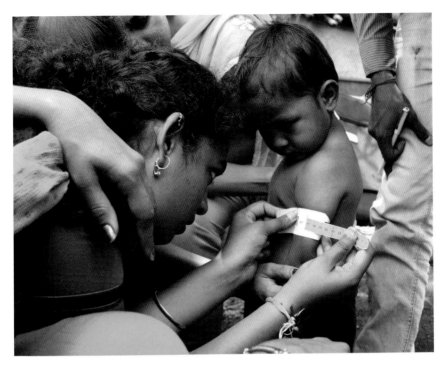

Plate 7   Measuring arm circumference

Plate 8   Schoolchildren at midday meal

Plate 9   Local SEWA leader with schoolchildren

Plate 10   Farmer standing near her cornfield

Plate 11 Members of fishermen's cooperative in Bhil tribal village

Plate 12 Farm labourer with newly purchased goat

Plate 13 SEWA organizer and woman with new sewing machine

Plate 14 SEWA rally

Plate 15 Mother receiving basic income on behalf of mentally challenged son

Plate 16 Elderly woman selling in the weekly market

The Mid Day Meal Scheme has long faced particularly severe misman-agement. The absence of local ('barefoot') functionaries for some public services, such as census enumeration, places an enormous burden on teachers because they are expected to help out, thus compromising the quality of primary education, which already is not at a high level.

Irrespective of administrative failure, the existence of these schemes makes it harder to isolate the effects of the basic income, although they do apply in all the villages equally. Our primary hypothesis is that the basic income helps to improve the *effectiveness* of schooling and could complement the government schemes in several respects.

Before we address the impact of basic income, it may be useful to look at the rubric of Madhya Pradesh's education system. At the time of the baseline survey, three features of the state's schooling system stood out. It was clear that government interventions had helped to increase the number of government primary schools; they had come to cover all parts of the state, including rural and tribal areas, thereby addressing the problem of low enrolment at primary school level.

However, the quality of public schooling and the high drop-out rate (more so for girls) remained critical challenges, while the spread of public schools had been matched by an increase in private commercial schools, unfunded by government (Narula, 2012). A growing number of students were enrolled in these schools.

The rapid proliferation of private schools since the 1990s is largely explained by the state government's liberalized registration guidelines. Legislation in 1994 meant that permission was no longer required to open private schools up to grade 4. Subsequent regulations liberalized secondary schooling, while taxes were made the same for government and private schools. The justifi-cation given at the time for liberalization was that strict regulations would be bypassed, and that privatization would reduce the burden on the public sector, which could then focus on students who could not afford private schooling (Leclercq, 2003).

The growth of private schools was checked by the Indian government's Right of Children to Free and Compulsory Education Act, which prescribed minimum requirements for private schools. But it did not reverse the trend. The Annual Status of Education Report of 2012 estimated that 20 per cent of rural primary-school students in Madhya Pradesh were registered in private schools in 2012, a four percentage point increase from 2010. The report also documented an increase in private tuition.

Hence a mixed public-private schooling system has emerged in rural Madhya Pradesh, with a few religious schools as well. Government schools are mostly used at primary level by low-income families, and compete with a growing number of fee-paying private schools; the latter are used not just by affluent families but also by a growing number of lower-income families.

While government primary schools have been established in many villages, schools above grade 10 or high schools are often located further away. For instance, the local government schools went up to grade 8 in the tribal villages of Ghodakhurd and Bhilami and up to grade 5 in Datoda. For further education, students had to travel to other villages. A similar situation applied to the general villages in the pilot, with the average distance being greater in the basic income villages.

There were a total of 3,061 children of school-going age (6–18 years) in the 20 general villages covered by the larger pilot. Nearly 45 per cent of them lived in basic income villages; 51 per cent were boys; nearly 36 per cent belonged to SC/ST households; 42 per cent were of primary school-going age (6–10 years), 27 per cent were in the 11–13 age cohort, and the remaining 31 per cent were of secondary school-going age.

So what were the effects of the basic income, bearing in mind that it was paid individually and unconditionally to all, including the children, and that the schooling system was essentially the same in all the villages? To examine this, detailed questions were asked in all the evaluation surveys. The findings reported in this chapter refer only to families with children who were usually resident in households in the basic income or control villages.

Questions about schooling and school-related spending were addressed to the mothers or surrogate mothers in all households in both basic income and control villages in the larger general pilot and in the tribal villages. In addition, data were gathered from a Teacher Perception Survey conducted in a sample of villages, with teachers interviewed about their perceptions of their students' attendance and performance. Data on actual school attendance and grades were also obtained from records in the schools where the children studied.

Recalling the hypotheses from studies of cash transfer schemes in other parts of the world, we start by considering the impact on spending, before turning to behavioural aspects. Strangely, the former has been given relatively little attention in the numerous studies elsewhere.

Basic income and school spending

Although government primary schools in Madhya Pradesh are nominally free, in that there are no fees to be paid, schooling always costs money, and many rural families cannot afford the direct or indirect costs associated with sending children to school without considerable difficulty. But it seems the basic income may have helped to unblock some of the constraints for many of those households.

The first set of findings came from the Interim Evaluation Survey, which showed that families with children in basic income villages were far more likely to have increased spending on schooling than similar families in control villages (Table 7.1). And many of those in the former attributed the increased spending directly to the basic income.

The Final Evaluation Survey essentially reproduced these findings, even if the differences were less pronounced, as shown in Figure 7.1. In most respects, SEWA did appear to have had a small independent effect, particularly with regard to private tuition.

By the end of the pilot, total expenditure by families on schooling was significantly higher in the basic income villages, by about 43 per cent on average. A particularly encouraging sign was that expenditure on schooling of girls was decidedly higher among households receiving the basic income. This effect was even greater among those in SEWA villages, where spending on girls' schooling increased by over 100 per cent, compared with just over 50 per cent in non-SEWA basic income villages.

The amount was still lower than that spent on boys, but the gap was substantially smaller, with expenditure on boys' schooling up by about 25

Table 7.1 General villages: Percentage of households with increased spending on school items, by receipt of basic income

Area of spending	Receiving basic income		Chi-square
	Yes	No	
School uniforms	47.7	28.6	34.025***
School fees	44.6	29.3	21.936***
Shoes for going to school	52.2	42.1	8.944***
School books, pens	58.5	45.3	15.474***
Private tuition	19.7	7.1	29.059***

Source: MPUCT IES, 2012; n = 893

Figure 7.1 General villages: Percentage of households with increased spending on school items, by type of village

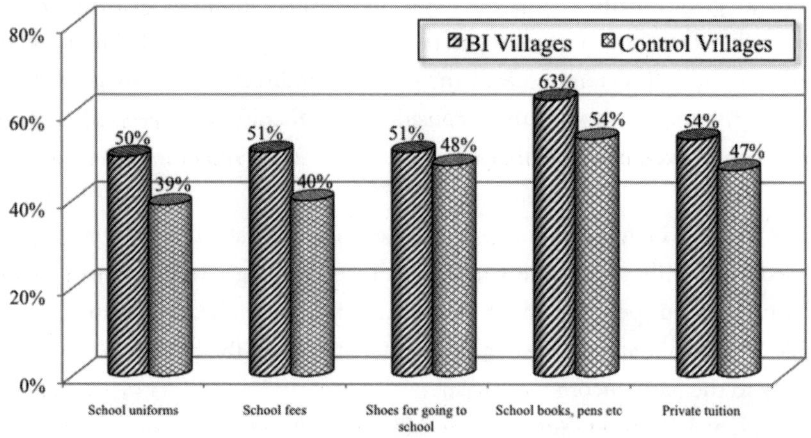

Source: MPUCT FES, 2012; n= 1337

per cent in SEWA basic income villages and no change at all in non-SEWA villages.

A similar positive development occurred among the relatively vulnerable scheduled caste and scheduled tribe families. The basic income was positively linked to spending for all caste groups. But while still not spending as much on sending their children to school as those from other groups, SC/ST households receiving the basic income in SEWA villages spent more than their counterparts who did not receive the basic income. And the increase occurred for all age groups, as shown by Figure 7.2.

In the tribal village pilot, similar findings were observed. Whereas there was no difference in the total spending in the two villages at the outset, by the time of the final evaluation there was a 17 per cent difference. This was entirely due to an increase in spending on girls in the basic income village, which increased by a remarkable 88 per cent. Spending on school fees for girls more than doubled.

Meanwhile, spending on boys' schooling actually fell a little. The main reason seems to have been that more families sent their boys to stay in a government hostel outside the village. The big decline came in fees, whereas spending on transport to school and on school uniforms actually increased.

In sum, the most striking finding is that spending on girls' schooling was significantly boosted by the basic income. One contributory factor was a practice monitored by the evaluation surveys, that of pooling money from the individual

Figure 7.2   General villages: Percentage of households spending more than Rs.500 on schooling, by age cohort and type of village

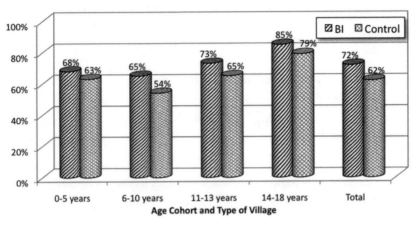

Source: MPUCT FES, 2012

basic incomes. Teenage girls were the primary beneficiary. Without the basic income, teenage boys were given priority in limited spending. The basic income allowed the girls in that age group to catch up, and this was achieved in many cases by families pooling part of their basic incomes to pay for it.

In some cases, implicit pooling of money took place, in that families allowed their offspring to use their basic incomes for school-related spending while using their own to pay for other expenses. A moving case was that of a 55-year-old Bhil woman, an agricultural labourer by trade, who was asked how the basic income money was being spent in her household. Asked by the enumeration team about her elder son, who had physical disabilities but who was studying in 10th grade, she said firmly:

> I don't take his money at all, sir! He studies, so he needs that money for his books and conveyance to go for tuition. He withdraws from the bank whenever he wants money for his studies. So far he has withdrawn twice: 600 Rupees and 500 Rupees. With the 600 Rupees he had his tricycle repaired. It has been lying around because we didn't have money to have it repaired. With his second withdrawal, he bought clothes and paid tuition fees.

Her case nicely illustrates the power of individual autonomy, emancipation. Another common practice was more coordinated pooling, and this was often to enable girl teenagers to gain what they were otherwise denied. One mother covered by the case studies told the enumeration team:

I have two daughters who are studying in Indore; they live in my brother's house where my father also lives. Until the cash transfer money came, my father used to bear all their expenses. But now, since cash transfers started I have been contributing to their upkeep, and also paying their monthly school fees from the cash transfers. The annual expenditure is 15,000 Rupees for stay and food.

That is not to say that only teenage girls benefited from family pooling their basic incomes. Another typical case involved what seems to be a common trend of sending children out of the village for schooling. A grandmother described her family's decision-making:

My daughter's son, who stays with us, studies in Choral-Dam school, where the school fee is 4,000 Rupees. This year we paid his fees by saving up the cash transfer money. Last year we had to sell wheat to pay the fees.

Note one point about that family's behaviour, highlighted in Chapter 3, which shows the emancipatory value of the basic income. It helped them to avoid having to sell their one marketable commodity at a time that might have been inconvenient or when it could not be sold at a good price. The basic income had given them greater control over their decision-making, lessening the strain of having to decide between food, in the form of the wheat, and extra schooling for their children.

School registration or enrolment

The next set of considerations concern school enrolment, school attendance and school performance. The impact on the first could be expected to be limited to secondary school level, since registration is mandatory at primary school level. But even primary school enrolment is worth examining, in that not every child is registered in reality.

It is generally recognized that primary school enrolment or registration is now close to universal in most of India. The Ministry of Human Resource Development estimated that across India, the non-enrolment rate of young children aged 6 to 10 years was merely 3.7 per cent in 2008 and 5.2 per cent for those aged 11 to 13 years, although non-registration was greater in rural areas.

We found non-registration at primary school level to be minimal in the villages covered by the pilots. Even so, by the end of the pilot registration was higher in the basic income villages, for both boys and girls.

The most striking development was that the extent of secondary school enrolment was significantly higher in the basic income villages, as shown by Table 7.2. Clearly, the major difference was that teenage girls were taken out of school much more than boys in the control villages.

The FES data suggested that the basic incomes checked the tendency for teenagers, particularly girls, to drop out and it did so quite strongly. While only 36 per cent of girls of secondary school-going age in control villages were enrolled in school, 65 per cent of girls of the same age cohort were going to school in basic income villages. We regard this as a major beneficial effect of the basic income, and a testament to the rationality of village families.

Secondary school enrolment levels, particularly for girls, were highest in SEWA basic income villages, compared with both the non-SEWA basic income villages and the control villages. While there were no differences for younger age groups, SEWA was positively associated with a bigger increase in secondary school enrolment by girls.

These positive results should be appreciated as coming from a context in which drop-out rates for teenage girls have traditionally been very high, due to early marriage, distance to schools, lack of separate toilets in schools, lack of female teachers, concerns about safety and demands for their time in household chores, including looking after younger siblings. According to research, across India about one-third of teenage girls drop out for these reasons (UNICEF, 2011, p. 22). So, the positive effects of the basic income are particularly significant.

There were also modest differences by social groups. The basic income seemed to have aided enrolment of teenagers in all social groups, with those belonging to SC/ST households benefiting slightly less than those from other category households, as shown in Table 7.3.

Table 7.2 General villages: School enrolment by type of village, age and gender (percent of age group enrolled in school)

Age (in years)	Male		Female		Total	
	BI villages	Control villages	BI villages	Control villages	BI villages	Control villages
6–10	98.0	93.5	97.3	94.3	97.6	93.9
11–13	94.8	96.7	96.5	83.6	95.7	90.1
14–18	84.4	65.6	65.0	36.1	76.0	51.3

Source: MPUCT FES, 2012; n=3061

Table 7.3   General villages: School enrolment by type of village, by age and social group (percent of age group enrolled in school)

Age (in years)	Scheduled caste/tribe		Other groups	
	Bi villages	Control villages	BI villages	Control villages
6–10	97.7	91.4	97.6	95.4
11–13	95.6	88.4	95.7	91.4
14–18	73.3	51.4	77.1	51.2

Source: MPUCT FES, 2012; n=3061

While secondary school enrolment was higher by nearly 25 percentage points for children from 'Other' category households in the basic income villages, the difference for SC/ST teenagers was about 22 percentage points. Again, the major underlying trend seemed to be that the basic income reduced the tendency of children to drop out at the end of primary school.

Similar results were found in the tribal village pilot. There was a drop in overall enrolment rates in both villages, which may have had something to do with a relative shift in the number of teenagers compared to the number of younger children. However, the key point is that whereas overall enrolment was higher in the control village at the baseline, it was substantially higher in the basic income village by the end of the pilot.

Finally, to test the effect of the basic income more systematically, we estimated a set of logit functions in which the dependent variable was the household's self-reported enrolment of their children expressed as a binary variable.

The standard statistical practice is to calculate odds ratios using the enrolment rate as the indicator of success (Baird et al., 2013, p. 24). However, in the general pilot, for reasons explained earlier, we made sure that everybody in one set of villages received the basic income and nobody in others did so. This implies that there is a possibility of intra-cluster correlation in the outcome variable, which may lead to smaller standard errors, so overstating the precision of the estimate.

With this caveat, and acknowledging that we cannot trace causality fully, we estimated a multivariate logistic regression to assess the determinants of the probability of enrolment. The vast international literature on schooling suggests that key determinants to be taken into account as control variables are age, gender, land ownership (as a proxy for poverty), household size, gender and education of the household head, as defined in the Appendix.

Table 7.4 reports the odds of being enrolled in school, with the first column being for the whole sample, the second and third reporting the results for girls

Table 7.4   General villages: Odds of children being enrolled in school

Variable	Coefficients		
	Overall	**Girls**	**Boys**
Constant	9.3927***	5.8317***	4.818***
Basic income	2.7675***	3.3868***	2.3469***
Land ownership	1.7345***	1.0930	2.9634***
Household size	1.0749***	1.0750**	1.0838*
Gender	0.3845***		
10–13 years	0.5491***	0.3690***	1.0363
14–18 years	0.0600***	0.0365***	0.1137***
Female-headed household	1.2576	1.6188	0.9865
Household head's education	1.7199***	1.9220***	1.4697*

Source: MPUCT FES, 2012; n= 3061

and boys separately. The results show that the basic income had a significant positive effect on enrolment, particularly for girls. Indeed, the basic income seemed to more than double the odds of a child being enrolled in school. If receiving the basic income, girls also had higher odds of joining or staying in school as compared to boys at both primary and secondary school age.

Land ownership, a proxy for wealth, was a greater predictor of the odds of children being in school than household size, particularly for boys. Separate regressions were run for SEWA and non-SEWA villages, to test for the effect of Voice. The results were similar, except that in the SEWA villages, the probability of a child in a female-headed household going to school was higher.

In sum, the data and case studies show that the basic income improved school enrolment rates, most dramatically in the case of teenage girls.

School attendance

Across India today, at both primary and secondary school levels, non-attendance by children represents a much bigger challenge than non-registration. The Annual Status of Education Report of 2009 concluded that on any particular day only about 75 per cent of all those registered in primary school were actually attending school (UNICEF, 2011).

A primary hypothesis is that a basic income would result in an improvement in school attendance. The results from the IES suggested that this took place quite quickly. School attendance, as reported by mothers, was significantly more likely to have increased in basic income villages in the initial period of the pilot.

Nearly two-thirds of those in basic income villages reported an improvement, compared with less than a quarter in the control villages.

Although it does not do so as dramatically, this difference was also brought out in the FES (Figure 7.3). Table 7.5 shows that the difference was statistically highly significant, and that there was also a statistically significant difference between SEWA and non-SEWA villages.

Attendance was improved in both scheduled caste/tribe households and in others, with 30 per cent reporting improvement in both groups in the basic income villages. This represented a bigger improvement for the scheduled caste or tribe households, as only 12 per cent of their counterparts in the control villages reported an improvement compared to 17 per cent for other groups.

Census and NSS data show that school attendance rates have been much lower for scheduled caste and scheduled tribe children (UNICEF, 2011, p. 25). So, the results are encouraging, in that they show a progressive impact, being greater for the more vulnerable social categories. There was no difference by gender, with an equal proportion of boys and girls reporting improvement in attendance in basic income villages.

As is well known, various intermediary factors, such as health and nutrition, affect school attendance, and a basic income raises attendance through affecting

Figure 7.3   General villages: Percentage of households reporting higher school attendance in past 12 months, by type of village

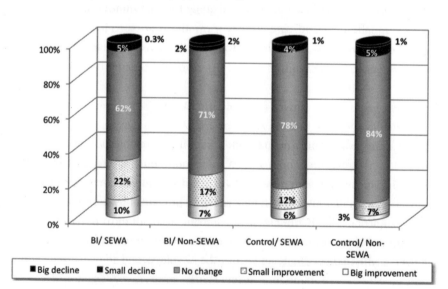

Source: MPUCT FES, 2012; n=1369

Table 7.5   General villages: Percentage of households reporting higher school attendance in past 12 months, by type of village

	Yes	No	Chi-square
Receiving basic income	29.0	13.5	49.243***
SEWA village	25.2	16.6	15.082***

Source: MPUCT FES, 2012; n=1369

some of these factors. In basic income villages, illness was reported by parents as the main reason for school absenteeism, followed by the claim that the child lacked interest in school. By contrast, in the control villages the most common reason given for absenteeism was lack of interest, followed by illness, being required to work for the family and transport issues.

One may speculate on the underlying dynamics, without being able to go beyond that. One could say that illness was the most common reason for absenteeism in the basic income villages mainly because other impediments had diminished. We know that illness was less common in the basic income villages, as shown in Chapter 6. But lack of interest as the main reason prompts the question: was it a rationalization by parents, a reflection of inadequate schools or teachers, or because children in the control villages were less likely to have good home breakfasts and healthcare?

Besides parental reports of changes in attendance, we consulted school attendance ledgers that both government and private schools are meant to maintain. Because of the cost and protracted work involved in mining the attendance ledgers, data were taken from a sample of eight villages for this purpose (four basic income, four control). Records for the school year 2011–12 were used to assess any change in attendance. Using these, it appeared that while absenteeism actually increased in control villages, it remained more or less the same in the basic income villages during 2011–12. So, there was a relative improvement in the basic income villages.

The decline in absenteeism in the basic income villages was concentrated among scheduled caste and scheduled tribe schoolchildren. If they were attending school more regularly, this can only be regarded as a progressive development. And the decline in absenteeism was exclusively found in government school records (falling from 23 per cent to 17 per cent, compared with no change in private schools), suggesting that this was one way by which the basic income was actually strengthening a public social service.

School registers are not very reliable. Regrettably, there is a reason for schools to falsify attendance records, as they can be penalized or even closed if the authorities deem that they have been remiss in their management. However, we may presume that the degree of falsification is random across the villages and the extent of falsification would not have changed systematically in the period covered by the pilot. And in cross-checking the registers with the reported perceptions by parents, we found a general consistency in the responses.

Furthermore, many students in the basic income villages were going to schools that were some distance away from their homes and the children were scattered over many schools. So there was unlikely to be a systematic bias in the records. To add further credence to the data, children from the basic income villages, on average, had further to go to schools, particularly those going to secondary school. So, their lower absenteeism is doubly impressive.

The higher attendance rates shown by the evaluation surveys and by the school registers probably reflect the prior influence on nutrition and health and the immediate effect of extra spending on such items as transport, shoes and uniforms. No longer dirty or having an unkempt appearance, children were more likely to attend school without a sense of shame.

We must acknowledge that we did not find any difference between attendance rates in the two tribal villages; just under a third of households with school-age children in both villages reported a big improvement in attendance.

Returning to the general villages, a set of three logistic functions was estimated, with the same variables as for the enrolment probability. These showed that for all children and for boys and girls separately, controlling for other household factors, the basic income was strongly and significantly associated with high attendance.

School performance

The third dimension is actual performance in school, which we had antici-pated would be less affected, in that it takes time to change. But already by the time of the IES, by comparison with control village families, many more of those receiving the basic income reported that their children's school perfor-mance had improved in the previous six months. The relative figures were 68 per cent and 36 per cent, a highly significant difference (Chi-squared= 61.516***).

While more parents in basic income SEWA villages said the performance of their children had improved considerably over the period of the pilot, when those reporting a small improvement were included, there was no difference

Figure 7.4   General villages: Percentage of households reporting improvement in school performance in last 12 months, by type of village

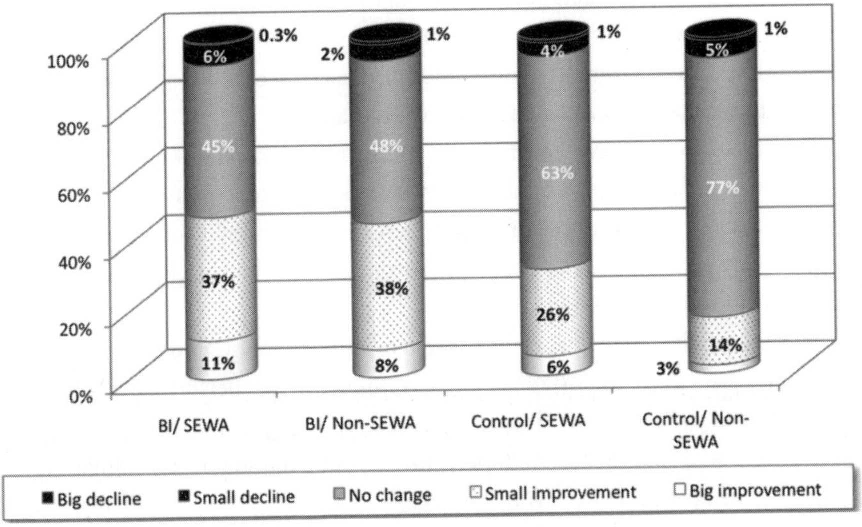

Source: MPUCT FES, 2012; n=1290

between SEWA and non-SEWA villages. By the time of the FES, slightly more parents in SEWA villages receiving the basic income than in non-SEWA villages reported an improvement in school performance (Figure 7.4). But the main story was the strong positive effect of the basic income.

As with school attendance, the difference in perceived improvement in performance was slightly higher for SC/ST children than for children from other categories. No differences were observed by gender.

Again, we can obtain a clue to the dynamics from the range of responses to the question addressed to parents of children who were not performing well in school. In the basic income villages, about 40 per cent of mothers attributed this to poor teaching. That was the most common reason given. By contrast, in the control villages about 60 per cent attributed poor performance to their children's lack of concentration or lack of interest. So, we may speculate that in the basic income villages, the children were more prepared for school, able to concentrate better or were more motivated.

We also studied the performance records for children from a sample of the villages. School records were obtained for both half-yearly and annual evaluations at four points – October 2011 and October 2012, to compare performance records at the half-yearly evaluation stage, and February 2011 and February 2012 to compare annual performance records and changes.

Overall, the register data revealed no significant differences in performance of children coming from basic income villages over the 12-month period. However, children from ST households in basic income villages seemed to record the greatest improvement in terms of grades.

Private schools tended to grade the performance of children higher than government schools. This could suggest leniency on their part to show better performance to attract more children. In government schools too, performance records may be suspect because of the pressure to show that children make it to the next grade.

In the tribal villages, a slightly higher proportion of households in the basic income village reported an improvement in the performance of their children than in the control village. The share reporting that their children were performing well rose by nearly 20 percentage points in the former, compared to 17 percentage points in the control village.

In sum, the basic income was associated with an improvement in performance in school, due almost certainly to the effects on factors like diet, transport, better clothes and better morale. It may also have had something to do with changes in the type of school, which we consider now.

Basic income: Accelerating school privatization?

In recent years, in the rural area covered by the basic income pilots, there has been a huge expansion in the number of private fee-paying schools, covering all three divisions of the Indore District in which the villages are located, Depalpur, Indore and Mhow (Narula, 2012).

Justifiably or not, the simple idea has spread that government schools are bad, private schools are good. This has been helped by aggressive marketing by private schools and by the apparent apathy in the government school system. Private schools have adopted novel and energetic marketing strategies, including making calls on parents to discuss their children and sending teachers to visit homes to enquire about their children's studies. Some private schools have begun to send buses to pick up the children in the morning and drop them back after school, cutting out the need to walk or cycle long distances.

The research team also heard of some private schools offering 'discounts', such as charging no fee for a third child if two siblings were enrolled in the school. We were also told how easy it was to open a private school up to grade 4. These establishments were usually ramshackle and small, run from the home of an educated village youth. No doubt the ease of setting up little units has contributed to a related phenomenon that exists in rural Madhya Pradesh, which is considerable movement between private schools.

The fact was that, although there was already a trend towards going to private schools, it seemed to have been accelerated by the basic income. There were many examples. Thus, one scheduled tribe landholding family told the enumeration team:

> All the four children of my *jeth* [elder brother-in-law] go to school. The elder son Yashvant stays in a government hostel near Mahu where he is studying. Everything including food and lodging is free of cost there. And the education is good. Yashvant is in 6th grade. The other three children go to private school at Choral-Dam. We only put them in private school this year, thanks to the cash transfer money.

In this case, the private school seems to have provided cost-saving extras. However, often private schools were found to be charging a considerable amount in bits and pieces for their services. In one used by children in the tribal control village, we found a graduated school fee structure, in which children in nursery, lower kindergarten (LKG) and upper kindergarten (UKG) levels were charged Rs.200 per month, 1st and 2nd grades Rs.220, 3rd and 4th grades Rs.240, 5th and 6th grades Rs.260, 7th and 8th grades Rs. 300, 9th and 10th grades Rs.350, and 11th and 12th grades Rs.400.

This was in addition to the enrolment fee, and there was an additional exam fee of Rs.500 to permit the student to take the high-school examination, a 'development charge' of up to Rs.800 annually and the cost of books and stationery of up to Rs.600 a year. One wonders if parents realize in advance the full extent of the costs once they have enrolled their children in such schools.

Against their unquestionably high costs, some private schools are playing a positive role in their wider communities. The remarks of the principal of one private school deserve to be quoted verbatim:

> It has been 8–9 years since the school was opened. Children from all the local villages come here. Our school is from LKG to 12th grade. We have to run the school on two shifts. Our fees are less than other private schools around here. The annual fee for the LKG-UKG children is just 1,500 Rupees, with no other fee for admission and so on. We ask for the fee on a half-yearly basis during the

soybean/corn and wheat harvest seasons. But a lot of people do not deposit the money even during the harvest. If we ask the children about the school fee, they may stop coming to school for 8–15 days. That is why we do not pressurize them too much about the fee, especially for girls. We don't say anything about the school fee to the girls because their parents anyway don't send them to school and if we pester them about the fee they won't send them at all. So we take from them whenever they have money and can pay.

At our school we give a full fee concession to one child if two other children from the same family are paying fees. And if a woman is a widow, we only charge half the actual fee. Because I am from a nearby village, I want the children of our area to study and become able persons.

The cash transfers have made a difference. But my suggestion is that you deposit the money in the children's bank accounts for their education, so that the money can be used only for their education. When parents come, they tell us about the cash transfer money and say they will deposit the school fee.

The latter sentiment, while understandable, would necessitate extensive bureaucratic interventions that would be costly and intrusive. Who would determine whether the money was spent on schooling? Limiting choice on spending would also be clumsy and probably counterproductive. A constraint to a child attending school might be an illness requiring the purchase of medicines. Or the child might lack shoes that fit. Paradoxically, if the money could be spent only on school items, that might actually be to the child's disadvantage if something else was the real constraint.

Returning to the trend towards private schooling, the difficulty of analysing the effect of the basic income is compounded by the fact that there is a trend in that direction across rural Madhya Pradesh. Moreover, in the non-tribal villages, the share of children going to private schools was higher in the basic income villages than in the control villages before the pilot began. That meant there was less scope for a shift to private schools.

In the tribal villages, although there was scarcely any shift from government to private schools in the control village, in the basic income village the share of children in private schools rose from 19 per cent to 29 per cent during the course of the pilot. It surely had a pronounced effect.

The reality of schooling in Madhya Pradesh is that there is disillusion with government schools as they are perceived to exist. Many villagers described them as poor and as having unaccountable or absent teachers. In one of the basic income villages where SEWA was operating, we witnessed a mass protest by women against a teacher from the government school. They were demanding that SEWA should do something about the teacher, claiming she slept during the day and was rude to the children and parents.

There was anecdotal evidence that the basic income raised the villagers' aspirations for their children. People reported that after the cash started many parents took the decision that they had previously contemplated but found too daunting or expensive, to move their child from a government school to a private school. This might not have been anticipated, since it represented a decision with longer-term implications. It seems some believed that somehow they would be able to sustain that extra cost.

There were of course some parents whose children were studying in government schools who were adamant that they could not afford to shift them to a private school. An example was Santoshbhai in Sahavada village, who told the case study team that she could not afford to send her children to a private school, and did not even aspire to send them there.

However, quite evidently, the general trend towards privatization was strengthened by the arrival of the basic income. That should be a clarion call to the government school authorities that they need to improve.

Private tuition

There is one form of private schooling that is a potential complement to both mainstream government and private schooling. Private tuition is a growing and potentially valuable phenomenon in Madhya Pradesh villages. It can enable some children who have been set back in school by illness, or by other demands on their time, to catch up on missed school. It can also help slow learners and enable some bright children to learn more on selected topics that interest them. The reasons are usually creditable. Typically, one father told the case study enumeration team:

> Last year, one of our children in 12th grade failed at maths. He then took private tuition with the help of the cash grants, and passed his 12th grade exam.

More generally, the evidence from the FES suggests that the basic income had a small but significantly positive effect on spending on private tuition. Such tuition seems destined to play a major role in the future of Indian education.

Transport and hostels

There remains one general constraint to schooling to consider, transport to and from school. As many secondary-school students must go a long way to their school, most must be able to pay for acceptable transport. And because of the shift to private schools and the rise in enrolment in secondary schools, many teenagers have further to go.

The data from the evaluation surveys showed that a rising share of pupils were travelling more than six kilometres to reach their school; this development had taken place only in the basic income villages, where the share doing so rose from 6 per cent of the total to over 15 per cent. There was also an increase in the relative number of children going to school by bus.

This was shown most dramatically in the tribal villages. At the time of the baseline, the proportion of children walking to school was roughly the same in both tribal villages. But by the FES, many more children in the basic income village were taking a private bus to school, nearly 16 per cent compared to just 2 per cent in the control village, where the proportion walking to school had actually increased.

There was also a trend towards more children staying in school hostels. According to the FES, this was occurring in both the basic income and control villages, without much difference. But in the basic income tribal village there was a sharp increase in the number doing so, which was not replicated in the control village. There was also a significant increase in school-related migration in the basic income tribal village, which was also unmatched in the control village.

So, in sum, the basic income facilitated a shift to more commercialized schooling and helped parents select from a wider range of school options. That could be said to have benefited their welfare and development potential.

Concluding reflections

The unconditional basic income facilitated and encouraged more intensive schooling and helped to unblock some major constraints. The data testify to the diverse ways it did so, as did some of the poignant stories related to the case study enumeration team.

An example was Chandaben, a 45-year old widow who was a wage labourer from the SEWA village of Jagmalpipliya, whose circumstances showed how the basic income had helped:

My husband passed away two months ago due to a kidney failure, and because of that our condition has become very bad. My only source of income is casual labour, which also is not available regularly. Our main expenditure is on food. I buy food items for only five to ten days because I have very little money. My eldest son is 20 years old. He and I are the only two people who go to work in my family. My three other sons go to school. They get lunch in the school, and they recently got money for their uniform. After my husband's demise, my son Narendra and I increased our hours of labour, but one of my sons is mentally challenged, so he is not able to do much labour. Employers easily exploit him. Three of my boys are studying and we have to bear the expenditure for their education. This money has helped us a lot. If it were not for it, we would have had to send our children for labour work. But because of this money we were able to send them to school.

However, not everyone was able to use the basic income to overcome the pressures. The research team also came across children dropping out of the school system, in spite of the basic income. An example was Mamatabai of Panthbadodia, whose youngest child was on the verge of dropping out of school when the basic income started. From subsequent interviews with her, it was noticed that despite the payments, she was resigned to taking him out of school in the following year.

Another woman, Ramkanya in Panthbadodia, told us that her daughter had to drop out of school because of the terminal illness of her husband. The basic income helped the family improve their food intake, and also helped her two sons live by themselves, studying and working in Indore. However, it was unable to stop their daughter from dropping out from studies.

Ironically, in Mamatabai's case, she was thinking of taking her youngest son out of school but, when we met her, had not decided to take her daughter Anita out of school. Anita was 15 and was studying in 7th grade in the government school in the neighbouring village of Rolai, three kilometres away. The point is that the basic income influenced the dynamics of decision-making and was doing so in generally positive ways.

The case studies highlighted how individual family circumstances influence the decisions to enrol a child or maintain him or her in school. The basic income might have changed the calculus. Or it might have had its effect indirectly, in enabling families to pay for medicine or food. It may not have had a direct effect on some, since a family would have known that the additional costs of schooling would remain once the basic income stopped.

Although a more prolonged pilot would be needed to assess the impact of a basic income on sustained learning, the evidence from these pilots is generally encouraging. The impact of unconditional income on schooling depends also on the amount of basic income relative to household income.

The short period covered by the pilots makes it impossible to trace the effect of basic income on related behaviour, such as early marriage or teenage pregnancy among girls, that determine schooling. Other studies have found that unconditional transfers do tend to lead to delayed marriages and make a difference to pregnancy (Baird et al., 2013).

The clearest effects of the unconditional basic income were on school-related spending and secondary-school enrolment, particularly of girls, and most in SEWA villages. The basic income also seemed to improve school attendance and performance of children from vulnerable scheduled tribes, who are under most pressure to put their children to work on family farms or as household help, given the abject conditions in which these families live.

It is for these children that the individualized basic income seems to make the most difference. In that regard, it could be said to have had a significant development effect, while being emancipatory in breaking constraints on children's learning.

8

Work, Productivity and Growth

Introduction

A basic income has usually been discussed as a way of reducing poverty and economic insecurity, as a welfare measure. To the limited extent that it has been considered as a development measure, it has been regarded dismissively, as reducing labour supply.

However, suppose it had powerful pro-growth qualities. This would not only promote development; it could also do so in a way that is consistent with the *Swadeshi* Principle outlined in Chapter 1. In this regard, it must be emphasized that economic growth can take several forms.

The conventional variety relies on large-scale production, with export orientation or import-substituting industrialization. But there is another way that respects the *Swadeshi* Principle, one involving steady additions to production in and around agriculture and small-scale production of basic goods and services. Many of these go unmeasured by national economic statistics and some go unrecognized as productive but add to personal and community development.

There is a common opinion among the comfortably well-off that if the poor were given some money they would become lazy, would reduce their supply of time and effort to labour and work, and would thus cause a decline in economic production. It is a comforting opinion, since it can be used to justify treating the poor with disdain and to justify paternalistic policies based on a presumption that 'the poor' cannot make rational decisions for themselves.

This returns us to one of the most controversial aspects of a basic income. Would it lead to less production and work or would it break constraints and promote a circle of growing productivity, greater energy and thus more rapid and sustainable economic growth? These pilots were a way of testing the impact. The outcome was not easy to disentangle or one-dimensional.

Let us start by recalling the pattern of economic activity in Madhya Pradesh villages. Across India, there are supposed to be nearly 650,000 villages, and they vary considerably in character. So we cannot be sure that what might be observed in the survey villages would be replicated everywhere else, even though they were selected randomly. However, the findings we will be reporting do seem likely to occur in other villages, simply because they reveal patterns of rational human behaviour.

The main activity in all the 20 general villages and in the two tribal villages was farming, growing a mix of wheat, soya and various vegetables combined with livestock rearing. Over four out of every five households were either landless or, more likely, owned a smallholding of under two hectares. Alongside these smallholdings, about one in every hundred had farms of more than ten hectares and a few landlord farmers had imposing estates of much more than that.

These landlords had pulled the economic strings for generations, controlling wage rates for agricultural labour and setting prices for local produce. One way or another, they had put many villagers into their debt and bolstered their economic position by luring a significant number of families into a form of bonded labour, discussed in Chapter 3. This had shaped the character of labour force participation, since under the *naukar* arrangement anybody trapped in it had to be on standby to provide labour on the landlord's farm whenever required, thereby acting as a considerable constraint on what they might do with their time.

Beyond the *naukar* system, most families traditionally tried to survive with a mix of farm labour, own-account farming, a little other non-farm work in and around their homes, and seasonal and other migration for labour.

Labour migration

The amount of migration in the 20 villages covered by the larger pilot had tended to be very low and seasonal in character. The basic income did not seem to have made much difference to the extent of out-migration among most groups. However, seasonal migration in tribal villages was as high as 25 per cent, which fluctuated over the year.

Superficially, the impact of the basic incomes on migration seemed minimal, in that the overall level of migration hardly changed during the course of the pilots. However, on closer inspection what happened was that the nature of the migration changed. In the basic income villages, labour-related migration declined a little but was compensated by an increase in school-related migration. This was particularly pronounced in the tribal village, by comparison with the control village. But it applied in general across all villages.

As one woman, Harlibai, from a scheduled tribe household, told the case study enumerators:

> Now because of the cash transfers, we rarely go outside the village for work. This has a positive effect on the children's schooling and health as well … Earlier, villagers had to go out of the village for labour; now they work only in the village.

Going out of a village for labour may have a detrimental effect on the children's schooling since the children often have to travel with their parents. We discussed the schooling developments in Chapter 7. But we can tentatively conclude that the change in type of movement was potentially beneficial, particularly if the decline in labour-related migration reflected productive developments in the villages. Travel for schooling replaced some travel that was disruptive of schooling.

The impact on economic activity

The inflow of the basic incomes seemed to result in a significant increase in local income-earning activity. By the time of the FES, many more households in the basic income villages had increased their earned incomes than was the case in the control villages, and many fewer had experienced a fall in earned income than in the control villages.

Figure 8.1 shows this for the four types of village. It is clear that the change was associated with the basic income rather than with SEWA, although a small positive effect associated with SEWA is possible. This is a testament to the growth-augmenting impact of a basic income, which should be factored into any estimate of the fiscal cost of it.

Among those households that had increased income-earning activity, nearly three-quarters (73.4 per cent) attributed that to the basic income. And among those that had experienced a decline in earned income, almost all said that the reduction had nothing to do with the basic income.

The increase in earned income could have come from increased investment – seeds, fertilizers, other raw materials and the purchase of tools and equipment. Or it could have come from increased work and labour. Or it could have come

Figure 8.1   General villages: Households with change in household income, by type of village

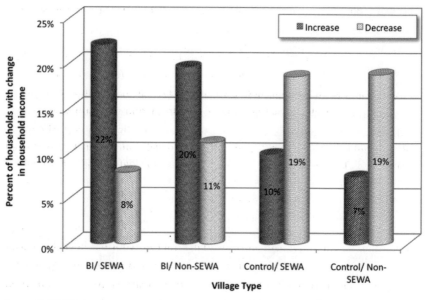

Source: MPUCT FES, 2012; n=2034

from some of both. We will come back to the impact on investment later in the chapter. The initial intriguing story relates to how the basic income induced a set of changes in work and labour that were almost transformational in themselves.

Child labour and work

Before going any further, it is worth considering the impact of the basic income on child labour and work, which is both a welfare and developmental matter, with implications for economic growth. Child labour is an emotive issue, and remains pervasive across India. In 2012, the Indian government announced that it intended to introduce a complete ban on the employment of children under the age of 14, tightening the restrictions in the 1986 Child Labour Act.

Unfortunately, as long as impoverishment continues, children will be used economically by their families, if they can. The questions most pertinent in the pilots were whether or not the basic income would lead to a reduction in child labour, and if so, of what types of work and labour?

Traditionally, child labour has been either a substitute for schooling or a complement to it. In the former case, it has obviously blocked off any development of the children's learning capacities, beyond the important ability to survive in difficult circumstances. In the latter case, it has typically limited their intellectual development if it has been extensive and arduous.

As it turned out, the extent of child labour in the general villages, in terms of wage labour, was not substantial, although many children did some farm work on family landholdings and many also did household chores. The latest official survey showed that 4.8 per cent of children aged 5 to 14 in Indore District in 2010 were doing some form of economic activity, for cash or in kind. So, while not very extensive, child labour was persisting.

In rural areas, even when attending school, most children are expected to help the family if there is work to be done. Most girls do some housework or childcare. Both boys and girls participate in grazing the animals and work on family farms during harvest time. Those families who are living mainly by wage labour often take their children with them to help earn a little more. Traditionally, in Indore District, schools have adjusted their schedules and holidays to accommodate the planting and harvest seasons, when the whole family is typically in the fields from dawn to dusk.

For both the general and tribal villages, the baseline and both evaluation surveys probed the extent of child labour and work, covering activities done for wages, activities done to help on a farm, activities done to produce something for sale or barter, and activities done in and around the home, including care work.

As expected, the probability of a child doing any form of work was closely linked to their age. Accordingly, children were divided into three age groups – 5–8, 9–14, 15–18 years – and the probability of doing any labour rose with age.

In the general villages overall, by the time of the IES, only about 12 per cent of households had children doing wage labour. There did not seem to have been any significant changes since the basic incomes had begun. But of those that reported a reduction in child labour, most said the children had increased the amount of time devoted to schooling.

However, by the time of the FES, there was evidence that child wage labour had been cut in households receiving the basic income, with over a third doing so, compared with under a quarter in the control villages. The SEWA villages in particular saw a reduction in children's work, in both basic income and control villages. This occurred in both wage work and work on the family farm.

Overall, among families with children, of those who had children doing labour at the outset, 26 per cent of families in the basic income SEWA villages and 13 per cent in the basic income non-SEWA villages reported that their children had stopped wage labour. Those figures compared with less than 6 per cent saying that in the control villages. This was encouraging.

In most of the families reporting an end to child labour, their children had been doing wage labour. And the major result in the basic income villages was a shift from wage labour to own-account farm work. Such work is more complementary with schooling, or at least potentially so.

As so often, the changes were particularly pronounced in the tribal village. In the basic income village, there was a pronounced shift from wage labour to own-account farm work and to own-account non-farm work. This explained why only 16 per cent of basic income families said that their children's economic work had a disruptive effect on their schooling, compared with 37 per cent of comparable families in the control village. One could conclude that the basic income had a beneficial effect on the type of work and indirectly also on schooling.

Among older teenagers, there was a similar story. While there was not much change in the overall level of economic activity during the pilot, in the basic income villages there was a shift from wage labour to own-account work on family farms.

Child work will not disappear in the near future. One should not dismiss its contribution to economic growth, partly by freeing up time of adults to do other productive activities. What is vital is that work done by children should not disrupt their learning opportunities. In this respect, the basic income seemed to be doubly beneficial.

Main and second economic activities

Turning to the overall picture of labour and work, we may begin by reminding ourselves that the complex links with basic income – or any policy intervention – are very rarely considered in anything like their entirety.

The usual practice has been to look at one variable as a proxy for labour supply, such as 'labour force participation', a binary for being in economic activity or not, where the status is defined usually as 'main' activity. This project has tried to go further than that.

To analyse what happens, work and labour should be disaggregated into their components. Thus to start with, there is work in and around the home, in caring for children or others, and in doing 'housework'. Beyond that, there are two types of what is regarded as 'economic activity', namely own-account production – whether for oneself or as part of family production – and labour done for wages or for some form of non-monetary payment from somebody outside the household.

These distinctive activities can be sub-divided by whether they comprise the individual's main activity, defined by the relative amount of time devoted to it, and their 'second main' activity. In principle, it is possible for the second main activity to be economic work yet not be the main one, even though it results in more 'income' than the main activity.

This is particularly true for women, many of whom habitually say their main activity is 'housework'. In villages, often their second main activity is animal husbandry, which brings income into the family through the sale of milk, meat or animals, or which results in increased consumption. Standard statistics that only take account of main activity will systematically underestimate economic activity and economic growth.

In these respects, the story coming through the evaluation data was intriguing and very clear. In terms of main activity in the larger pilot, the basic income appeared to have just a small positive effect overall, due to a modest increase in women's economic activity. The share of the adult population doing a main activity for income or family gain was about the same in the basic income and control villages at the beginning of the pilot.

However, the primary finding was that in the basic income villages there was an increase in the number of adults having both a main and second main economic activity. This dual economic activity was significantly greater than in the control villages.

That dual activity had a double advantage, providing both two sources of income and a degree of informal insurance, so that if one activity suffered a setback the other could provide some income. We conducted a test of the probability of having a second and a main economic activity by the end of the pilot among those who had only one economic activity at the beginning. Controlling for other factors that influence work activity, such as landholding, schooling, gender and household size, a set of logit functions showed that the basic income had a significantly positive effect on the probability of doing two work activities.

This is where the big change took place. And it was strongest among those in their early twenties (20–24) and for those aged 25–54. Even more intriguing, it was greater for women in the latter age group than it was for men. As we will see later, that had something to do with the type of assets women acquired with the basic income.

Days and hours of work

Most data on days and hours of labour and work are of dubious value since they are collected long after the work or labour is done and, usually, are collected for long reference periods. Asking somebody how many hours they worked in a past month is to ask for a guess. Most of us do not keep records, and only if we have a formal job with contractually agreed hours and days of labour can we be reasonably sure. Even then, we are likely to forget hours working off the workplace or days when we did not do such work.

Asking somebody to recall what they did a year ago is even more unreliable. We do not recommend that approach. Unfortunately, a long reference period was used for the baseline survey for the 20 general villages, and we feel the resultant data were useless. What we can do is use the Final Evaluation Survey data from the question about how much time was spent on various activities in the past month and report the respondents' reflections on whether they had increased or decreased the amount of time spent in various activities over the past year.

In general, as far as wage labour is concerned, while there did not seem to have been much change, the average number of days spent doing wage labour was slightly higher in the basic income villages. But the average number spent doing own-account work was significantly higher. These figures refer only to those doing any economic activity. Given that slightly more were doing that in the basic income villages, the averages are slight underestimates of the positive relationships between the basic income and the amount of work and labour.

Again, we have more faith in the data from the tribal villages, because the sample size was smaller, because the surveys were done after refinements had been introduced based on lessons learned from the surveys in the general villages, and because identical questions were used in the baseline, interim and final evaluation surveys. An expectation of more observable effects may also reflect the fact that the basic income was higher relative to subsistence and average incomes in the tribal village.

The results in the tribal villages showed that the basic incomes led to more days of labour and work. Bear in mind that labour migration is widespread in these villages, and that many villagers spend a lot of time waiting for labour. It is in this context that the share working more than eleven days in the past month rose from 85.5 per cent to over 90 per cent, whereas the share doing so in the control village fell from 84 per cent to 79.5 per cent. There was an increase in the number of people doing some work in that period, with some doing just a few hours a day. But the effect was an increase in the extent of economic work.

Villagers may be 'under-employed' in that they obtain only low incomes and have to do sporadic bursts of intense labour in between periods of slack. But when they have labour or work to do, they tend to self-exploit in overworking at what are tiring manual tasks. In that sense, an encouraging finding was a reduction in the extent of what could be called 'over-employment'. In 2011, at the outset of the pilot, nearly 41 per cent of those who went on to receive the basic income worked over eight hours a day; that had dropped to 19 per cent by the end of the pilot, a drop that was much greater than for the control group.

Overall, there was a net decline in wage labour, but if anything that was less pronounced in the basic income villages (about 12.5 per cent versus 15 per cent). Meanwhile, there was an increase in own-account work in the basic income villages. It was this latter shift that was so dramatic.

To conclude this analysis, a set of logit functions was run to assess the impact of basic income on the change in days and hours of work. Controlling for age, gender, caste, landholding, schooling and household size, the basic income had a significant positive effect on hours worked in main and second main activities combined.

This result was due solely to the positive effect on women's work, since the coefficient for a function run solely for men was statistically insignificant. The results for a similar set of logit functions run on days worked in main and second main activities showed very similar results.

We reiterate our initial caveat about the reliability of figures on reported working time. Nevertheless, all the data are consistent with a perception gained from the case studies and from the other measures of work and labour that the basic incomes were associated with an increase in the extent of economic work.

A modest transformation

What was most intriguing of all was that the basic income was associated with a shift from wage labour to own-account work. And it was really mainly a shift from casual wage labour to own-account work, representing a double improvement. Some would say that this was more than a modest transformation, since it points to a greater sense of sustainable livelihoods and a greater sense of autonomy and independence.

If we take just the main activity, we find that by the end of the pilot, while the economic activity rate was slightly higher in the basic income villages, the share doing casual labour as their main activity was considerably lower

(17 per cent compared to 22 per cent), while the share doing own-account work was much higher (33 per cent compared to 27 per cent). In other words, the proportion of households being relatively self-directed was substantially greater, putting them in a better position to contribute to local economic growth.

The impact of the basic income in the tribal village was similar. As in the general villages, at the outset of the pilot most tribal families owned some land but most of the plots were regarded as small and unproductive, mainly because of a traditional lack of investment in irrigation, good seeds and fertilizers. The result was that many families earned most of their living from wage labour, rather than as farmers on their own land.

The basic income – perhaps because of the liquidity, perhaps because of the security provided by it – seemed to enable more families to farm their land more intensively, in the process converting themselves from being primarily wage labourers competing for limited opportunities and uncertain wages into being primarily farmers.

In the basic income village, the proportion reporting own-account farming as their main occupation rose from 40 per cent to 62 per cent during the pilot, the share reporting animal husbandry rose from 1.2 per cent to 4 per cent, while the share reporting they were a wage labourer fell from 55 per cent to 27 per cent, a remarkable drop. By contrast, in the control village, the shares doing the three types of occupation hardly changed, falling for being a farmer from 42 per cent to 36 per cent, rising for wage labour from 50 per cent to 51 per cent, and staying at 1 per cent in the case of animal husbandry.

It is reasonable to assert that given the opportunity, tribal villagers would prefer to cultivate their own land rather than do casual labour or, worse, bonded labour, which many have traditionally had to do, often in brick kilns in distant towns or on the farms of landlords. The shift from labour to own-account farming seems to have been due to their ability to spend on seeds, fertilizer, irrigation and livestock, as we will see.

The shift from wage labour to own-account farming in the tribal village is also important because it represents a reversal of the powerful trend taking place across Madhya Pradesh and all the other six central states of India, whereby scheduled tribal families have been losing land and abandoning cultivation. More than 5.6 million tribals joined the ranks of agricultural labourers between 2003 and 2013 (Varma, 2013). They have been losing their capacity to sustain their economic base, and thus in an unheralded way were losing their capacity to contribute to the country's economic growth.

By 2013, 48 per cent of all tribal workers were categorized as agricultural labourers, compared with 38 per cent a decade earlier. In Madhya Pradesh, tribal cultivators declined by 15 per cent and the number doing agricultural labour rose by an astonishing 63 per cent. So, the reverse trend in the basic income village should be regarded as particularly significant, especially as the general state trend persisted in the control village.

Overall, the essential story is that the basic incomes were associated with an increase in double (or even treble) economic activities and a shift from wage labour to own-account work. This has implications for the nature of the surrounding labour market. If low-income households can do more on their own farms or in small-scale informal production for income, they can also strengthen their bargaining position in the market for wage labour.

Again, this implies an emancipatory effect, a modest mechanism for the redistribution of income at the local community level and a clear means by which the local community could boost economic growth, in the *Swadeshi* spirit. Replicated elsewhere, it would be a low-cost way of accelerating economic growth. Development is about removing constraints to sustainable economic dynamism. A basic income is one way of doing precisely that.

New assets and new work

One of the expected effects was that some households would use their basic incomes to purchase low-cost productive assets. The biggest change was due to families putting some of their basic income money together to buy small or large livestock. Indeed, the outcome was nothing less than dramatic.

Again, this came out most in the tribal village pilot. In the village where the basic incomes were paid, there were 424 small livestock (chicken and goats) at the time of the baseline. By the end of the pilot, there were 633. By contrast, in the control village there were 466 at the outset, and 355 at the end. In the case of large livestock (buffaloes, cows or oxen), the number rose from 259 to 323 in the basic income village and fell from 207 to 190 in the control village. These shifts coincided with the reported increase in animal husbandry as a main or second main economic activity.

That is, while the number of cows and buffaloes declined in the control village by 23 per cent, due to sales or deaths, the number increased in the basic income village by the same percentage, seemingly almost entirely due to households buying more livestock, which then started to breed.

In the basic income village, the share of families owning large livestock increased from two-thirds to 81 per cent, whereas in the control village the share fell from two-thirds to 51.5 per cent. In the case of small livestock, the share rose from 62 per cent to 78 per cent in the basic income village, while rising only slightly from 59 per cent to 61 per cent in the control village.

The data speak for themselves. However, it was also shown by practical experience. The case study team reported that at the time of the baseline they were very rarely offered tea by respondents, because few had enough milk. During the final evaluation survey, they were offered tea in most places, with cow and goat milk. The general change was clear. As one SEWA leader in the tribal village put it:

> As everyone in the village was receiving the basic income, some paid their debts, some bought cows or oxen worth 6,000 Rupees each. Some bought goats for 5,000 Rupees. About 15 people in the village bought goats in this way. Eighteen people bought hens, eight bought cows, to give milk for home consumption.
>
> We bought the goats for rearing. One goat produces at least two kids in six months and four in a year. We sell the male kids and keep the females. The goat milk is used to make tea. One kid can be sold for 6,000 Rupees. We go to Mahu and Maanpurhaat [bazaar] on Saturdays and Tuesdays to sell the kids. In the same way, we sell the chickens; one can sell for 400 Rupees. Overall, in the two harvest seasons, we earned over 2,000 Rupees in the village from all this.

Simple really. The obvious question is why they did not do this before the arrival of the basic income. The only feasible answer is that they lacked the liquidity to make the series of transactions and 'investments'.

In the general villages, significantly more purchases of large livestock were reported in the basic income villages, and slightly more purchases of small livestock were reported in them. So, whereas at the baseline, only about 12 per cent of households set to receive the basic income had any large livestock, by the time the pilot concluded over 40 per cent did. The number of large livestock increased considerably in the basic income villages, especially for households that had owned just a couple of bullocks or cows at the outset. Although control villages also saw some expansion among those with small numbers of large livestock, there was an overall decline due to cuts among those that initially had more. In sum, the basic income seems to have enabled households to scale up their livestock holdings.

Livestock are vital in these villages. Listen to how one woman, Lakhan Dholi, a *dhol* (drum) player in Datoda village, described her family's actions:

> This year our family has received the basic income. With that money, I bought four goats. These have had five kids. I bought the four goats for 14,000 Rupees by pooling our basic income money. The intention was to increase our income. But they also give milk for our children to drink and for us for tea. Earlier we had to buy milk, but now the goat milk is enough. So we don't have to buy milk. I'm thinking of paying off my debts by selling these goats now.

While an increase in livestock is surely a sign of rising living standards, as noted at the outset, significantly more basic income households reported an increase in income-earning work or production. Among those that did so, nearly three-quarters attributed that directly to the basic income. Part of this reflected a small entrepreneurial initiative, as exemplified by Babitbai, a casual labourer of the Malviya caste, living in Gogakhedi village, who told the enumeration team:

> When we began getting the cash transfer, we started a business making *chudas* [large bangles] that are worn on the arms. We get the raw material and make them at home. We are able to earn about 1,000–2,000 Rupees a month from this work … We also bought a second-hand motorcycle in instalments … We paid three of the instalments – 1,200 each – with money from the basic incomes. Apart from that we have used the basic income money to buy stuff for daily household needs.

A particularly encouraging aspect of these small-scale entrepreneurial activities is that they occurred across all castes. Thus, over 19 per cent of scheduled caste households with basic incomes increased their economic activity, compared to only 7 per cent of such households in the control villages.

During the course of the pilot, there were also increases in the purchase of productive assets, with more wells, tractors and sewing machines in the basic income villages than in the control villages. Another common occurrence was families pooling some of the basic incomes so as to buy a sewing machine to add a supplementary income-earning activity.

Perhaps the most striking development was that in the tribal village where the basic incomes were paid no fewer than 41 new wells were dug, whereas beforehand only four existed. There was also an increase in the control village, but nothing like as many were dug.

These purchases increased the productivity of land, suggesting another means by which the basic incomes were growth-inducing. Along with wells, households also invested in pumps and pipes, enabling them to bring water from the village pond to their fields as well as to their dwellings. Over one in every five households invested in irrigation and another one in five did so jointly with neighbours. Overall, the number of families possessing an electrical water pump for irrigation purposes increased by 45 per cent, whereas there was no increase in the control village.

Moreover, in the basic income tribal village, 57 new ploughs were bought during the pilot, a 48 per cent increase. Again, this was much greater than in the control village. There was also a growth in the number of machine tools and carts in the basic income village.

In both the general villages and the basic income tribal village, the basic income was associated with more purchasing of seeds, fertilizers and pesticides, and the vast majority of those who acquired more of any of these reported that the purchase had resulted in increased production and income. And in most cases they said the increased production had resulted in increased consumption.

In sum, there can be little doubt that the basic incomes had increased productive activity and made it more profitable in the most meaningful sense of raising living standards.

Women's labour and work

The impact of the basic incomes on women's work and labour was also fairly clear. First, comparing the baseline and final points of the general village pilot showed that the overall female labour force participation rate rose in the basic income villages (from 35 per cent to 36 per cent), while it fell in the control villages. This finding is consistent with the impact of cash transfers in Latin American countries, notably Brazil and the *Bolsa Família* scheme (Soares et al., 2010).

In this regard, according to official NSS data, the female labour force participation rate in Madhya Pradesh has been low relative to other parts of India, although studies have shown that the NSS data systematically undercount women's work participation, especially own-account work on or around the farm (Banerjee, 1998).

However, as with the general story on labour and work, the impact on main economic activity only tells a small part of the story of what happened. For women were the primary beneficiaries of the growth of secondary economic activities.

A revealing tale that emerged in one of the case studies highlighted the potential importance of individual basic income payments compared with monetary transfers that are family-based or directed at either the nominal head of household or one particular woman ('the mother'). It was a report from a 45-year-old woman who is a scheduled caste farmer from Padlya village. Her name is Shakuntalabai.

> With the basic income money, my husband and I bought a goat, and my three daughters pooled their money and bought a sewing machine. They want to learn and start a tailoring shop. All the three girls are married; the eldest one's husband is a drunkard, so she has decided to stay with us. The other two are yet to reach their puberty, and then will be sent to their husbands. When they go there they want to continue their tailoring. My son and daughter-in-law spent their money on their children's education. Their children are studying in a private school. My daughter-in-law has gone to her maternal home for child-birth. She has taken her diary with her so that she can use the money there. Her child is fifteen months old now.

These are the sort of behavioural and emancipatory dynamics a modest policy change can induce. An individualized basic income led to an independent work opportunity for these young women. Without that individualized cash payment they would have been unable to do any income-earning work or would have been obliged to work in a dependent position in the household economy. We will consider this further in the chapter on women's agency. Another woman told how her daughter-in-law had bought a sewing machine with savings from her basic income money that had been combined with a monetary contribution from her son. She reported, 'She stitches all the household clothes now. Perhaps in the future, she can earn an income from it.'

Many women used their basic income money to improve their own income and production status and, very specifically, that of their female family members, usually their daughters. For instance, the data from the IES showed that the basic income caused a change in the patterns of working days of women, with those in basic income SEWA villages increasing their days of work both on their own farms and as wage labourers.

Naukar labour

We return, finally, to that scourge of village life, bonded labour, in the form of the *naukar* and *gwala* labour relationships. A typical case was that described by a low-income woman from the Bhil scheduled tribe. The family of two adults and four offspring possessed an AAY ration card. She was aged 35, her husband aged 40. This is how she described their situation:

In my house three people work for wages, my husband and my two older sons. About three years ago, I was working in the field and I climbed a tree to collect firewood. I slipped and fell, and broke my right leg and hand. They have put a rod in my leg. Since then, I can no longer work outside; I just do the housework.

My eldest son, Vinod, who is 17 years old, works as a *naukar* for a big farmer. He receives 15,000 Rupees a year. And my second son, Laxman, works as a *gwala*, and receives 10,000 Rupees a year. My husband does casual labour on the farm. My sons go to work early in the morning and come back only in the evening. Vinod was just a *gwala*, but now has become a *naukar*.

So he does all the work relating to cattle and also works on the landlord's farm, whereas Laxman does only cattle-related work. They don't even send them home for lunch. They give them lunch so that they can make them work even during the time that they would spend in coming home for lunch.

A finding from the FES is that by then fewer households were trapped in such situations in the basic income villages, as shown in Figure 8.2.

The link between the basic income payments and the weakening of the *naukar* system does not stop there. Consider the statement of Gumaan Singh,

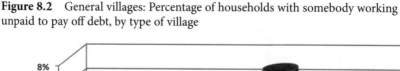

Figure 8.2   General villages: Percentage of households with somebody working unpaid to pay off debt, by type of village

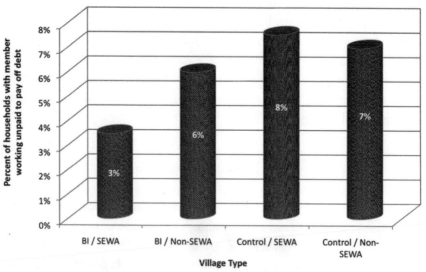

Source: MPUCT FES, 2012; n=2029

a scheduled tribe man from Gogakhedi Village, speaking at the end of the pilot to the case study enumerator:

> We were much helped by the basic income money that we were getting. If we didn't get any labour work, then we didn't have to think about where to get food. We could go to the doctor for treatment whenever required. Earlier it wasn't like this. I'm not a bonded labourer anymore, and if it weren't for this money, then perhaps I'd still be working as a bonded labourer. After all, one needs money to run a household, and there is almost no labour work available in our village. So far it was all fine as we were getting the money. Now that it has stopped, let us see what happens.

What this personal story suggests is that the modest payments had provided a safety valve, enabling him to avoid or escape from the *naukar* trap and thus helping him to take other decisions to his family's benefit. There can be little more emancipatory than that.

Collective economic activity

One hypothesis on basic income is that it increases cooperation and collective action. Within the family, of course, there was pooling of funds sometimes for education and more often to improve the home. There was anecdotal evidence of pooling money within and between families. For instance, two teenage women in two villages pooled their cash to start a stitching class, and some families pooled their funds to buy seeds and fertilizers collectively.

However, the most transformative collective action that was observed occurred in the basic income tribal village Ghodakhurd, where households used the pond in the centre of the village as a common resource to increase their incomes.

The basic incomes began in February 2012. When the rainy season came in June and July, some of the villagers started to discuss the possibility of buying fish roe so as to start fish farming. They announced the idea to the villagers and asked people to join the venture, set up on a cooperative basis of shared costs, shared work and shared income. Thirteen people came together and pooled Rs.2,000 each from their basic income.

With this money, they bought fish roe and began farming. By the start of the harvest season, they were able to sell fish both within the village and in the market in the local town of Mhow. The proceeds were used to buy more fish roe. This process, illustrated in Plate 11, continued in the next year. Thus, an informal fish cooperative was formed that gave not only income to its members but also made fresh fish available to the villagers.

By the end of the pilot, it was clear that fish had been added as a regular item of the village diet. So, as a result of the basic income, incomes, collective action and consumption were all improved. As the famous saying goes, 'Give a man a fish, and he will be hungry later. Enable a man to fish, and he will improve his life.' In this case, there was the added benefit of cooperation and strengthened social solidarity. It was another form of emancipation induced by the basic incomes.

Concluding reflections

We initially feared that the actual level of the basic income would be too low to have a major series of effects on work and labour. However, we soon realized that the liquidity effect was likely to mean that the real value of the money was greater than it seemed and that it could unlock constraints to create mini-multiplier or transformative effects through the influence on work and labour.

Overall, the effects were positive, reducing the extent of short-term labour migration, changing the nature of child work, raising economic opportunities for women, curbing *naukar* labour, and leading to a shift from casual wage labour to own-account farming and non-farm economic activity. The money helped households to buy more productive assets, which helped to increase economic security as well as raise incomes.

There are also indirect effects to bear in mind, such as the impact of improved health and nutrition that make work and labour more feasible and less onerous. And one should not ignore the possibility that by providing a steadier, more predictable income, basic incomes reduce the adverse shock of temporary periods of unemployment. Households are also less likely to default on debt repayments and thus are less likely to fall into an asset loss cycle.

We believe the effects of the basic income on the pattern of work and labour were positive. Overall, there was an increase in economic activity and thus a beneficial effect on economic growth and incomes. That is eminently desirable.

However, the shift from reliance on a single source of income to two or more also had a beneficial effect on socio-economic security, while the shift from wage labour to own-account activities also tended to have a modest redistributive effect via the impact on the capacity of people to escape from the *naukar* relationship and to bargain for better wages if they wished to enter the wage labour market.

Meanwhile, the impact on child labour, although modest, was in the direction we should all wish to see. We will consider what happened to the elderly and those with disabilities in a later chapter. But in sum, we can reasonably say that the impact on work and labour was rather transformative, raising incomes in an emancipatory way, almost unlike any other policy that we could envisage in rural India.

There has long been a debate among economists about achieving structural change in the course of economic development. No single policy can achieve that. But the argument that should emerge from this analysis is that a basic income can be part of a realistic package of reforms that would unlock the development potential in most of village India.

9

Women's Status: Empowerment, Identity and Citizenship

Introduction

Women in India are taught not to have an identity of their own, but to be subject to the decisions of others within and outside the family. Most have few choices on how to live and few opportunities for personal development. There are caste and class dimensions to the freedoms that women enjoy, but most women struggle against social barriers restricting their individuality.

Many younger women have freer lives than their mothers and grandmothers, but change is slow. Patriarchal values remain strong. To indicate the depth of the challenge, let us begin by hearing from a 70-year-old woman, Surjibai, from one of the pilot villages:

> I was born in Kishanganj. We were two sisters and my father married me off when I was very young. I was sent to my husband's home after puberty but did not have any children. Because of that, his family did not want me. After a while my husband sold me to someone in Rajasthan. I lived with him for many years, but it was a hard life. After my mother-in-law died I returned to my husband's village Malibadodia and he decided to begin living with me. I did labour work, earned and looked after him as he was not well. But he died 15–20 years back. Now, I have no assets but earn a little by working in other people's houses. I do their household work (cleaning the house, utensils and wheat). I don't get any money from the government. I glean the leftover wheat from fields during the harvest in order to eat. My main problem is that I have eczema all over my body, but do not have the money to go for treatment.

Surajbai's experience may have been among the most extreme but her very presence testified to a social environment of deplorable oppression. The complete control of her life by her father and husband, even to the point of selling her to another man, and her destitution in old age, is a reflection of the life among many poor women in India.

As lack of choice about how to live is pervasive, any policy intervention that increases women's choices must bring about a greater sense of empowerment and begin a process by which they can exert control over their lives (Kabeer, 2000; Strandberg, 2001). The basic income, just by increasing individual access to cash, provided a route to new opportunities.

It could only make a small difference. The amount provided was modest and the duration of the pilots was too short to have a major impact. But the bar of judgement should be set lower. If it modestly improved women's welfare and personal development, and if it enabled them to contribute to economic growth, for themselves and their communities, and if it was emancipatory in the process, it would surely be worthwhile, and stand favourable comparison with many other social policies.

The pilots on which this book are based tested for the effects of basic income and Voice, the separate impact of a collective body able to represent the interests of women and articulate their views and aspirations. The presence of SEWA was measured by a controlled experiment in this pilot, with half the villages having SEWA members and the other half having no contact with SEWA. The design of the pilots was intended to enable us to distinguish between the effects of SEWA and the effects of the basic income. Earlier studies (e.g. Carr, 1996; Jhabvala, 2010) have shown that joining a voice agency increases women's effectiveness in the public sphere and enhances citizenship. Did the presence of SEWA combined with the basic income have an impact on women's lives, increasing their choices and their standing in the community, at work and within the family?

Empowerment and citizenship

There are many studies on women's empowerment and agency, with numerous competing, if not conflicting, definitions and measurements. We cannot do justice to that literature, and will not try. Some scholars (e.g. Golla et al., 2012) have differentiated between empowerment and agency, others between empowerment, agency and well-being. Ibrahim and Alkire (2008) listed 32 different definitions, centred mainly on 'agency, autonomy, self-direction, liberation, participation, mobilization and self-confidence'.

For our purposes, the following sections examine women's empowerment, which may be summarized as transformative changes in individual consciousness and capabilities. We further look at women's citizenship rights within the villages, with citizenship being expressed through the exercise of civil, social, cultural, economic, financial and political rights.

Empowerment and the exercise of rights derive from *individual* resilience and from *collective* strength, the latter being the capacity to exercise resilience and undertake action as a group when perceived as necessary. It may be said that empowerment is the outcome of changes within the individual and of shifting relations within families, whereas exercise of rights depends on opportunity structures in communities and the wider society. These are often mutually reinforcing, with empowerment and changing family relations often leading to assertion of citizenship rights, while new opportunities within the wider society combined with a collective voice may bring about a transformation in individual consciousness.

Identity as a sense of self

Most women in India, particularly those in villages, do not have an identity separate from their household. They are generally known in relation to their 'head of household', as wife, daughter or daughter-in-law, or in relation to their children, as mother or grandmother.

This may sound normal. After all, everybody is partially defined by their relationships to others. But it is the degree to which a woman's personality and self-perception are submerged in the norms of traditional relations that is so suffocating and debilitating. Emancipation is ultimately about having a separate set of identities, understood by the woman herself and by others in their dealings with her as a human being.

The idea of identity involves four dimensions – as an individual, as someone within the context of a family or household, as someone participating within the public community and as a worker in workplaces. When commentators refer to women's 'invisibility', they really mean that they lack identity and citizenship – the capacity to be an individual with equal rights – in all or most of those respects.

What the pilots were trying to do was to see whether the basic income, particularly when combined with membership of SEWA, enabled women to develop a greater sense of empowerment and a broader identity. To return to our overriding theme, it was about enhancing women's sense of emancipation, while helping in capability development and enabling women to participate in economic growth.

Another way of putting the challenge is to postulate the desirable and optimal situation as where men and women enjoy equal citizenship rights. Citizenship has several dimensions – financial, civil, social, cultural, economic and political. It is about rights in all these respects. Just as men and women of different classes and castes have to struggle to obtain and maintain equal rights with their equivalents in other social groups, so women in general have to struggle for equal rights, as individuals, within their households and wider families, and outside in various public spheres, including workplaces.

This is partly a struggle within the mind, requiring an escape from a subordinated consciousness that stems from generations of diverse forms of oppression. No single policy or institutional change by itself could be expected to break that psychological barrier to emancipation. All one could hope is that it would begin to do so.

Within the family

A person's identity is closely tied up with the relations within the family, with an individual's sense of self being formed in childhood. A woman's low status starts as soon as she is born, with the sex ratio at birth being 904 girls born per 1,000 boys according to the 2011 census. Although in general more boys than girls are born to a family, the ratios are abnormally low in India. In most countries of the world (other than South and East Asia) the ratio is much higher. In the United Kingdom, for example, 952 girls are born per 1,000 boys.

The structural discrimination continues with higher infant mortality rates for girls – 113 girls under five per 1,000 compared to 104 for boys – and then to lower school enrolment, especially in secondary school and higher classes.

Girls are also married earlier, and have fewer opportunities to participate in the labour force. These figures reflect deep-rooted attitudes and beliefs within the family, where girls and women are treated as inferior to boys and men, and decision-making and control remains out of their reach. The main decision-maker in the family is the 'head of household', usually a man; over 80 per cent of the household heads in the pilots were men, with female-headed households mainly appearing with widows or when there was no older male in the family.

Basic income, SEWA and changing identity

The following assesses the impact of the basic income and SEWA's involvement on women's agency through the prism of various forms of citizenship, considering the three vital dimensions – the individual woman, the woman as a member of families and households, and the woman as a member of the wider social community.

The pilots involved four features rarely found in social policy, which taken together provided women with increased choices. The first was that they were designed to test the effects not just of the basic income itself but also those of a *Voice* organization, SEWA, whose main objective is to bring women together to increase their sense of empowerment and solidarity. The underlying hypothesis was that SEWA would enhance the positive effects of the basic income.

A second feature was that the payment of money was *individual* – given to women and men separately, as individuals. A question was whether the woman retained control over the money, or at least enough to be able to have a strong influence on how the money was spent. Implicitly, it also meant asking whether the distributional effects would have differed had the money just gone to a household 'head' or to the family as a unit.

Third, the amount was *equal* for men and women, which made it progressive in gender terms, since the average income of women was lower. So it was worth more for them. If they were mothers, the women received the basic income of their children as well, giving them greater control, potentially, over spending decisions on behalf of their children.

Fourth, as the basic income was *unconditional*, in principle women as well as men had a choice on how to spend the money. Women were not told by any external agency how to spend it. Given the nature of intra-family decision-making, it remained to be seen if they were actually able to exercise choices. In sum, the design of the pilots meant it was possible, in principle, to trace the impact of the basic income, and that of SEWA, on women's sense of agency. The hope was that the data from the evaluation surveys and case studies would show, first, whether they enabled women to develop their capabilities and obtain more resources; second, whether they enabled women to participate more effectively in social, economic, cultural and political life; and third, whether they could increase women's decision-making roles within their families.

Social citizenship

Being a social citizen means having equal rights to develop and remain a viable member of society. This encompasses the right to be born, to be adequately fed, to be able to go to school on the same basis as others, with as good facilities, to be able to live as healthily as others, to be able to obtain healthcare on the same favourable basis as others.

All of these are partly the result of family norms and attitudes, partly the result of social and community pressures and structures, partly the result of the design of government policies and special schemes, and partly the result of women's own consciousness, shaped by generations of stereotype images and behavioural norms and expectations.

Being a social citizen is also about having equal rights to social benefits, social services and opportunities to develop and maintain capabilities. In the pilot villages, some of the many government schemes were targeted on low-income women or on all women. The trouble was that most remained on paper.

Social services included access to the Public Distribution System, to subsidized public healthcare, to free public schools, to *anganwadis* for children under five and to subsidized infrastructure in the form of water and sanitation.

Food and nutrition

Access to adequate nutritious food is a social right. But traditionally, nutrition for girls and women has been considered less important than for boys and men. Women eat after the men have finished, and girls are required to serve their brothers before they themselves eat. All this results in more malnutrition among girls and a situation where women accept lower status.

However, there is encouraging evidence that girl infants benefited from the basic income. As shown in Chapter 5, the basic income led to a fall in child malnutrition, which was greater among girls. This was followed by an improvement in girls' participation in secondary schooling. But, besides the effects of the basic income itself, were these signs of increased female empowerment, changing beliefs, or the influence of SEWA?

The changes were due to a combination of factors. A woman having an individual account and an individual basic income, which included those of the children, allowed her to make decisions in favour of the girl child that she was unable to do beforehand. The influence of SEWA made a difference. In the background, Indian society is changing, and traditional beliefs are waning. A modest source of security allowed many families to change their pattern of spending.

The z-score index outcomes showed that girls experienced a greater drop in malnutrition than boys of the same age. This was particularly true for girls who had begun solid food, from the age of seven months, suggesting that more of the cash gained by mothers was used to increase the nutrition of girls, not just boys.

While the proportion of girls with normal weight for their age increased considerably in all basic income villages, the improvement in SEWA villages was significantly greater, rising from 34 per cent to 61 per cent, an increase of 27 percentage points, compared to an increase of 20 percentage points in non-SEWA villages.

There was a reason for this extra effect. By the age of seven months, most children had shifted to solid food and between the age of two and five years most were receiving some food from the *anganwadi*. So, nutrition often depended in part on how well the *anganwadi* was run. In SEWA villages, activists became participants in making the system work better. To repeat an example given in Chapter 5, Lakhina, a SEWA *agewan* in the village of Jagmalpipliya, summed up a common situation:

> In our village there is lot of casteism. The *anganwadi* teacher was a Brahmin and she did not allow scheduled caste children in the *anganwadi*, so children who needed it most were deprived. I met the teacher and tried to talk to her. But instead of listening to me she started threatening the families in the scheduled caste locality and told them to not to complain, as she had connections with higher-ups, and that she was not afraid of the SEWA workers. So at our next meeting of SEWA in Indore, I brought this up and a written complaint went to the local supervisor of ICDS. Later, along with the SEWA organizer and some women from the village, I met the supervisor and we said she should resolve the issue; otherwise a written complaint would be sent to the Principal Secretary of the department and the concerned minister. Hearing this, the supervisor got scared and immediately went to Jagmalpipliya and convinced the *anganwadi* teacher. The next day we sent scheduled caste children to the *anganwadi* and monitored the issue afterwards. The midday meal was also not cooked daily, inadequate food was being cooked and the food was not properly cooked. With the supervisor's help, this issue was also resolved and I was asked to supervise the cooking each day. I ensured that the children were having enough food every day.

Although this story was not about girls per se, the intervention of local SEWA activists enhanced the effect of the basic income. It exemplified collective agency. Such efforts, made in all SEWA villages, made a minor difference in the control villages, but a pronounced one in the basic income villages.

Schooling

Education is a social benefit rather than an economic one; it means so much more than is conveyed by the term 'human capital'. Madhya Pradesh was the first state to pass a Right to Education Act, which ensured government-funded primary schools near each village. The schooling is practically free, children receive a midday meal and the government provides support for uniforms and books. This has ensured a very high enrolment rate in primary school for both girls and boys.

Yet, as noted in Chapter 7, the lamentable fact is that girls' enrolment drops sharply at secondary-school level, that is, after age 13. Secondary schools were usually further from the village. The Madhya Pradesh government has been trying to encourage girls to go to school by providing free uniforms, books, bicycles and scholarships. But the data showed that few girls or boys received such items.

There are various reasons for the low enrolment of girls. Parents complain that teachers do not come in time, leave early, sometimes do not come at all, do not teach properly or are rude to the children. In some schools there is inadequate infrastructure, with overcrowded or non-existent classrooms. Many secondary schools are too far to walk from the village and there is often no proper transport. All this has tended to reduce girls' schooling. And many families do not value education for girls. Rather than spend money on educating them, they prefer to marry them off early.

What Laxmi Yadav, a small-scale farmer from the Yadav community, said in an interview reflects this attitude:

> Only the two boys in my family go to school. We prefer the private school to the village government school, because that does not provide good education. My daughters do not go to school as there is no school in the village and no means of transport. I want my sons to study well and get good jobs.

In short, this family rationalized that it could afford transport for boys but not for girls.

However, as shown in Chapter 7, the basic income induced more families to send girls to secondary school or keep them in it. By the time of the FES, while only 36 per cent of girls in control villages were enrolled in secondary school, in basic income villages nearly 65 per cent of girls of that age were enrolled. And girls' enrolment in SEWA basic income villages was significantly higher than elsewhere. Further, while still lower than for boys, expenditure on girls' schooling was higher among households receiving the basic income, and was highest of all among households in SEWA basic income villages. Significant differences were also observed in schooling variables between the basic income and control villages, showing better attendance, or less absenteeism, among both boys and girls.

While the basic income increased girls' enrolment in secondary school and prompted a big increase in spending on girl's schooling, both were higher in SEWA villages. This may be due to SEWA's efforts to ensure that government schools, where girls were more likely to go, performed better. In one village, for example, the teacher rarely came to the school and had engaged a youth on his behalf, to whom he paid Rs.1,000 per month. The teacher came once in a month to obtain signatures on the attendance register by visiting every household. A written complaint was lodged with the Education Department, which transferred the teacher. SEWA *agewans* proposed that the youth apply for the teacher's job. He obtained it, the school started functioning properly and more children went to school regularly.

The emphasis on sending children to school also helped reduce the incidence of child labour. Where children were working on the family farm, the amount of work by the child fell. Here too SEWA seems to have played a part. About 37 per cent of SEWA basic income households said that child labour had stopped or been reduced, as compared to 17 per cent in villages where there was neither a basic income nor a SEWA effect.

In short, the positive basic income effect on girls' schooling was further enhanced by SEWA. This was a dimension of social citizenship where women made tangible gains.

Healthcare

Another indicator of women's low status is that when, as is usual, a family has scarce resources for healthcare priority is given to men. Healthcare tends to use up much of a family's resources. So when a woman falls ill, she is less likely to see a doctor and be more likely to wait out her illness. This emerged in the tribal villages. In the baseline, when respondents were asked what form of medical treatment was first taken, 22 per cent of women said that they tried 'home remedies', whereas only 8 per cent of men did.

However, by the FES, only one in every 50 women receiving the basic income said this was their first option. By then, just like the men, they were going to local medical practitioners or to a private or public hospital. This is a form of empowerment, even though there were still differences, as more women were receiving medical advice from a chemist, while most men were going to a doctor.

The combination of the basic income and SEWA membership seemed to make an impact on healthcare. Households in basic income SEWA villages were the most likely to report an improvement in their health. But the SEWA effect was most visible in the increase in regular taking of medicines. Some 17 per cent of households in basic income SEWA villages reported this, compared to 12 per cent in the other basic income villages, 10 per cent in the SEWA control villages and just 4 per cent in the non-SEWA control villages.

As far as health and healthcare are concerned, the chief beneficiaries seem to have been disabled women who were able to use their basic income to gain greater priority in access to treatment and medicine. This is a group that is too often neglected.

In sum, the basic income and SEWA combined to narrow the healthcare differences between men and women, and in this respect as well, they acted to improve women's social rights.

Financial citizenship

To be a financial citizen – admittedly an unfamiliar term – is to enjoy the rights of having access to financial services on an equal footing to others around you. And it makes a difference to living standards, being both emancipatory and developmental.

Financial citizenship is an underestimated part of society. Increasingly, the financial sector shapes economic, social and even political structures, and exclusion from accessing finance curtails the exercise of other citizenship rights. Although access to financial systems is a *de jure* right of every citizen, the financial structures across the country have ensured that poorer villagers and most women are unable to access these rights *de facto*.

In 2012, across India only 59 per cent of all households had any bank account and only 54 per cent of rural households had one. Where a family had an account, it was usually in the name of the man or 'household head'. Only 26 per cent of bank accounts belonged to women and only 14 per cent of Indian women had a bank account.

Implicit in the project was a question whether the basic income would enhance women's financial citizenship. Recall that the larger pilot required recipients to open a bank or cooperative account, and so it almost imposed a need to develop a financial identity. During the first few months of the pilot, separate bank or cooperative accounts were opened for all men and women. It inevitably involved teething problems, but financial citizenship was an implicit objective.

The lack of an independent identity is closely tied to exclusion from the financial system. In Indian villages, the most difficult part of opening a bank account is the 'Know Your Customer' requirement that the person must produce proof of identity and proof of residence. For most women, this would have been the first time they had to prove they had an identity. A voter ID card was perhaps the only proof, but this was often packed away somewhere and had to be retrieved. As many women did not have a voter card, they had to rely on a ration card, which merely listed them as one family member. Some did have school certificates, but the name on those would have differed from their ration card name, as after marriage their first name would have been changed by their husband's family.

The struggle to overcome all these factors was protracted. But one positive result was that women said they realized the importance of having their own identity. Many became determined to obtain *Adhaar* cards for themselves. In villages where it was active, SEWA worked towards helping to create this identity. Its involvement was captured well by Ramabai, who described herself to the case study team as a garment stitcher:

> My neighbour brought me to a meeting in SEWA; it was the first time that I had come to a meeting. We were asked to introduce ourselves and I was struck dumb, I could not say my own name. You know, in our families no one calls us by name. My mother-in-law calls me bahu, my children call me mother, and other family members call me bhabhi. I had almost forgotten my name! And in my father's house my name was Leela, after marriage my name was changed to Ramabai. Now when I stand up and say my name in meetings, I feel a change has come over me.

Having a named identity is taken for granted by middle-class people, but in a tradition-bound rural context, gaining one can represent a personal breakthrough with life-defining ramifications. An 'account of my own' is an important step towards identity and independence for a woman. There was a larger significance too, in that not only did she own an account, she also became part of the country's financial system.

One objective of those wishing to roll out cash transfers across India is to extend financial inclusion through inducing more rural and low-income people to open and use bank accounts. A widely held view in policy circles is that there is resistance to opening bank accounts, from the banks themselves as well as from poorer sections of society, who supposedly find banks difficult to use. Indeed, in November 2012, it was reported that at least four state governments said they could not operationalize direct cash transfers because of difficulties in opening bank accounts.

In that context, a basic income could be a trigger for action to open accounts that could be of more general benefit for villagers. Within a few months of the start of the pilot, almost all adults had accounts. In SEWA villages, the number of women having savings accounts before the project started was relatively high, because long before the project SEWA had mobilized women in villages where it worked to open savings accounts with its Thrift and Credit Cooperative. Before the pilot started, only 63 women in non-SEWA villages had a bank account, although 305 in SEWA villages had one. But within a few months, 1,660 women had opened accounts, meaning that financial inclusion had been rapid and extensive.

Women in all strata are structurally disempowered. But changed circumstances could move them to action. Women in richer households were no exception. There was considerable inequality in the pilot villages. A few households owned large tracts of land, had big houses and businesses in the city. Some of these refused to take the basic income, saying it meant nothing to them. However, within a few months the women in such households in one village contacted the team to say they wanted to open accounts and wanted the money even though it was modest. 'We have enough material goods', one said, 'but we do not own anything ourselves, not even a bank account. It is a small independence for us.'

We know that basic income households were more likely to save. But equally important is the *form* of savings. The most common forms in India are keeping cash in 'the home' and purchasing gold or jewellery. But as we saw earlier, the basic income induced many households to shift to saving in banks or the Cooperative.

In the FES, respondents were asked about the form of saving. Among basic income households who saved any money, 53 per cent said they saved in a bank, compared to 30 per cent of control village households who saved. A typical situation was that of Ramkayabai, a woman in the Boyi caste:

> I put the money back in my account. I have saved the money for the past four months. My husband and I are vegetable vendors. We leave at 4am each morning in the milk van to Indore. We go to the market, buy vegetables and sell them at various places in the city and return home. I want to save my money so that I can use it to set up a shop. I want to have a settled shop in one place instead of changing places each day. It is so difficult to walk around all day. Each day I buy vegetables worth 1,500 to 2,000 Rupees. We stay until the stock is completely sold and only then return home. Sometimes we return after 8pm. It costs 15 Rupees by shared auto-rickshaw to come from Indore to Malibadodiya.

In effect, the basic income contributed to a securitization of saving, a benefit in terms of security if one accepts that savings in banks are more secure and so more valuable. The basic income boosted savings directly by providing more money and indirectly by inducing more financial inclusion.

In the evaluation surveys, saving was considered as a household activity but also as an individual one. Women now had their own accounts and were able to save individually. Women often hid savings from other family members and used them for purposes that the household head might not approve. Sangeeta Chouhan, an *anganwadi* worker, said that she wanted her daughters to study and be independent, although that was not a part of the household plan. She said,

> We did not plan for my daughters' studies because there is not enough income. The girls know about the cash transfer, but they never ask for this money. However, I wanted to spend it only on them. I had to do it quietly. I have two accounts, one opened for the cash transfer in Bank of India and the other in State Bank of India as an *anganwadi* worker. I withdrew the money in my Bank of India account and put it in my State Bank of India account. This is because when my husband saw the Bank of India passbook, he demanded that money. So to save it, I used to take it out and put it in my other account; and with the help of this money, my daughter did a beauty parlour course. Now she can start her own beauty parlour in Indore. This course cost 5,000 Rupees and I used the cash transfer money to pay for it.

Being part of the financial system enabled more women to borrow at reasonable rates of interest. But even if they have bank accounts, women are less likely to obtain loans from financial institutions as they do not own assets and so cannot offer security. Banks have no incentives to offer them loans, and, although the government stipulates that a certain share of loans must go to women, it is just 5 per cent. Alternative forms of financial institution – self-help groups, microfinance institutions and cooperatives – empower women more. As shown earlier, loans through the SEWA Cooperative increased economic opportunities and choices.

Opening individual accounts requires carving out an independent identity. Controlling and operating an individual account leads to empowerment. Recall that respondents were asked whether they preferred a family or individual account. Fewer women preferred a family account – 41 per cent as compared to 48 per cent of men. Upper-caste women were the most independent-minded, with only a quarter of them preferring a family account. In the tribal villages too, women were keener on individual accounts. Whereas 52 per cent of women said they preferred individual accounts, only 38 per cent of men said so.

The question of whether the money should be given to the household head or the individual yielded a similar pattern of responses, with over 40 per cent of women preferring individual transfers compared to 34 per cent of men. An equal number, about 18 per cent, said it did not matter.

SEWA's role was important here, because women who could open a cooperative account had more choice than those who had a bank account. Bearing in mind the high illiteracy among women, fewer women using the Cooperative had difficulty in opening accounts, with only 30 per cent saying they had difficulty, compared to 56 per cent who had difficulty in doing so with a bank.

While most women were able to deal with banks without difficulty, some did have difficulty. Nearly 60 per cent of those said the main difficulty they faced when they went to withdraw or deposit money was an inability to fill out forms. Many relied on other customers or brought along literate family members; just over a quarter said bank staff helped them. By contrast, most illiterate women using the Cooperative said staff helped them fill out forms.

Women also had easier access to the SEWA Cooperative. Due to its visits to villages, 86 per cent of women in SEWA villages used their account frequently, compared to only 44 per cent of women who had a bank account in non-SEWA villages. At the time of the FES, almost all respondents who had SEWA accounts said they had no difficulty in withdrawing money, whereas nearly a third of women who had bank accounts said they faced some difficulty. Problems included being told to come back later, being told that money had not arrived in their accounts or being told that they had to maintain a minimum balance, even in no-frills accounts.

The picture was partially captured by the experience of Maanguben, who worked mainly as an agricultural labourer:

> The Cooperative comes to my village twice in a month and we can withdraw or deposit our money. The banks are far from our village. So, we have to walk three kilometres to reach the point of Tata Magic [private bus] and then go to the bank. It takes lots of time and money in travel. The bank staff do not behave well. My husband has an account in the bank and, without checking in the computer, they tell him that the transfer money has not come. Also, we always have to ask other customers for help in filling out the withdrawal form. But with SEWA the staff help us. The Cooperative also provides us with loans at a very low interest rate, minimum documents and repayment in monthly instalments. It is our Cooperative. It believes that we, the poor, will repay the loan, and of course, we will.

So far, we have focused on access to financial institutions. But financial citizenship starts inside the home, with an understanding of power and control within a family. Control may be revealed by, first, how intra-family resources, including money, are allocated; second, on how decisions are made; and third, what degree of support is given to meet individual needs or foster opportunities. Although these are hard to measure, several proxy indicators of intra-family decision-making were considered in the evaluation surveys and case studies.

One indicator was a self-assessment of how earnings were shared within the family. By the end of the pilot, as revealed by the FES, those who had received the basic income were much more likely to report that they were sharing earnings, with 55 per cent of basic income families saying they shared earnings equally compared to 36 per cent in the control group. This represented a clear gain for women.

The shift occurred in all social groups, including the poorest, notably among scheduled tribe households, where 60 per cent of basic income families shared compared to just over 40 per cent of the control group. Among the better-off general (upper) castes, 63 per cent of basic income families shared equally, compared to just over 30 per cent of the control families.

Women who earned an income were more likely to say that family earnings were shared. But regardless of that, the basic income made a difference. Over 50 per cent of non-earning women who received it said that all earnings were shared in the family, as compared to under a third of similar women in the control group. Evidently, the basic income strengthened women's voice on domestic finance, especially among those who were previously not able to contribute income to the family. As one woman, Harlibai, a labourer from the Bhil tribe, put it:

We use the cash transfer money mainly on food, then on health, and on clothes if any money is left. There is a lot of change happening in our family, in terms of food and health aspects. Now even the children are well aware of the cash transfer. We have had discussions about it with all the family. Everyone asks questions.

Respondents were also asked whether the basic income had changed their role in decision-making within the family. Roughly the same number of men and women, over 60 per cent, thought it had enabled them to have more influence on household spending. One might interpret this as reflecting the fact that the increased availability of money enhanced their ability to make consumption decisions rationally.

What is encouraging from a gender equity perspective is that most women thought decisions on spending their basic income were shared within the family. It appeared to have tilted decision-making in the direction of gender equity.

Similarly, in the tribal villages, between the start and end of the pilot, in the basic income village there was a shift from a strong norm of the household head deciding on how income was spent to a weaker norm, with a shift towards shared decision-making. In the baseline, 71 per cent of respondents said decisions were made by the household head, whereas at the end only 52 per cent said this. The change within basic income households as compared to control households was highly significant statistically. Some even felt that decision-making had shifted to the wife.

In sum, financial citizenship was enhanced by the twin effects of the basic income and SEWA activities, which were probably more influential on the institutional side than on domestic behaviour.

Economic citizenship

Economic citizenship is about having equal rights to earn income, to pursue the sort of work and labour one is capable of doing, and to have economic security through access to resources and assets. In these respects, there are several dimensions of economic activity to consider when assessing women's economic status. As shown in Chapter 8, women who had received the basic income increased their labour and work relative to women who had not received it, particularly in the tribal village where women's labour participation increased by 16 per cent, while it scarcely changed for men.

One reason for the increase in women's income-earning was simply more opportunity, where the role of SEWA in mobilizing became relevant. This may even have extended to access to public works. According to one SEWA coordinator:

> In our village, we all have MGNREGS job-cards but no work has come to the village. After we started getting the cash transfer we were discussing and thought we should apply for work. So we all got together and applied. Fifteen people got some days of road construction work, 15 got work making hedging and 15 got work under the *Kapildhara* [well-digging] scheme, but in all it was not many days.

A much more important reason is that many women had increased own-account activity. While casual labour was uncertain, involved hard manual work and paid women less than men, own-account work gave them more control of their time and production. The shift to own-account work was particularly significant in the tribal village where the share of women doing it rose from 40 per cent to 60 per cent, while in the control village it actually shrank.

One reason for the shift was that small-scale and marginal farmers were able to farm their land. They used the basic income to buy seeds, fertilizers and other inputs. The presence of SEWA freed them from exploitative moneylenders, allowing them to borrow at reasonable rates. The results were amazing. The share of women whose primary activity was farming almost doubled, rising from 39 per cent to 66 per cent (see Table 9.1). This was a much greater increase than for men. It was both emancipatory and developmental, helping to boost work and economic growth.

Usually, small-scale tribal farmers with about three bighas cultivate soybean for sale and wheat and maize for consumption. But as they lack capital to purchase inputs, they must borrow at very high interest. So, traditionally, many left the land fallow, migrating for labour rather than take the risk of farming.

Actions to break this debt cycle, or offering loans at lower interest rates, helped to disrupt a structural impasse. SEWA's intervention here was crucial. Apart from the fact that its loans were usually for six months with a monthly repayment schedule, the interest rate was much lower and on a declining

Table 9.1 Tribal villages: Main occupation of women (percentage distribution of responses)

Occupation	Baseline		FES	
	Basic income	Control	Basic income	Control
Farmer	39.1	34.8	65.7	33.3
Wage labour	55.4	56.5	25.4	50.6
Other	5.5	8.7	8.9	16.0

balance, making repayment more feasible. In the basic income tribal village, loans of up to RS.6,000 coupled with the basic income made a big difference to sustainable incomes.

The combination of loans from SEWA's Cooperative and the basic income seemed to prompt more cultivation. Altogether, 33 families opted to take loans in the basic income tribal village during the course of the pilot. As one woman included in the case studies, Radhabai, who had two bighas of land, put it:

> My husband has taken a water contract with a landlord in Bassi Pipri. He is away most of the time. I manage the house and also do the farming. We have some land but don't have legal documents [*patta*], so we are not eligible for credit from the Farmer Credit Society. Earlier, we took loans from the money-lenders from other villages for seeds and fertilizers and had to pay 5 per cent monthly interest. This year we took a loan of 5,000 Rupees from SEWA and are saving money due to the lower interest. With that and the basic income, we purchased seeds and fertilizer and produced 10 bori [10 quintal] of maize. We are repaying monthly, so the interest cost does not keep going up. Before, we had to repay to moneylenders at one go with capital and interest, so almost nothing remained after we sold the grain. That is why we used to prefer to do labour rather than farm our own land. Now we have maize for consumption and also to sell.

Here was a case of the emancipatory effect of the basic income and the SEWA facility, which in turn had a positive effect on local economic growth. Loans for such purposes were also made in the control village, but there were fewer of them. It seems the basic income made villagers more confident in taking the risk of borrowing for production. A similar trend was observed in non-tribal SEWA villages, where a combination of the basic income and access to cheaper cooperative credit seemed to result in more spending on farm inputs and hence an increase in income.

Many households started a business or economic activity, which was more common in basic income villages where SEWA had been operative for some time. And there was other evidence that much of the new economic activity was geared to women, such as small shops and the purchase of sewing machines and livestock, especially cattle and goats.

While average earned income rose in all basic income villages, there were fewer cases of a fall in SEWA basic income villages and more cases of a rise. Although the differences were modest, in net terms they were equivalent to five percentage points. Reflect on what Babitabai, a 30-year-old woman in the tribal village, said:

We don't have any land and we make our living only through labour. As only agricultural labour work is needed in the village, we find work only during the harvest season. During the wheat harvest, we are paid in kind [wheat] instead of cash. During the soybean harvest, the wages are 100 Rupees a day for women, 150 Rupees a day for men. From the harvest labour, we collect enough wheat to last 8–10 months. We must buy the rest from the market. When we started getting the cash transfer, we started a business of making *chudas* [large bangles] that are worn on the arms. We get the raw material and make them at home. We are able to earn about 1,000–2,000 Rupees a month from this work. We have been greatly helped by the cash transfer money. We started the work of making *chudas* in order to increase our income.

Initiatives such as this were described by various women, typically involving the acquisition of small-scale assets. The links between asset acquisition and retention, production and women's economic citizenship are complex. But the data from the evaluation surveys and case studies point to a positive set of outcomes.

They showed the purchase of small capital goods and the construction of facilities for women to work, notably involving home-based shops. Households in basic income villages also purchased sewing machines, with the maximum happening in SEWA villages. There was a 6 per cent increase in households owning sewing machines among basic income households, whereas the number fell among the control group. Having an asset like a sewing machine spurs the desire to start an income-generating activity.

As Laxmibai, a 43-year-old woman who was an own-account farmer and reared animals, described her situation:

All of us used the cash transfers to buy our own things. We bought some clothes and shoes. We were thinking of buying a sewing machine for a long time for our daughters. Now we have been able to buy one for 3,000–3,500 Rupees after saving some of the cash transfer. The men's share mostly gets spent on transport fares and petrol, so all the women's share was pooled.

Without the individual cash transfer it is unlikely that those sewing machines would have been bought. As 26-year-old Leelabai, the wife of a bus driver, said:

These men always make arguments, so that they don't have to buy a sewing machine. How feasible is your project of tailoring? Will it get you income? People will not pay for your clothes. I say, 'Why will they not pay?' Look at how much I pay to get my blouses and children's clothes stitched. But I have stopped arguing and now I am buying my sewing machine with my own money.

However, as shown in Chapter 8, the major shift in assets came from the purchase of livestock. Although they are household assets, in reality it is the women who spend their time and energy in looking after the animals, in collecting fodder, cleaning and milking them.

In sum, through increasing and diversifying their economic roles and through acquiring assets oriented to women as workers, there was a significant improvement in the economic citizenship of women in these villages. There was no doubt a long way to go to reach anything like equality. But the emancipation was there, while women had been enabled to contribute substantively to economic growth within these communities.

Civil and political citizenship

The other great rights and forms of citizenship are civil, political and cultural. The nature of the pilots and the data give us relatively little on these dimensions. But there are some indicators. Civil rights stem from being treated as an equal before the law. This is a matter for government. But whatever the laws might be, exercising one's claim on rights depends on having the confidence and means to do so. Having a basic income did have a positive effect on these; belonging to SEWA must surely have had similar effects.

Political rights come from being entitled to vote and to participate as an equal in the political, decision-making spheres of society. We have seen how the basic income induced more financial citizenship, and in doing so must have had some positive effect on the capacity to be a public person in other ways. But women suffer from lack of political rights in being frozen out of public amenities.

In some villages, women were effectively banned from using public places. The village *choupal* or square is used for meetings, or to just sit together, relax and talk. But this right was reserved for men. Women were not allowed to use the *choupal*. On rare occasions when an all-village meeting was called, some were summoned to sit at the edges. Women have to cover their faces when they go out. And higher-caste and richer women are not allowed to leave their houses. This changed through the basic income, especially when SEWA was involved and when women laid claim to the *choupal*. As one SEWA organizer described what happened in one village:

> I had noticed that women in Jagmalpipliya were not allowed on the *choupal*. Men used to sit on it, talk and gamble. We needed a place to have the awareness meeting and for the first three months we needed a place to give out cash. The

sisters from the Cooperative also needed to operate. So we chose the *choupal*. We started cash transfers there and women began coming. At first the men tried to stop them from climbing onto the *choupal* but we sat right in the middle so they had to come. Then meetings were conducted by SEWA there and slowly the *choupal* was used by all. However, it remains a partial victory. Today, all are allowed to come when the SEWA Cooperative comes to the village, but for other occasions only older women are allowed.

There also remains a great deal of untouchability in these villages. Dalit and Adivasi families are still very poor, and are ostracized by higher castes, who do not allow Dalits into their houses or to eat with them.

SEWA had tried to tackle this issue. Some *anganwadis* were not encouraging Dalit children to come or made them sit outside. After SEWA intervened, all Dalit children were admitted to the centre and a Dalit helper was appointed, enabling them to eat food cooked by her. In some *anganwadis*, Dalit children were made to wash their own plates. This practice was stopped when SEWA objected.

SEWA organizers also raised the issue of temples. Dalits were not allowed in the main village temples, so for opening accounts SEWA organizers sat outside the temple where there was open space. Slowly Dalit women and then men came. Some higher castes objected. But Dalits came to the space and prayed in the temple itself.

Although Indian laws criminalize all forms of violence, many women have to endure violence within their homes. According to the National Family Health Survey of 2005–6, 51 per cent of women and 59 per cent of men believed domestic violence was justified if women did not respect their in-laws or if the husband suspected infidelity. Questions of violence were not included in the project, but anecdotal evidence suggests that SEWA helped some women to deal with domestic violence.

Finally, there is surely a right to basic amenities to ensure a disease-free life. Most villages are unclean, with garbage piling up, stagnant water breeding mosquitoes, open defecation and lack of clean drinking water. These circumstances, especially open defecation, are most harmful for women as they can only go under cover of darkness and so suffer during the day. Worst affected are older women, pregnant women and sick women. The basic income did bring about some changes, as more households invested in toilets and in drinking water. However, much of the problem is due to lack of public sanitation, and here the SEWA effect was beneficial as well, as demonstrated by what happened in the village of Malibadodiya.

Sareeta, who ran a small shop in the village, and Maangu, who earned her living from agricultural labour, told the enumeration team that in their view the main problem in their village was lack of drainage. Dirty water collected in front of their houses or in public places, and was mixed with urine. Mosquitoes, flies, dengue and malaria were rampant. People had to wade through filthy water to travel out of the village. Sareeta said that after the basic income started, she became more active and confident and decided to make a drain in front of her house for disposal of dirty water. She made it herself, from her house all the way down to the outside of the village.

Her neighbours asked her why she was doing all that work, even implying that this was only done by low-caste persons. She replied that it was for the health of her family and the village. When they had seen the effect, others began making drains as well.

Maangu said that the dirty water from their village would run downhill and collect in a hollow in front of the shop. She convinced the shopkeeper to cooperate in putting some rubble there so that puddles did not form. The collective action resulted in sand and rubble covering the hollow. But as there was still no place for the water to go, it collected in other hollows. So when Annapurna, the SEWA organizer, came to the village the women went to the *sarpanch*, who is from another village, and on their urging, he used money from the *panchayat* to put rubble all down the main path.

Still there was no proper drain, which required real investment. So again all the women in that neighbourhood went to the *sarpanch*, apparently many times. In the end, he had a resolution passed in the *panchayat* and a request for drainage funds was sent to the *tehsil*. By the end of the pilot, that had been sanctioned and the road was dug up. It was hoped that drain lines would be laid soon.

This is a powerful example of collective agency, and one can surmise that it was aided by the confidence gained by having a greater sense of individual economic and social status.

Concluding thoughts

A woman lives as an individual, as a member of a family, and as a participant in society. Individual strength is reflected in her dealings with others within the family. A supportive family atmosphere builds up individual resilience. Participation in society needs family approval or support as well as opportunities in the public sphere, which has traditionally been the preserve of men. But the strict rules that bound women's behaviour are being loosened; today there is more scope for individual choices.

Many women experience a moment or an incident that leads to a transformation in consciousness. It can be in their family, in a meeting, at a public function or even in their thoughts. Empowerment grows as women use opportunities that arise, and as they become more willing to face up to obstacles.

During the course of the pilots, several of the authors had some eye-opening moments in conversations with women in the villages, some reflecting a sense of genuine emancipation, often arising from little opportunities to participate in economic or social activities. In some cases, this was due to their husbands, fathers or children giving them encouragement, perhaps for economic reasons. In some cases, it was in reaction to prejudiced behaviour by someone in authority, as one woman told the case study team:

> I am a *panchayat* member. In a public meeting the *sarpanch* said to me, 'You need not come to meetings, we will come to your house and take your signature. Women have no brains, so you will not understand anyway.' It made me angry, and I thought I would show him. I had to convince my mother-in-law and husband. But after that I became very active and made sure that we brought a school, a road and drinking water to the village.

Breaking the mould of prejudice takes time, but often starts with a burst of confidence, which itself derives from a new source of basic security. After the pilots had ended, in the Post-Final Evaluation Survey, all respondents, men and women equally, were asked who in their households had benefited particularly from the basic income. A majority said working-age women had benefited the most (59 per cent), and a majority also singled out elderly women as major gainers. Particularly revealing was what one woman said in a group conversation with the research team in Panthbadodia, a non-SEWA village:

> We women have felt the difference more than the men now that the cash transfers have stopped, because when the men are in need of money, they borrow from here and there in order to buy what they need for themselves. But where do we women borrow from? Earlier when we were getting the cash transfer we were able to buy things for our personal needs, household provisions and for our children. Now we have to ask our husbands for money. Sometimes we cannot buy the things that we require for the household. We women do not get wage labour easily so often we have to stay at home and live completely dependent on men. Compared to when we were getting the cash transfer money, we go to

the market less frequently. When we were getting this money, we used to feel empowered; we could go out and buy the things that were required.

By way of conclusion, we may return to Surajbai, the elderly woman cited at the beginning:

> I was helped by this money [basic income] immeasurably. I used it for my treatment and feel better. Now, I have no outstanding loan to repay and I could buy monthly ration from the village shop. I borrow groceries from the shop when I need and am not charged any interest. I have relatives who come to help me when my sickness becomes severe, but otherwise nobody cares. I only cook food for myself. I live by myself, and I take all decisions by myself. I am old but independent.

10

No Longer Last nor Least ... The Elderly and the Disabled

Introduction

In India in general, in both economic policy and social policy, two groups receive very little attention. Yet both encompass many millions of people and comprise a growing proportion of the population. Estimates of the number of people with disabilities vary very widely, from an unbelievable low of just over 2 per cent revealed by the Census of 2002 to about 16 per cent of the total population. Some have claimed it is higher.

The World Bank has guesstimated that there may be up to 90 million people with one or more disabilities (O'Keefe, 2009; Shenoy, 2011), and the WHO (2011) has estimated that the average percentage of a population having disabilities is 15.6 per cent, which would put the Indian number much higher. Yet, whatever their number, their needs tend to be neglected in public discussion of social policy.

Most of us have disabilities of one sort or another, latent or visible. Some face chronic disability and can barely function. Some face a life of episodic disability, that is, they have conditions, such as diabetes, which afflict them from time to time, incapacitating them temporarily. They are difficult to categorize, making it hard to design social policy oriented to helping those classified as 'disabled'.

Meanwhile, the elderly are a growing proportion of the total population. As mortality rates drop, and as morbidity among older people declines, this growing group is not just a dependent one requiring some formal or informal pension, but is also a substantial group of productive people, giving a new meaning to the idea of the 'elderly'.

The disabled and the elderly share some deeply ingrained problems linked to cultural and social prejudices. Typically, they are regarded as involving families and communities in additional social and economic costs. Almost by definition, they have a higher probability of experiencing a shock in the form of a medical crisis that precipitates a financial crisis, simply because dealing with a medical crisis tends to be very costly.

Those with visible disabilities also tend to be regarded as having a lower expected income, in the short term and in the longer term. If they also require attention and care from others in their households, they also tend to lower the potential income of the household and, in particular, that of those who provide the care, typically a woman or adolescent.

A village community typically responds to these realities by supporting moral codes of behaviour and by various sharing practices. But households struggling to survive tend to behave, to a greater or lesser extent, in ways that maximize the probability that they will be able to maintain themselves.

That is likely to mean that priorities will usually be decided within families, explicitly by decisions made by the nominal household head or implicitly, over time, by rationalization of little acts of preference, such as giving larger portions of food to those seen as offering the highest probability of producing more or bringing the most income into the family. This is all understandable, and is what happens the world over.

Add cultural prejudices and there are the ingredients for a pattern of discriminatory decisions that inevitably affect the welfare and development of individuals. In this cruel dilemma, it is surely common for those with disabilities, and those aged and frail, to be the least favoured. This will not be the case all the time, because sympathy, pity and empathy play a part, leading to moral pressure on family members to compensate for their relative's disability or past contributions. But the sheer survival instinct must be strong in such circumstances.

Bearing these behavioural and attitudinal concerns in mind, it is important to consider how individualized basic incomes affected them, and affected the welfare of those with disabilities and the elderly. We will do this briefly in this chapter, hoping that the tentative findings prompt more detailed analysis.

The disabled enabled?

Examining the data from the evaluation surveys and relevant case studies, there was reason for thinking that those with disabilities would tend to gain nutritionally more than others, mainly because the basic income represented a higher proportion of their previous living standard, which would have been below that of other members of the household.

So, as the disabled tended to be disproportionately concentrated in lower-income households, receipt of their Rs.200 or Rs.300 basic income would have raised their relative as well as absolute standard of nutrition. It is also notable that scheduled caste households had a higher incidence of disabled members than others.

The basic income also had a particular emancipatory value for the disabled, because in gaining access to more food, the individualized basic income gave the person more bargaining strength within the household. It was their money.

The same reasoning is applicable to access to schooling. In a cash-scarce community, in which certain costs associated with schooling act as barriers to regular attendance in school, such as the cost of transport and clothes, the tendency will be for families to give priority to paying for those costs for children who have what they perceive as the greatest probability of turning schooling into income-earning activity.

Those with what families will tend to see as having a low probability of bringing income into the family are more likely to face discriminatory treatment by their own families. Again, this is not heartlessness but cruel pressure. In addition, the actual costs of ensuring school attendance would tend to be higher for children with disabilities.

Laws and regulations cannot fully overcome these self-discriminatory tendencies. A basic income could not be expected to do so either. However, the very existence – and the community's knowledge of its existence – of the individualized basic income would surely help improve the bargaining position of the disabled and induce moral pressure from others to ensure they have equal treatment.

Nanuram, a Bhil tribal agricultural labourer in one of the pilot villages, had a physically disabled son due to polio. Aged 20, he was studying in 10th grade at a private school and taking private tuition at a local town. Talking about the basic income, Nanuram said:

> I don't take his money at all, Sir! He studies, so he needs that money for his books and transport. He takes from the bank whenever he needs money for his studies. So far he has done so twice – 600 and 500 Rupees. With the 600 he had his tricycle repaired. It has been lying broken because we did not have money. With his second withdrawal, he bought clothes and paid for his tuition fees.

Beyond nutrition and schooling there are, of course, the several effects on health and healthcare. Cruel decisions have always had to be made in cash-scarce situations. And the individualized basic income must have unambiguously positive effects, even if they are modest. Happily, there is evidence from the evaluation surveys that this was indeed the case.

The health impact was strong. Households with disabled members were just as likely to report a lower incidence of ill-health as other households compared with those without the basic income. Thus, whereas 68 per cent of households without it and with disabled members reported some illness in the past three months at the time of the FES, only 56 per cent of equivalent households with the basic income had an illness.

Among households receiving the basic income, those with disabled members were more likely to have increased spending on medicine (68 per cent versus 56 per cent) and more likely to have done so than households with disabled members without the basic income. And among those with the basic income that increased such spending, those with disabled members were more likely to attribute that directly to the basic income.

Among the basic income households, those with disabled members were relatively more likely to have shifted to private treatment, 37 per cent of them having done so, compared with 26 per cent of other households.

And among the basic income households, those with disabled members were more likely to report having taken medicine more regularly in the period (24 per cent versus 14 per cent). This was more than double the share of households with disabled members that did not receive the basic income.

However, the biggest impact was in inducing more of the disabled to go for hospital treatment. Although the range of disabilities was broadly similar across all the 20 general villages, it was remarkable that in the year covered by the retrospective data collected for the FES, 48 physically disabled persons in the basic income villages had hospital treatment, whereas only two did so in the control villages. It is extremely unlikely that this difference came about by chance.

Moreover, when hospital treatment was needed, the average number of days between the need arising and going to hospital was much lower in the basic income villages. In short, the disabled and chronically ill were not only more likely to go for the treatment but were more likely to go in a timely way.

Kamlabai, a 70-year old disabled woman in Datoda village, was one of many disabled persons to have benefited from the basic income payment. Recounting how the money had helped her, she said:

> All my basic income money was spent on my treatment itself, because I have such physical weakness that every month I have to spend up to 500 Rupees. We

go to Ghata-Billod for medical treatment because it is nearer. We go to a private doctor. He takes 200 Rupees.

Like Kamlabai, a majority of the disabled within basic income households perceived their situation to have improved. At the time of the Post-Final Evaluation Survey, a census in two of the basic income villages, 120 individuals said they had a disability or chronic illness that affected their ability to work or study, of whom 95 per cent said they needed regular treatment, medicine, aids or prosthetics for their condition.

Among the 120, 87 per cent believed the basic income had improved their personal living conditions, 80 per cent believed that it had helped them take medicines more regularly, 73 per cent said it had helped them to go to a doctor or clinic more regularly, 81 per cent said it had given them a sense of independence, and 76 per cent said that it had helped them pay attention to their health problems more than a year ago. Remarkably, it had an even bigger positive effect for women with disabilities (Table 10.1).

Similar findings emerged in the tribal villages, where nearly two-thirds of those receiving the basic income mostly went to hospital within two days of falling ill or needing treatment, compared with just over a quarter of those in the control group. The duration of stay in hospital was also less, suggesting that they went at an earlier stage.

Households with disabled members tended to experience more financial crises than others. There is nothing surprising in that. They were also more likely to have experienced a rising level of debt and were slightly less likely to have had any savings. But as with so many aspects of their lives, they reported that the basic income had lightened the load.

Table 10.1   General villages: Percentage of disabled and chronically ill persons reporting improvement due to basic income, by main reason and gender

	Disability		Chronic illness	
	Male	**Female**	**Male**	**Female**
Improved personal living conditions	91	100	86	88
Helped taking medicines more regularly	73	100	69	86
Helped visiting doctor/clinic more regularly	73	85	69	78

Source: MPUCT PFES, 2012; n=120

Debt, saving and financial crises

The effect of the basic income on the financial situation of households with disabled members was a mixed one. A majority of such households (58.5 per cent) reported an increase in debt over the year covered by the FES, compared with 45 per cent of other basic income households. But they were less likely to have experienced increased indebtedness than households with disabled members that had not received the basic income (64 per cent).

A similar pattern emerged with saving. For those receiving a basic income, households with disabled members were less likely to have saved in the past year (16 per cent versus 21 per cent). But nevertheless, they were more likely to have saved something than equivalent households that had not received the basic income (10 per cent).

The impact on work among the disabled

The disabled tend to be grossly neglected in analyses of labour and work, and much else. As emphasized earlier, they make up a significant proportion of village populations, and deserve far more analytical and policy attention than they receive.

It is difficult to isolate the effects of a basic income on work activity. Clearly, it was likely to help those capable of working to do so, enabling them to buy more raw materials or small tools or instruments, and so doing activities that they might have wished to do but lacked the resources. Thus, several people opened a little shop. Again, this is an emancipatory effect.

A poignant case was that of Saloni, pictured on the front cover of this book, a disabled 30-year-old landless woman from a backward caste, whose husband, Devnarayan, was also physically disabled, and who lived in the village of Malibadodia. She told the case study enumeration team that her disability meant she could not work outside the home, but added:

> From the basic income money we saved and bought a hand-operated sewing machine. With the help of that, we started sewing work for the villagers. This has added to our income. In the past year [when receiving the basic income], we have increased the intake of vegetables, as compared to the year before. With the help of the cash, I also bought bangles, clothes, *chappals* and household utensils, and we paid the school fee for our daughter. For health expenses, we started taking our medicine regularly. The main benefit from the basic income

has been that of buying the sewing machine, which has increased our income, and as a result we are able to fulfil our family needs.

In effect, the basic income had released a constraint on her capacity to work and on her capacity to be a productive member of the community. It is this sort of small but vital liquidity effect that comes across in so many respects.

In terms of the statistics from the evaluation surveys, the FES revealed that households containing one or more disabled people were more likely to have increased their income-earning activity in the past year than similar households not receiving the basic income. The impact on households with disabled persons in them was remarkably similar to the impact on households without disabled members. In effect, such households were also able to take advantage of the opportunities afforded by the basic income.

Perhaps what was most striking was that households with disabled members who did not receive the basic incomes were the most likely to have experienced declines in income-earning – 27 per cent, compared with 12 per cent that had received the basic income.

A related finding from the FES is that the basic incomes appeared to have the same positive effect on the number of days of farm work done by households with or without disabled members, 14 per cent compared with 13 per cent for basic income households that did not have disabled members.

So, in net terms the change was actually bigger for those containing disabled members (i.e. comparing those with and without basic incomes). This latter finding was a reflection of a decline in own-account farm work by households with disabled members that were not receiving basic incomes.

In sum, one may conclude that at least some of the disabled, presumably those with least impediments, had been able to participate in the local economy and had thus become contributors to its growth and development.

The subsidy and labour lines

How did the disabled fare with respect to the two major welfare policies pursued over recent years? The subsidy line should be of concern. Households with disabled members were slightly more likely to have a BPL card, but still only a minority of those had one. They were less likely to have an APL card or to have an AAY card.

There was no difference between households in their use of the PDS ration shop. Over the past year covered by the FES, among those receiving the basic income, more of each type of household reported using the PDS less. Thus, 10 per cent of households with somebody disabled in them used it less, compared with 5 per cent using it more. But more of the control households with disabled reported using it less, 11 per cent, compared with 2 per cent using it more.

In sharp contrast, 47 per cent of basic income households with somebody disabled reported using the market more, precisely the same as among other households receiving the basic income. That was significantly more than for equivalent control households. In sum, over half (52 per cent) of disabled basic income households reported shifting more to the market.

If the disabled were just as likely to be moving away from the subsidy line, their experience of the labour line was predictably dispiriting. A smaller proportion of households with disabled members were aware of the MGNREGS. And of those who were aware, only a minority had registered with the scheme, and of those only a very small minority had actually had any labour on it. Evidently, the scheme was effectively discriminating against those with disabled members.

The elderly

The elderly also tend to be neglected in discussions of social policy. That cannot continue with any credibility, because their numbers are growing. And in that regard it is welcome that a big enquiry was conducted in 2014 on the status of the elderly across India (NCAER, 2014). They presently comprise just over one in every 12 rural inhabitants in Madhya Pradesh, roughly the national average. Only about 16 per cent were receiving any money from government benefits.

In terms of assessing the impact of the basic income, there are two ways of looking at older people in the villages. One can look at them as individuals and one can compare households made up of elderly persons with those made up entirely or predominantly of younger people.

In dividing households into types, we may define an 'elderly' household as one consisting solely of persons aged over, say, 55, or as one consisting of a majority of persons over that age, or as one in which the average age is 55 or over. We have done all three. There is a rather extraordinary effect that emerges from examining the impact of basic income. In some crucial respects, the basic income had a bigger relative effect on outcomes in elderly households than in 'younger' households, whichever way one measured the difference.

Because the basic income was paid individually, its impact could have been high for similar reasons as for the disabled, by strengthening their voice in decision-making and because the cash probably accounted for a larger-than-average share of their total income. But neither could be taken for granted, simply because the elderly tend to be frail and dependent on younger relatives.

According to the FES data, and using the first definition of an older household (all members aged 55 or over), more of the older households preferred the basic income to rations of equivalent value, although the difference was greater for young households. Of those older households that had received the basic income, 43 per cent preferred the basic income in cash and 39 per cent preferred rations.

The experience of basic incomes and the attitudes to them were quite similar to those of younger households. More preferred family accounts to individual accounts than was the case among the younger households. But most of both the old and younger households reported having no difficulty with operating bank accounts, while the take-up rate of the basic income was actually slightly higher for the older households.

In the year leading up to the FES, more elderly households that had received the basic income made at least some improvement to their dwelling or living conditions than their equivalent households that had not received the basic income. They were less likely to have done so than the younger households that had received it, but more likely than younger households that had not received the basic income. A similar pattern emerged with changes in energy and lighting.

It was a similar story for nutrition. The share of old-age households that received the basic income which reported having too little income for their food needs was just 16 per cent, which was higher than for the younger households that had received the basic income (12 per cent) but much lower than for old-age households without a basic income (31 per cent) and also lower than for younger households without a basic income (25 per cent). This is surely a striking finding. Very similar findings emerged using the other two definitions of old-age households.

The old-agers were most inclined to use their basic incomes for food and to try to save something for emergencies. Recall Surjibai, a 70-year-old woman whose plight was seen in the previous chapter. Her experience was typical in that respect if not in others:

> Then the basic income started, with cash. I used this money for the treatment of my illness and for regular household things like tea, sugar, oil, salt, chilli, turmeric, etc. I smoke one bundle of *biri* every day, so I used to get that also. I glean the leftover wheat from the fields during the harvest season in order to eat.

First, I went to Borsi village for treatment of my eczema and then I went to the private doctor at Jambudi village. Later I also went to Indore for treatment but still there is no relief from the condition. Because of this illness I now have 1,000 Rupees of debt. But I have no other outstanding loan to repay. I borrow groceries from the shop when I need. I am not charged any interest. I repay the debt by working at houses, but I am not a servant. I don't save anything and I am not associated with any unit. I live by myself, and I take all decisions by myself.

I eat twice a day. For my last meal I had *kheer-puri* from the *anganwadi*. I eat three *rotis* at a time. I do get enough food. I don't drink milk. I am vegetarian and eat vegetables occasionally, when I can afford it. Otherwise, I eat only *dal-roti*. The food I get from the *anganwadi* is good enough. It is better than nothing. I get food to eat, but I can't say it is nutritious food. I don't have money for nutrition. I go to the market [which is 10 kms away] once or twice a month. I don't buy anything from the ration shop.

I was helped by this cash transfer money immeasurably. I could buy food from the village shop and use some for my treatment. I have relatives who come to help me when my sickness becomes severe. But otherwise nobody cares. I only cook food for myself. I don't get any other help from my relatives. Since the coming of the money, women of our village have started saving through small units. The villagers have also decided to build the roof of the temple from the last instalment of the cash transfer money. I feel SEWA is doing good work by trying to make women self-reliant.

Clearly, this is a tough survival existence. But the little more had enabled her to gain a modicum of control over her life, and buy extra food from the local shop. It was notable too that she did not use the ration shop.

Indeed, among those receiving the basic income, more old-age households reported buying less from the ration shops (13 per cent) than young-age households (10 per cent), whereas hardly any reported buying more in these shops (3 per cent compared with 5 per cent). In this respect, there was little difference between old-age households by whether or not they were receiving the basic income.

However, the real differences came out in the shift to use of the open market. Significantly more old-age households with basic incomes increased their purchases in the market compared with older equivalents without the basic income. In neither case was the shift as great as for younger households. All groups had shifted from the ration shops to the market.

Health and access to healthcare are the most crucial issues for the elderly. Here again the results were encouraging and similar. So, the share of old-age basic income households having had at least one illness in the past three months was much lower than in equivalent households that had not received the basic income (52 per cent compared to 67 per cent) and also lower than in non-old households without the basic income.

And fewer had been hospitalized than their equivalent old-age households without the basic income. Meanwhile, old-age households with the basic income were the most likely to have increased spending on medicines. And as the control households were also more likely to report having spent less, the net difference was even greater.

Anandibai, a scheduled caste wage labourer, described how her mother-in-law, an asthma patient, was able to use her basic income to pay for injections and medicines, which cost her Rs.150–200 every month. Another old person, when asked what he did with the basic income, had this to say:

> On account of my old age the money was utilized for my injections. Twenty Rupees would be spent just on transport. The rest of the money was given to the doctor.

Similarly, more old-age households with the basic income reported increased spending on doctors' fees, and the difference was greater for the old-age households than for younger ones. There was no significant difference between the aged and other households in terms of spending on private treatment. But the spending increase due to basic income was greater for old-age households.

Households with elderly persons were actually not more likely to have substantial debts than other households. The fact was that debt was pervasive, although the share of old-age households with substantial debt was lower than average. Some 58 per cent of old-age basic income households had debts, compared with 72 per cent of other basic income households. What was also striking, however, was that very few old-age households that did have debts were able to reduce them. And fewer old-age households managed any saving, whether or not they had received the basic income.

Many old-age households regarded the basic income money as a source of increased security. Consider another fairly typical account, by a 73-year-old man, Mohanlal, from the Teli-Rathor community (a designated backward caste), who lived with his 70-year-old wife, Parvatibai:

> We have three children, all of whom are married. They all live separately from us. I have three acres of unirrigated land. We rent out this land on a yearly rent, for which we take 15,000–20,000 Rupees a year. We distribute this money among the three children. I do the work of herding the cattle of my three children. In return, they give us stuff required for the running of our household,

for example milk and groceries, etc. They don't give us cash. My wife goes to do wage labour in the fields of the village farmers. She goes for 8–10 days in a month, which provides us for the month.

Only my wife and I stay in our house; the children live nearby. I only do the herding of the children's cattle. We have an APL ration card, on which we buy wheat and kerosene. We both eat twice a day. We ate *sabji-roti* at our last meal. We both eat 2–3 *rotis* at a time. Food is sufficient and we don't face problems regarding food. The market is four kilometres away. We don't buy stuff in bulk; we go and buy things that are required at home. We buy vegetables from the vendors who come to sell in the village.

Both of us are in good physical health except for the usual seasonal illnesses. We go to Ghata-Billod for medical treatment. Our government hospital is at Betma, and it costs 20 Rupees to go there as it is far away. This is why we go and get the treatment in Ghata-Billod, which is nearby.

We sieve the water before drinking. We sometimes use soap for bathing and washing, but it is not obligatory. In order to repel mosquitoes we smoke the house; nothing other than that. We have a toilet in the house, which is shared by our children as well. The roads in the village are not at all good and there are no drains. All this causes a lot of dirt and filth in the village.

We have a bank loan to be repaid. We had taken this loan on land, from the Bank Society for Fertilizers and Seeds. I used that to go for a pilgrimage. We will pay it back by taking loans from here and there, and then we will take it out again after repayment.[1] It works like this only. At present we don't have savings of any kind. We have saved only the cash transfer money that has been coming. We have saved this so that we can use it in case of emergency. It will be useful if either of us falls sick. Fortunately our bodies are still in working condition, but as old age advances, this money will be useful to us. For this reason, we have not taken out any of the money.

Intriguingly, old-age households were significantly less likely to have experienced a financial crisis in the past year. They were just as likely to have had to borrow to meet a crisis if it arose, but at least among those receiving the basic income they were the least likely to have had to sell or mortgage any assets to deal with it.

Regarding access to selective and targeted social policies, the old typically have certain disadvantages. Old-age households were more likely than their younger counterparts to have a BPL or AAY card, and correspondingly less likely to have an APL card. But they were slightly more likely to have no card at all, presumably reflecting their difficulty of obtaining or re-obtaining one. Unsurprisingly, they were less likely to be aware of MGNREGS and, if aware, much less likely to have had any labour on it. As with the disabled, that labour-based scheme of social security has been a discriminatory policy against older people.

Finally, there is the impact on the work and labour of the elderly. Here there is a very mixed picture. The problem is that with this age group, there is an income effect and a substitution effect. The increased income represented by the basic income should have enabled some to reduce their labour, particularly bearing in mind that among the elderly the productivity of manual labour would presumably be low. At the same time, the influx of the cash may have enabled them, like younger villagers, to obtain more seeds or small-scale equipment to enable them to conduct an income-earning activity.

In general, the data pointed to a slight drop in labour force participation among the elderly who received the basic income, although in the overall multivariate analysis the coefficients were not statistically significant. Taking the age group 55–59, the male economic activity rate as conventionally measured remained the same over the period of the pilot, whereas it dropped by about seven percentage points for women in the same age bracket.

This should not be interpreted as women doing less work per se, since they reported doing more housework and care work. Men reported doing less of such work. The changes in all these respects were greater than observed in the control groups.

As with all age groups, among those aged 55–59, those receiving basic incomes tended to shift from casual labour and construction labour to own-account work, and this was greater than in the control villages. For both men and women, there was a greater amount of animal husbandry. And for both, there was an increase in the number reporting that they were working what might be described as full-time, more than 20 days in the past month, whereas for the same age group there were declines in the control villages.

For those aged 60 or more, there were no discernible changes that could be linked to the basic income. But it seems as if for the age group 55–59, the basic income had a small positive effect on work activity, not the negative effect that one might have envisaged.

Concluding reflections

At the end of the pilot, in the PFES, a set of questions was asked about which person in the household had benefited most. The disabled were often mentioned.

Respondents who had some disability were just as likely as others to report that the basic income had made a difference – more reporting a big difference – to their influence on decision-making within the household. However modest it might have been, it was empowering for them.

In spite of the encouraging outcomes, it must be emphasized that the disabled continued to experience the greatest hardships, being in general the least likely to have increased their earned income, less likely to have saved and less likely to have reduced their debt, and more likely than average to have experienced a financial crisis. But in all those respects, the disabled with basic income did better than those without it. Even for them, it had proved emancipatory and had helped improve their general welfare.

Note

1   It is a reference to the bank loan given by the government to landowning farmers. The bank loan is 'renewed' every year after the repayment. Usually this happens during the harvest season. However, in the case of Mohanlal, who used this money for his pilgrimage instead of farming, he had to take other loans in order to repay the bank loan.

11

The Transformative Potential

A little more, how much it is
A little less, what worlds apart

Robert Browning

Dictated by financial constraints, the period for the general pilot was originally limited to 12 months. Just before the end of that period, UNICEF was able to supplement the funding, enabling the pilot to be extended for another six months. Immediately, the fieldwork team visited the villages to inform residents through another round of what had been dubbed 'Awareness Visits'. The coordinator sent us the following account:

> In the last three months, whenever we went to villages, there have been queries about cash transfers, and villagers would ask us if they would resume at a later date. Our standard reply had been that we didn't know, and if there were any likelihood of continuing, we would inform them. In Malibadodiya, when we announced a meeting, some 50 women assembled, and a dozen or so *bidi*-smoking men stood at a distance.
>
> An old woman sitting in the front said, 'I had a dream last night. You are going to continue the cash transfers.' Some laughed and made fun of her; some nodded in agreement. When we announced they would get transfers for five months, in three instalments, people clapped and laughed. An old man came forward and said to the old woman, who had a dream, 'Ma, have more such dreams!'

Perhaps our coordinator used poetic licence. We cannot be sure. However, although sceptics might not be convinced by such accounts, we can say we are convinced that a small amount of extra money in the form of a very basic income can and did make a great deal of difference. A little more, how much it is.

And for reasons given earlier, the emancipatory value of that little amount was and is greater than the monetary value. We conclude that this makes it doubly more valuable than indirect schemes, since more of the total money reaches the recipients.

New times

In 2014, the Indian population elected a new government, the first with an absolute majority of seats for 30 years. It took office with high hopes and new energy, amidst some well-known fears. Nevertheless, given that it should have a full term, the new government has a rare opportunity to reshape social policy as well as the economic development model. Reforms should start soon and be what is called 'evidence-based'.

All the old policies seemed set for review. The new government had made a commitment to pursue the security of all groups. In doing so, it is to be hoped that the options will be evaluated by reference to the sort of social justice principles enunciated in the first chapter of this book. They should be judged too on whether or not they facilitate economic growth and sustainable development. It is in that context that modest basic income schemes should be considered objectively and dispassionately.

People's preferences

People the world over tend to prefer the security they know over the security they might obtain from something else. The average human being tends to be risk-averse. We adapt to what is known, and have anxiety about what is not. This is highly relevant to assessing attitudes to basic income.

If, for generations, people have been receiving some modest benefits in a particular form, they are likely to cling to them even if somebody assures them that something else would actually provide them with more security, income or satisfaction. This psychological barrier to something new is well known and rational. But it should be taken into account in assessing people's attitudes to basic income.

In that context, social policy analysts have repeatedly asserted that Indian villagers prefer subsidized food to basic cash income. Take the well-known critic, Jean Dreze (2011):

> The most common argument for cash transfers is that cash makes it possible to
> satisfy a variety of needs (not just food), and that people are best judges of their

own priorities. Fair enough. But if people are best judges of their own interest, why not ask them whether they prefer food or cash? In my limited experience, poor people tend to prefer food, with a gradual shift from food-preference to cash-preference among better-off households.

Similarly, in a vehement defence of the PDS, Reetika Khera (2011a) reported on a survey, considerably smaller than those in the pilots, whereby only those actually possessing a BPL or AYY card were asked their opinions on the PDS and cash transfers. A decision was made in that project to exclude anybody without a card. Since those denied a card are much more likely to be dissatisfied with the PDS system, excluding them gave a strong bias in favour of supporting the PDS. If you exclude those most likely to be dissatisfied, it is quite wrong to draw a conclusion that people are satisfied!

In the FES, the question was asked of every respondent, 'Would you prefer to have subsidized goods in a ration shop or to receive cash equal to the value of the subsidy so that you can decide what goods to buy and where, or do you not mind which?'

Note that all options were given, so the respondents were not led to any desired answer. The responses given are interesting for two reasons. First, more respondents said they preferred to receive cash benefits than subsidized goods in a ration shop. Overall, the figures were 40 per cent for basic incomes, 34 per cent for subsidized goods from the ration shop.

Second, there were differences in attitudes between those who had received basic income and those who had not. Those who had experienced receipt of basic income were more likely to support basic income rather than subsidized goods compared with those who had not experienced basic income. So 44 per cent of households preferred cash in those households which had received the basic income, while 34 per cent of those who had not preferred cash.

If one puts aside those who were unsure which option they preferred, 58 per cent of those with an opinion who had received it preferred basic income. In other words, there was a learning function. Of those who had actual experience of both types of assistance, significantly more preferred the cash option.

In sum, those who gain experience of having a basic income come to realize its value, and more people prefer that to subsidized items.

Welfare and social justice

The claim we have been making is that a basic income would be transformational, in having three integrated types of effect. Let us start with a brief review of the impact on welfare, or 'well-being', and in doing so see how well or badly it does by reference to the social justice and SEWA principles set out in the opening chapter.

Welfare covers nutrition, schooling, health and living conditions. Consider what happened in terms of the first of the justice principles, the Security Difference Principle, and SEWA's closely related Most-Vulnerable-at-the-Centre Principle. It is apt that the sentiments expressed in the report of our fieldwork coordinator came from elderly villagers. For among the strongest findings from the pilots is that it was the most insecure who benefited most, including the elderly, women of all ages, notably young girls, and the disabled.

The elderly tend to be among the most neglected in rural low-income households. Too often they do not receive the pensions owed to them, and too often life insurance benefits are unpaid to widows and widowers. They are usually 'semi-destitute', they tend to be the last to obtain medical treatment and they lack Voice to demand social assistance. But as we have seen, the individualized basic income gave them an independent voice that improved their welfare.

We may argue further that the basic income would satisfy the Security Difference Principle, and its SEWA equivalent, more than targeted and selective alternatives, since each of these has high exclusion and inclusion errors, particularly the former.

This is particularly true of schemes that have relied on possession of a BPL or AAY card. Just recall how badly the MGNREGS did in terms of reaching women, households with disabled people in them, and older-people households. It effectively discriminated against the most insecure members of those villages. And the PDS with the BPL cards was demonstrably prone to high exclusion errors.

Also recall a few of the welfare outcomes. In terms of *basic living conditions*, a significant number of households made improvements to their dwellings and invested in improving their toilets. This was likely to have demonstration effects on others, encouraging them to save and take advantage of the Total Sanitation Campaign. Improved latrines have a beneficial effect on health, particularly for young children, women and people with illnesses of one kind or another. The improved health surely has a beneficial effect on learning in school and on productivity in work and labour, and reduces pressure on public social spending.

Then there is the positive impact on *nutrition*. The effects on children's weight-for-age, notably for girls, were among the most encouraging findings. Those positive effects tended to predominate after infants moved from breast-feeding to solid foods.

We also saw that vulnerable groups gained relatively the most, notably in gaining more food sufficiency, which had a progressive effect, particularly for scheduled caste and tribe households. The improvement in diets, with more vegetables, milk, eggs, fruit and fish, was particularly striking in the tribal villages. And the individualized basic incomes make it more likely that intra-family and community concerns for social equity will come to the fore, an advance over household-based subsidies, for instance.

The improvements in *health and healthcare* were marked by a greater regularity in the taking of medicines, an aspect of healthcare that tends to be underestimated. The key point here is that the basic incomes made it easier to take rational decisions on healthcare, through more prompt treatment, change of diets or whatever specific illnesses or mishaps required.

The cash, and the assurance of it over forthcoming months, combined with access to medicines, made it more likely that low-income people would take their treatment to its proper conclusion, rather than stop when feeling slightly better. Again, the relatively vulnerable, including the disabled, benefited relatively the most in terms of improved healthcare, partly because they were less dependent on the benevolence of others inside or outside the family.

There is one potentially controversial aspect of the observed changes in healthcare, which is the shift from public to private services. We believe this is partly a reflection of a shift from situations in which people lacked any treatment, or who had postponed treatment due to lack of money, to where they had the means to obtain some treatment or to resort to treatment sooner, which should be beneficial.

However, to the extent there was a shift from government to private commercial institutions and treatment, the interpretation should not be that there should be more privatization. It should be that the government healthcare system must be improved, so as to become a more attractive option for everybody.

In terms of the impact on *schooling*, a key point is the positive impact on school enrolment and attendance, particularly of girls at secondary-school level. As such, there may be no need to apply conditionality, especially as applying arbitrary rules requiring some high percentage attendance rate would be administratively burdensome and expensive, as well as be prone to unfairness in making judgements on whether non-attendance was the 'fault' of the mother or parents. There is also tentative evidence that the basic incomes helped improve school performance, although this requires more intensive research.

As with healthcare, the relative shift to private schooling can be interpreted in two ways, as reflecting an increase in schooling in general, particularly in the broad idea of 'private tuition', and as reflecting widespread concern over the quality of government schools as they exist and as they are perceived to exist.

In general, the pilots showed positive welfare effects, showing that conditionality was not required. As the Deputy Chair of the Indian Planning Commission, Montek Singh Ahluwalia, said at the conference convened to present the preliminary results of the project in May 2013 (as reported in *The Hindustan Times* (2013)):

> This project proves two things. First of all, cash transfers can be organised. Secondly, when you give the money directly into the beneficiaries' account, it is simply not wasted or used for the wrong things.

In sum, a basic income, being universal and unconditional and paid equally, improves the social and economic security of the most insecure groups, and does so by more than it does for less insecure groups.

Growth, development and social justice

There should be little doubt that the basic income was beneficial for economic growth and economic dynamism in the villages covered by the pilots. The money was not just used for welfare improvements, however important they were. It helped boost the productivity of the villagers' farmland, and helped generate new economic activities, the essence of economic growth.

Indeed, back-of-the-envelope calculations of the cost of income transfers almost always neglect to consider the cost-saving effects and the developmental impact that make the net economic cost much less than the simple transfer cost. If, for instance, a scheme lowers the incidence of ill-health, it will lower the cost of public expenditure on healthcare; if it lowers drop-out rates from school, it increases the productivity of public spending on schooling.

The main growth-enhancing effects of the basic income, as shown in the pilots, were the significant increase in production it induced, and the corresponding increase in the extent of adult labour and work, and even more intriguingly the change in the pattern of work.

As the new economic growth was a reflection of increased local production, the economic multiplier effects could be expected to be higher. This is consistent with the *Swadeshi* Principle of local production. In promoting higher economic activity, the basic income appeared to boost local food production, particularly of wheat (through more acreage and more productive use of land), and including an intriguing revival of local strains of wheat, millet and other cereals. And it generated investment in more storage facilities, particularly of wheat, thereby providing more food security through the barren months.

There was also a growth in the number of small and large livestock, which improved nutrition and income-earning options. That surely had feedback effects on health and the learning capacities of children, particularly in the tribal villages, which were the most deprived.

The impact on child work deserves further reflection. The basic income seemed to result in less child labour of the type that is generally regarded as more 'arduous' and disruptive. To the extent that it resulted in little change, and even an increase, in the extent of child work on family farms, a policy conclusion might be that more advice should be given in educating families on how to combine schooling with useful farm work and what pitfalls to avoid. There is nothing wrong with having children involved in productive work if it does not distract them from learning, expose them to dangers or leave them too exhausted to learn.

More significantly, contrary to popular prejudices, the basic incomes did not lead to a net reduction in adult work. On the contrary, it led to more work and to a shift from casual wage labour to own-account farm and non-farm productive work, as well as more reproductive care. The principles of *Swaraj* and Dignified Work seemed to be supported in this respect.

Own-account work allowed people to try to be more self-reliant and to gain more control over their own time. As individuals and families were working more for themselves, the work surely gave greater dignity than doing casual wage labour. All of that was surely favourable for the families and for the local community. And, if it resulted in a rise in local wage rates, it could reduce the extent of exploitation and oppression that are so characteristic of the casual wage labour and *naukar* labour markets.

In sum, the development effect of a basic income was seen in several ways, which should be taken into account in any calculus of the cost of implementing a policy of this sort.

Emancipation and social justice

One of the most striking aspects of the whole project is that one can conclude by stating that the emancipatory value of the basic income is greater than its monetary value. This arises primarily from the fact that for most villagers money itself is a scarce commodity. In gaining the basic income, people gained a source of monetary liquidity, enabling them to avoid using expensive credit and having to borrow so much at seriously high rates of interest.

There are also emancipatory effects on the status and agency of women. The fact that the basic income was individualized and unconditional enhanced the agency and identity of women, and they themselves recognized that it gave them additional strength in decision-making. In the villages where SEWA was active, collective action helped women gain more traction in village life.

In short, the evidence is strong that the individualized payments resulted in women and other vulnerable groups, such as the disabled and elderly, having more independence, more voice and more equitable treatment within the households and within the village communities.

There is another aspect of the emancipation that derives from the community coverage of the basic income, which is what might be called a social multiplier effect. Put simply, because others are sharing in the economic security, the overall effects for individuals are more positive, because optimism spreads and social norms and expectations evolve.

Emancipation is linked to the Indian idea of *Swaraj*, of self-rule or self-reliance. As Tilak famously asserted, '*Swaraj* is my birthright, and I will have it!' Gandhi's idea of *Hind Swaraj* means more than political freedom. It means being in control of one's work, undominated by exogenous forces. This sentiment has had its counterparts elsewhere, perhaps most notably in John Ruskin's celebrated essay, 'Unto This Last'. It is an abiding human value.

From emancipation to transformation

The most important conclusion is that 'the whole is greater than the sum of the parts'. It is this which makes the basic income potentially transformative. While the individual effects, on living conditions, nutrition, health, schooling, economic activity, agency and so on, were all major in themselves, the overall effect was transformative, in the sense that constraints on economic dynamism were weakened, inducing feedback effects, while the emancipatory outcomes were likely to lend local communities a developmental energy that the alternatives of targeted, selective subsidy schemes could not hope to achieve.

What is perhaps the most transformative outcome of all was the impact on debt and savings. The basic incomes helped families to reduce their debt and to increase their saving. But the key is that the emancipatory value of the basic income exceeds the monetary value because it gives individuals and families vital liquidity, and probably access to liquidity possessed by others, with which to confront shocks, hazards and the simple uncertainties of life. The ability to avoid or reduce dependence on usurious moneylenders and landlords, and in some cases escape from bonded labour or *naukar* relationships of exploitation and oppression, should be counted as among the most transformative aspects of all.

It allowed families and individuals to focus more on gaining control over their lives and becoming more economically productive. In this way, emancipation boosted economic growth, in the spirit of *Swadeshi* and *Swaraj*.

We have seen how emancipatory effects spilled into development effects. This is consistent with findings in other parts of the world. People who feel a sense of basic security not only feel more free but become healthier (Marmot and Wilkinson, 1999), more productive, take more entrepreneurial risks, have a longer planning horizon and act more responsibly, in large part because they feel more in control of their own lives.

The villagers speak

At the end of the evaluation questionnaires, every respondent in every village was asked a series of questions on aspects of social justice, although they were not put like that. Respondents were asked if they 'strongly agreed', 'agreed', were 'not sure', 'disagreed' or 'strongly disagreed' with several statements about social policy. All possible answers were presented to counter bias.

The first questions related to income inequality, posed in the following way:

In thinking of India, do you agree with or disagree with the following:
a There should be an upper limit on earned incomes.
b There should be restrictions to limit the difference in income between the richest and poorest.

On the first of those questions, the responses showed substantial public support for policies that would limit very high earnings, with 83 per cent of basic income recipients (with the same for SEWA and non-SEWA villagers) saying they strongly agreed or agreed and about 75 per cent saying that in the control villages. To the extent that the difference is statistically significant, one can only speculate that a sense of social solidarity had been strengthened.

When the distributional question was posed as a matter of limiting income differentials, slightly more of the basic income recipients supported this, but the overwhelming view was that there should be restrictions. Villagers have an orientation towards less inequality.

A third and more immediately relevant finding is that the vast majority of people in the villages supported the idea of a basic income (Figure 11.1). In this regard, there was only a small difference between those who had been receiving the basic income and those who had not.

There may be something else going on with implications for government policy. All respondents were asked about their general assessment of government policies in combating poverty. The villagers were not impressed. Only about 4 per cent thought they were a big success, and less than a third thought they were a small success.

Figure 11.1   General villages: Percentage of households judging whether there should be a basic income, sufficient to cover basic needs, by type of village

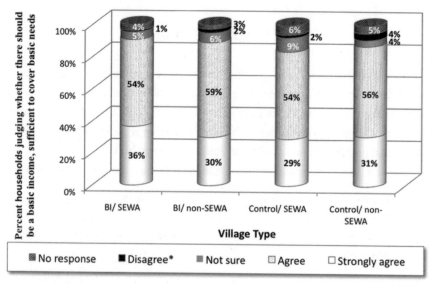

Note: *Due to very low levels (<1 per cent) of 'Strongly disagree' responses, they have been merged into the 'Disagree' category.

Source: MPUCT FES, 2012; n=2030

Figure 11.2 General villages: Percentage of households evaluating government achievement in poverty reduction, by type of village

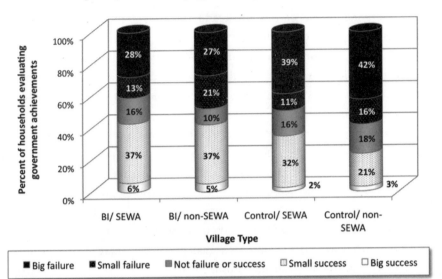

Source: MPUCT FES, 2012; n=1781

However, as Figure 11.2 shows, more were positive in the basic income villages and in SEWA villages. One may speculate that a policy, even though not associated with government, that provided improved economic security can prompt better public feelings about social policies in general, especially if there is a Voice organization playing its part in making it more effective.

One cannot divorce the failings of government policy in dealing with poverty and economic insecurity from the role of institutionalized corruption. Here again the villagers were not impressed, even by comparison with their views on poverty reduction. Less than one-third of those in basic income villages regarded efforts to restrict corruption as successful, and even fewer felt that way in other villages.

In sum, what these results imply is that villagers have a well-developed sense of social justice. Rural dwellers generally favour a progressive redistribution of income and a sense of universal basic security. Neither has been on offer. We may conclude that the basic income policy would prove popular, would be ethically appealing and would engender a general improvement in trust in government.

What next? The affordability issue

An underlying theme of this book and the weight of evidence obtained through these pilots lead us to believe that moving towards a universal basic income as an anchor of the twenty-first-century social protection system of India is desirable in itself, whether it is phased in as an additional social protection policy – as a social floor, as some would put it – or as a substitute for other schemes.

The first big question, therefore, is whether or not a sensible modest basic income would be feasible and affordable. Some critics would claim that it is unaffordable, because the gross cost would impose an excessive burden on the government budget and because it would require closure of other programmes.

At the heart of any answer is the matter of deciding on policy priorities. In that regard, several stylized facts stand out. First, apart from public works and subsidies, social security accounts for a small percentage share of GDP by international standards (Weigand and Grosh, 2008).

Second, subsidies account for a remarkably high proportion of GDP, and many are both regressive and unjustifiable for growth or welfare. In 2014, it was revealed that the cost of food subsidies, much of which does not help the intended beneficiaries, had more than quadrupled since 2004 to reach Rs.1.15 lakh crore, fertilizer subsidies had quadrupled to nearly Rs.68,000 crore and fuel subsidies had risen 18-fold (Sidhartha, 2014). These bare statistics indicate vast scope for substitution.

Third, the share of total spending on social development that actually reaches the intended beneficiaries is remarkably low. According to one official estimate (Mahapatra, 2011; Ahluwalia, 2005), in order to provide one Rupee of development spending, India spends 3.65 Rupees. There has been a lot of money going to waste.

Fourth, to return to a theme of Chapter 1, the complexity of the numerous social policies instigated over the years means that many, perhaps inadvertently, channel large sums of money to commercial interests rather than to low-income families and individuals. Social insurance schemes are particularly prone to suffer from this failing. Selective social insurance schemes in the realities of India today are bad cash transfers.

Two examples relevant to the feasibility of a basic income in Madhya Pradesh should suffice to illustrate the point. Social insurance for low-income informal workers is often covered by multiple agencies, since most earn their livelihoods through various means and occupations. Commonly an insurance premium on one person is paid by up to five government agencies or departments (Bhatnagar, 2013). But if a claim is made by a worker, it goes to just one agency.

Much more often than not, no claim for compensation is made at all, due to lack of awareness, ignorance of procedures, lack of confidence or some other reason. This is a concern that has exercised SEWA for years. But the main point here is that the state and national government are wasting money by paying multiple premiums for each person, even though there has apparently been some improvement in Madhya Pradesh since the beginning of this project. Who gains? Certainly the low-income workers do not.

Another example is life insurance. The Madhya Pradesh government pays out huge amounts each year to cover more than 4.3 million people under two insurance schemes. Under normal insurance industry outcomes, death claims should range from between 12 per cent and 15 per cent of the insured, according to reports of the Life Insurance Corporation of India and the Society for the Elimination of Rural Poverty, which run relatively successful schemes. But while the Madhya Pradesh government has been spending on life insurance, claims run at under 1 per cent. From a social equity and development point of view, the money is wasted.

One more pragmatic reason for recommending a shift to a basic income system is that the government system for delivering benefits resembles pipes that are choked up, and with growing government budgets the inefficiency of delivery has been increasing (Jhabvala and Standing, 2010). The expanding number of schemes is partly due to the paternalistic desire to extend selective, conditional policies into more and more spheres.

Often the motives for the selective targeting may be well-intentioned. But it is recommended that government should apply a practical rule, which is that such schemes should only be implemented where research has demonstrated social externalities, in the form of social costs if they are not implemented or having social benefits that would flow from such schemes.

It would be wishful thinking to claim that the schemes are only failing because of administrative deficiencies that could be overcome with due diligence. A policy that relies on something improbable to work even moderately well is not sensible. It is a waste of public funds that could be allocated to policies that do not depend on the improbable in order to work. This is a claim that can be made on behalf of a basic income.

However, the bottom line is that funding a basic income scheme is affordable, in principle. If the Rs.180,000 crore currently spent on centrally sponsored social schemes and subsidies on food, fertilizer and fuel were distributed equally among all low-income families in the country, it would have meant Rs.2,140 per household, which is more than the poverty-line income of rural families.

These figures come from the budget documents of the Government of India. We do not advocate a targeted system. But the figures give substance to the belief that even with existing expenditures, rural poverty could be drastically reduced through shifting to a system anchored by a basic income.

Another approach would be to replace subsidized items *en bloc*. One editorial in Livemint (15 November 2013) put this perspective starkly:

> The freed up money can then be used to provide UBI [Universal Basic Income]. The numbers are simple. If, to pick an arbitrary number, every Indian family is handed out 5,000 rupees every year, then for a population of 1.2 billion, the expenditure works out to Rs.1,20,000 crore every year. This is not a big, unrealistic sum. By comparison, the budgeted amount for total subsidies alone in 2013–14 is Rs.2,31,000 crore – almost double what is required to provide UBI of Rs.5,000 to every Indian family. The entire non-Plan expenditure stands at Rs.1,10,9975 crore, more than nine times what is needed for UBI. Now shaving off non-Plan expenditure in toto is not feasible, but surely if providing UBI is a political priority, the sum required can be easily found.

The writer went on to recognize that political feasibility is the big issue. More realistically, moving towards a basic income will have to be done in stages and by rolling out through a programme of selected measures, including converting some schemes.

Moving towards a basic income: Conversion of existing schemes

There are some options for helping to build towards a basic income, slowly and methodically, through a partial or complete conversion of existing schemes. Those that seem to be candidates for reform include all the extensive and costly subsidy schemes, including the fertilizer and fuel subsidies. They also include the major social policy schemes MGNREGS and the PDS.

Consider MGNREGS. In order to reduce the well-documented corruption due to the way labour was remunerated, the UPA government undertook campaigns to have bank accounts opened for people who held MGNREGS cards. Given the corruption in MGNREGS, the scheme's complexity and the number of layers involved, and the fact that it has not created much in sustainable infrastructure, an option might be to convert it to a straightforward unconditional basic income, for all those holding cards.

This would have the advantage of ensuring that the people for whom the MGNREGS has been intended actually receive the full benefit without them having to do unnecessary and unproductive physical labour. For this to happen, of course, the MGNREGS law would have to be amended.

As for the PDS, there has been a great deal of discussion about converting it to cash transfers. The National Food Security Act of 2013 seemed to move in the opposite direction, although it did allow for use of cash as an alternative to direct provision of food. In that regard, an option would be to provide communities with a Choice Policy, roughly along the lines SEWA and the Government of Delhi did in an initial pilot in West Delhi, where residents were offered the choice of continuing with the PDS-subsidized rations or receiving a cash transfer of equivalent value.

This would be financially feasible, and it would almost certainly put positive pressure on the PDS ration shops to improve their efficiency and quality. But of course there are inherent weaknesses in the PDS system, with the BPL cards, with the realization that some of the poorest do not have them, and with the selection of items provided. Care would have to be taken to encompass those who are left out of the PDS system through the many exclusion errors that exist now.

Tribal villages as game-changers?

The pilots have shown that the basic income has particularly strong transformative potential in tribal villages. As a result, it is strongly *recommended* that state governments should conduct expanded pilots in tribal villages, particularly in states where there are large tribal populations. Much of the money needed already exists, some in tribal sub-plans, and perhaps this could be supplemented by funds from national or international donor foundations and wealthy philanthropists. There are principled and pragmatic reasons for moving in this direction.

Tribal villages are among the most deprived and vulnerable communities in Madhya Pradesh and in India generally. Focusing on them as the next phase would be socially desirable. These communities have also been centres of social discontent, ripe for becoming recruitment centres for violent groups. The tribal village pilot has surely shown that a basic income would have a high probability of fostering economic growth while improving nutrition, health and schooling. In short, a universal basic income could induce a transformative development for all tribal villages, helping to defuse social unrest.

In 2013, the Chief Minister of Madhya Pradesh initiated Chief Minister *choupals* and held a series of *panchayats* on diverse social groups, including tribals. This is promising. And there would seem to be adequate funds available for a series of pilots that would fit that strategy. For the fiscal year 2013–14, the Government of Madhya Pradesh envisaged spending that implied a revenue surplus of Rs.5,215 crore, which was 1.3 per cent of the state's Gross Social Domestic Product.[1] That could be used wholly or in part to fund a serious pilot in at least two districts of Madhya Pradesh and/or cover a wide variety of tribal communities.

The pragmatic reasons for proposing a basic income scheme in tribal areas is that they are relatively self-contained communities and a pilot is thus relatively easy to administer. In the case of Madhya Pradesh, a scheme of this kind could allow the government to refine its *Samruddhi* three-pillar model of financial inclusion. And furthermore, tribal communities are already identified and recognized nationally as groups that deserve special assistance.

Roll-out recommendations

Moving towards providing basic economic security through a basic income is one of the great challenges that lie ahead for India. It cannot be done overnight. This does not mean it cannot be done. It means that if it is to succeed it must be rolled out slowly and methodically across individual states and across the country, step by step.

In this regard, as argued in an article written in the early stages of this project (Standing, 2011), it is *recommended* that if a system of social protection with a basic income as an anchor is to be constructed, it should be phased in before existing subsidy schemes are replaced or phased out. That was not done with the experimental schemes tried out in the latter part of the UPA government's tenure.

This approach would pay social dividends later, since it would mean that low-income families would not face the initial risk and potentially severe cost of not obtaining the cash transfers while they were losing access to subsidized goods. As with the UPA government's Kotkasim pilot mentioned in Chapter 1, mishandling the transition phase can undermine the legitimacy of cash transfers (Prasad, 2013). Making the two changes simultaneously is a recipe for chaos and social suffering (Kazmin, 2013).

This returns us to the limited, and some say diminishing, capacity of state bureaucracy to administer a vast array of complex social policy schemes, especially at a time of budgetary cuts and public deficits. The bureaucratic raj has generated a labyrinth of schemes, based on a castle of arbitrary rules of entitlement and disentitlement. It is vital that the number of such schemes is reduced and as many as possible amalgamated. Their internal rules should be simplified and made more transparent. In doing so, they could be converted to a more rationalized structure that could be combined with a basic income anchor to a genuine social protection system.

Financial facilitation: Business correspondents and 'door-step banking'

Coincidentally, while the pilots were taking place, there was an intense debate in the mass media on the need for financial inclusion, with the emphasis being on plans to extend banking to the whole country.

The pilots showed that a regular basic income could be combined with rapid opening of bank accounts. In fact, the introduction of a basic income induced people to be enthusiastic about opening accounts. This was greatly facilitated by SEWA acting as a financial intermediary to help open the accounts. Had that not been so, the cost in time and money would have been high for villagers, and the process would have been much slower and more difficult.

SEWA was able to lessen the transaction costs for villagers considerably, while helping the banks to incorporate thousands of new low-income clients. The banks in turn generally cooperated, and this should be acknowledged with satisfaction. However, in order to make financial inclusion a reality on a countrywide scale, financial facilitation needs to be encouraged and financed properly. Most state governments have been working closely with banks to try to make this happen. In underbanked areas, working with financial facilitators would hasten the process and help legitimize it more efficiently and equitably.

Financial inclusion, however, means more than just opening a bank account; it requires the capacity to operate that account, to be able to save in it, borrow from it and use it for financial planning. Since bank branches are far from villages and understaffed, what has become known as door-step banking is the only solution. Other than the banks, there are many financial institutions, such as cooperatives, self-help group federations and microfinance agencies, that do provide door-step banking. This experiment showed that using such institutions leads to more genuine financial inclusion.

The banks and the Reserve Bank of India (RBI) have been promoting 'business correspondents' all over the country. Unfortunately, we found this system to be non-operational; the 'correspondents' could not earn even a modest living from the work, and they did not obtain the full cooperation of the banks. To derive the full benefit of basic income, the banking correspondent model should be re-examined by the RBI and be made more remunerative and easier to operate.

Voice as agency

One unique feature of this project has been that the pilots were designed to identify the impact of both basic income and independent Voice, the hypothesis being that any positive effects of the basic income would be augmented by the existence of a collective body able to assist, advise and support vulnerable recipients.

In many if not all respects, the evidence has borne out expectations. We recognize that SEWA is a particular type of collective organization, and as such we anticipated it would have stronger effects on some issues than on others. But we are confident in concluding that the involvement of a body such as SEWA can ease the process of financial inclusion.

The use of the cash transfer is enhanced when it is linked to improving public services and better access to productive activities. The study shows that basic income meshed with SEWA activities to produce better results in families using health and education services. Being a member of SEWA also tended to make people less averse to taking risks.

In many ways, the involvement of a Voice organization can help make basic income work optimally. Its first role should be to help in the education of recipients on how to acquire and manage money and how to protect the economic and social right that an unconditional basic income involves. This educational function is vital in communities where cash in people's hands has been relatively scarce. Financial emancipation, not simple inclusion, should be the goal.

In some ways, the lack of an observable effect of the Voice body points to potential learning functions. If pilots were replicated or expanded, collective organizations should be integrated into the process, with training for their activists in helping advise recipients on how best to use the new liquidity. Collective involvement can make social policy so much more effective, particularly in safeguarding those who are most vulnerable inside families and inside any broader communities.

Concluding reflections

> I will give you a talisman. Whenever you are in doubt, or when the self becomes too much with you, apply the following test. Recall the face of the poorest and the weakest man whom you may have seen, and ask yourself, if the step you contemplate is going to be of any use to him. Will he gain anything by it? Will it restore him to a control over his own life and destiny? In other words, will it lead to *swaraj* for the hungry and spiritually starving millions? Then you will find your doubts and your self melt away.
>
> Mahatma Gandhi

This was one of the last notes written by Gandhi in 1948. It is a call to empathy, and a call to respect the Security Difference Principle and SEWA's foundational principle that the most vulnerable should have first claim on society's resources. A basic income, properly implemented and backed by the presence of a Voice organization that can defend 'the weakest', can give real effect to the hopes that Gandhi had in mind.

The basic income can be transformational. But for that to be realized, it will be crucial that policymakers handle what might be called the micro-politics of social policy reform with sensitivity. If the progressive principles of the individual, unconditional basic income are to be preserved and enhanced, it will be crucial to show that 'basic incomes', or whatever they turn out to be called, are not introduced as a means of lowering the level of state benefits, or reducing their reach, let alone as a means of rolling back the state commitment to improving the welfare of the Indian population.

They must be seen as progressive, in reducing the inequities and inequalities in Indian society, not as a step towards dismantling public and universal social services. They should be seen as helping to make public services function better. In this regard, the 'revealed preferences' of villagers should be interpreted correctly. Some used their basic income to turn to private schooling or private medical care. This does not mean that public schooling or healthcare is undesirable per se. It does suggest the quality and accessibility of those vital public services must be improved.

Indian villagers have a keen sense of social justice and generally favour a progressive redistribution of income and a sense of universal basic security.

And there is no reason to suppose that a basic income would not have a range of comparable positive effects in towns and cities across India, as the small SEWA-led pilot in West Delhi demonstrated.

We hope that the basic income as piloted in this project will be replicated and scaled up. We believe it would prove an ethical and popular policy, which would engender a general improvement in trust in government. Above all, it would liberate those constrained by debt and economic insecurity, and in doing so would surely promote sustainable economic growth and development in a way that policymakers coming from a wide range of ideological persuasions could support.

Note

1   These figures come from the Budget Document of the Government of Madhya Pradesh for the Financial Year 2012–13 and 2013–14. The figures are published on its website: http://www.finance.mp.gov.in

Appendix: Variables Used in Regressions

In logistic functions and multiple regressions reported in the text, the following were the independent variables typically used:

Household head's schooling/education: The level of schooling of the head of household. This was included as a proxy for wealth as well as for knowledge of financial management. It was measured by a binary (1 if the head had secondary schooling, 0 if primary or none). Alternatively, in some specifications it was also taken as an increasing function of the household head's education.

Disabled member: The presence of someone in the household with a disability, expressed as a binary variable (1 if having a disabled person, 0 otherwise).

Female head: A binary variable for whether or not the household was female-headed (1 if yes, 0 otherwise).

Child ratio: The ratio of children to adults.

School enrolment: Measured by a binary (1 if child was enrolled in a school, 0 otherwise).

School attendance: Parents' perception on whether there had been an improvement in school attendance of their children. It was measured by a binary (1 if parents' reported a big or a small improvement, 0 otherwise).

Middle school (11–13 years): Defined in relation to children in the primary school-going age cohort (6–10 years).

Secondary school (14–18 years): Defined in relation to children in the primary school-going age cohort (6–10 years).

Upper caste: A variable for caste of household, with Other Backward Caste (OBC) or general households given a value of 1, 0 otherwise.

Household size: Total household size, defined as the number of persons who were usually resident.

Basic income: 1 if receiving basic income, 0 otherwise.

SEWA: 1 if the household was in a SEWA village, 0 otherwise.

Land ownership: 1 if the household owned any land, 0 otherwise.

Age: Completed years of age.

Gender: 1 if female, 0 if male.

Bibliography

Adato, M. and Bassett, L. (2009), 'Social protection to support vulnerable children and families: The potential of cash transfers to protect education, health and nutrition', *AIDS Care: Psychological and Socio-Medical Aspects of HIV-AIDS*, 21, No. 1, Supplement 1, pp. 60–75.

Aguero, J. M, Carter, M. R. and Wooland, I. (2007), 'The impact of unconditional cash transfers on nutrition: The South African child support grant', Brasilia: International Poverty Centre.

Ahluwalia, M. S. (2005), 'Forward', *Performance Evaluation of Targeted Public Distribution System*, New Delhi: Program Evaluation Organisation, Planning Commission, Government of India.

Alatas, V., Banerjee, A., Hanna, R., Olken, B. A. and Tobias, J. (2012), 'Targeting the poor: Evidence from a field experiment in Indonesia', *American Economic Review*, Vol. 104, No. 2, pp. 1206–40.

Alkire, S. and Seth, S. (2008), 'Determining BPL status: Some methodological improvements', *Indian Journal of Human Development*, 2, pp. 407–24.

—(2012), 'Selecting a targeting method to identify BPL households in India', *Social Indicators Research*, Vol. 112, No. 2, pp. 417–46.

Alvarez, C., Devoto, F. and Winters, P. (2006), *Why Do The Poor Leave the Safety Net in Mexico? A Study of the Effects of Conditionality on Dropouts*, Department of Economics Working Paper, Washington, DC: American University.

Ariely, D. (2008), *Predictability Irrational: The Hidden Forces that Shape our Decisions*, New York: HarperCollins.

Attanasio, O., Battistin, E., Fitzimons, E., Mesnard, A. and Vera-Hernandez, M. (2005), 'How effective are conditional cash transfers? Evidence from Colombia', London: Institute for Fiscal Studies, IFS Briefing Note 54.

Baird, S. J., Chirwa, E., de Hoop, J. and Özler, B. (2013), *Girl Power: Cash Transfers and Adolescent Welfare: Evidence from a Cluster-randomized Experiment in Malawi*. National Bureau of Economic Research Working Paper No. 19479, September.

Baird, S., Ferreira, F. H. G., Özler, B. and Woolcock, M. (2013), 'Relative Effectiveness of Conditional and Unconditional Cash Transfers for Schooling Outcomes in Developing Countries: A Systematic Review', Campbell Systematic Reviews, 2013: 8.

Baird, S. J., McIntosh, C. and Özler, B. (2009), 'Designing Cost-Effective Cash Transfer Programs to Boost Schooling among Young Women in Sub-Saharan Africa', World Bank Policy Research Working Paper No. 5090. Washington, DC: The World Bank, October.

Banerjee, N. (1998), 'Household Dynamics and Women in a Changing Economy', in Maitreyi Krishnaraj, Ratna M. Sudarshan and Abusaleh Shariff (eds), *Gender, Population and Development*, New Delhi: Oxford University Press, pp. 245–63.

Bassi, N. and Kumar, D. (2010), *NREGA and Rural Water Management in India: Improving Welfare Effects*, Hyderabad: Institute for Resource Analysis and Policy.

Bastagli, F. (2009), 'From social safety net to social policy? The role of conditional cash transfers in welfare state development in Latin America', Brasilia, IPEA-UNDP Working Paper No. 60.

Benhassine, N., Devoto, F., Duflo, E., Dupas, P. and Pouliquen, V. (2013), *Turning a Shove into a Nudge? A 'Labelled Cash Transfer' for Education*, National Bureau of Economic Research, Cambridge, MA, July.

Besley, T. and Kanbur, R. (1988), 'Food subsidies and poverty alleviation', *Economic Journal*, Vol. 98, pp. 701–19.

Bhalla, S. (2013), 'Manmonia's FSB: 3% of GDP', *Financial Express*, July 6, http://www.financialexpress.com/news/column-manmonias-fsb-3-of-gdp/113822

Bitran, R. and Giedion, U. (2003), 'Waivers and exemptions for health services in developing countries', Washington, DC: Social Protection Discussion Paper Series No. 308, The World Bank.

Caldés, N., Coady, D. and Maluccio, J. A. (2004), 'The cost of poverty alleviation transfer programs: A comparative analysis of three programs in Latin America', Washington, DC: International Food Policy Research Institute FCND Discussion Paper No. 174.

Carr, M., Chen, M. and Jhabvala, R. (1996), *Speaking Out: Women's Economic Empowerment in South Asia*, London: Intermediate Technology Publications Limited.

Case, A., Hosegood, V. and Lund, F. (2005), 'The reach of the South African Child Support Grant: Evidence from KwaZulu-Natal', Research Program in Development Studies Working Paper No. 224, Princeton University.

Cecchini, S. and Madariaga, A. (2011), *Programas de Tranferencias Condicionadas: Balance de la Experiencia en America Latina y el Caribe*. Santiago: ECLAC.

Centre for Science and Environment (2008), *An Assessment of the Performance of the National Rural Employment Guarantee Programme in Terms of its Potential for Creation of Natural Wealth in India's Villages*, New Delhi.

Creti, P. and Jaspars, S. (eds) (2006), *Cash-transfer Programming in Emergencies* London: Oxfam.

Davies, S. and Davey, J. (2008), 'A regional multiplier approach to estimating the impact of cash transfers on the market: The case of cash transfers in rural Malawi', *Development Policy Review*, Vol. 26, No.1, pp. 91–111.

Deaton, A. (2008), *Instruments of Development: Randomisation in the Tropics, and the Search for the Elusive Keys to Economic Development*, The Keynes Lecture, British Academy, October 9.

Department of Women and Child (2011), *Indira Gandhi Matritva Sahyog Yojna: A Conditional Maternity Benefit Scheme, Implementation Guidelines for State Governments and UT Administrations*, New Delhi: Government of India.

Desai, S., Thorat, A. and Vikram, K. (2014), 'Is India's child malnutrition caused by hunger?', paper presented at the Annual Meeting of Population Association of America, Boston MA, May 1–3.

Development Pathways (2011), *Targeting the Poorest: An Assessment of the Proxy Means Test Methodology*, Canberra: Australian Government, September.

Dhar, A. (2012), 'Left out of benefits', *The Hindu*, September 20.

Dreze, J. (2011), 'The cash mantra', *The Indian Express*, 11 May.

Dutta, P., Murgai, R., Ravallion, M. and van de Walle, D. (2014), *Right to Work? Assessing India's Employment Guarantee Scheme in Bihar*. Washington, DC: World Bank.

Economic Policy Research Institute (2004), *The Social and Economic Impact of South Africa's Social Security System: Final Report*, Cape Town: Department of Social Development, EPRI Research Paper No. 37.

Engler, M. and Ravi, S. (2013), 'Workfare as an effective way to fight: The case of India's NREGS', retrieved from Social Science Research Network http://ssrn.com/paper=1336837

Evans, R. G. and Stoddart, G. L. (1994), 'Producing health, consuming healthcare', in Evans, R. G., Barer, M .L. and Marmor, T. R. (eds), *Why are Some People Healthy and Others Not?*, New York: Adine de Gruyter.

Filmer, D. and Schady, N. (2006), 'Getting girls into school: Evidence from a scholarship program in Cambodia', *World Bank Policy Research Paper 3910*, Washington, DC: The World Bank.

Fiszbein, A. and Schady, N., with F. H. G. Ferreira, M. Grosh, N. Kelleher, P. Olinto and E. Skoufias (2009), *Conditional Cash Transfers: Reducing Present and Future Poverty*, Washington, DC: World Bank.

Forget, E. L. (2011), *The Town with No Poverty: Using Health Administration Data to Revisit Outcomes of a Canadian Guaranteed Annual Income Field Experiment*, University of Manitoba, Canada.

Ghosh, J. (2011a), 'The siren song of cash transfers', *The Hindu*, 2 March.

—(2011b), 'The cash option', *Frontline*, Vol. 28, Issue 5, 26 February–11 March, www.frontlineonnet.com/fl2805/stories/20110311 0311280510900.htm

Golla, A. M., Malhotra, A., Nanda, P. and Mehra, R. (2012), 'Understanding and measuring women's economic empowerment', International Centre for Research on Women, http://www.icrw.org/publications/understanding-and-measuring-womens-economic-empowerment

Goswami, U. A. (2013), 'Business correspondents weak link in UPA's cash transfer plan', ET Bureau, January 23.

Government of Bihar (2011), Rural Development Department, Letter No. 3552/R11019/234/2010-Sec07, dated 31/3/2011.

Government of India (2011), *Working Group Report on Elementary Education and Literacy*, 12th Five Year Plan (2012–17), Ministry of Human Resource Development, New Delhi, GOI, October 2011.

Himanshu and Sen, A. (2013), 'In-food transfers – 1: Impact on poverty', *Economic and Political Weekly*, Vol. XLVIII, Nos. 45 and 46, November 16, pp. 46–54.

Himaz, R. (2008), 'Welfare grants and their impact on child health: The case of Sri Lanka', *World Development*, Vol. 36, No. 10, pp. 1843–57.

Hindustan Times (2012), 'Rotting grain has deprived food to 80 mn people', September 26, http://www.hindustantimes.com/india-news/newdelhi/rotting-grain-has-deprived-food-to-80-mn-people/article1-935807.aspx

—(2013), 'DCT will not lead to misuse of money: Montek', May 30, http://www.hindustantimes.com/StoryPage/Print/1068289.aspx

Hirschmann, A. (1991), *The Rhetoric of Reaction: Perversity, Futility, Jeopardy*, Cambridge, MA: Harvard University Press.

Hirway, I. (2003), 'Identification of BPL households for poverty alleviation programmes', *Economic and Political Weekly*, 38, pp. 4803–38.

—(2006), *Concurrent Monitoring of National Rural Employment Guarantee Act*, Ahmedabad: Centre for Development Alternatives.

Hirway, I., Saluja, M. R. and Yadav, B. (2010), *Employment Guarantee Program and Pro-poor Growth: A Study of a Village in Gujarat*, New Delhi: JBA Publishers.

Hoddinott, J. and Barrett, I. (2008), *Conditional Cash Transfer Programs and Nutrition in Latin America: Awareness of Impacts and Strategies for Improvement*, Washington, DC: International Food and Policy Research Institute.

Ibrahim, S. and Alkire, S. (2008), 'Agency and empowerment: A proposal for internationally comparable indicators', *OPHI Working Paper Series*, Oxford.

ILO (2005), *Economic Security for a Better World*, Geneva: International Labour Organisation.

India News (2013), 'Goa's Ladli Scheme Stoking Dowry System: Study', Indo-Asian News Service, India News, March 8, http://twocircles.net/2013mar08/goas_laadli_laxmi_scheme_stoking_dowry_system_study.html#.U1ogSeaSxXc

Indian Express (2013), 'Jairam Ramesh says toilets more important in India than temples', April 8, http://archive.indianexpress.com/news/jairam-ramesh--says-toilets-more-important-in-india-than-temples/1012719/

International Institute for Population Sciences (IIPS) and Macro International (2008), *National Family Health Survey (NFHS-3), India, 2005–6, Madhya Pradesh*, Mumbai: IIPS.

Jain, S. K. (2004), 'Identification of the poor: flaws in government surveys', *Economic and Political Weekly*, Vol. XXXIX, Nos. 46–7, November 13.

Jalan, J. and Murgai, R. (2007), *An Effective Targeting Shortcut? An Assessment of the 2002 Below Poverty Line Census Method*, mimeo, New Delhi: World Bank.

Jhabvala R, Desai, S. and Dave, J. (2010), *Empowering Women in an Insecure World: Joining SEWA Makes a Difference*, Ahmedabad: SEWA Academy.

Jhabvala, R., and Standing, G. (2010), 'Targeting to the "poor": Clogged pipes and bureaucratic blinkers', *Economic and Political Weekly*, Vol. XLV, Nos. 26–7, 26 June, pp. 239–46.

Jhabvala, R., Standing, G., Davala, S. and Kapoor, S. (2014), *A Little More How Much It Is: Piloting Basic Income in Madhya Pradesh*, New Delhi: SEWA-UNICEF.

Kabeer, N. (2000), 'Resources, agency, achievements: Reflections on the measurement of women's empowerment', paper presented at Conference *Power, Resources and Culture in a Gender Perspective: Towards a Dialogue Between Gender Research and Development Practice*, Uppsala.

Kabeer, N., Sudarshan, R. and Milward, K. (2013), *Organising Women Workers in the Informal Economy*. London and New York: Zed Books.

Kapur, D., Mukhopadhyay, P. and Subramanian, A. (2008a), 'India's poor: From raw deal to new deal', *Business Standard*, New Delhi, 15 January.

—(2008b), 'The case for direct cash transfers to the poor', *Economic and Political Weekly*, 43 (15), 12 April, pp. 37–43.

—(2008c), 'More on direct cash transfers', *Economic and Political Weekly*, 43 (47), 22 November, pp. 85–7.

Kapur, D. and Subramanian, A. (2009), 'Rahul's role? *Garibi hatao*', 23 May.

Kareemulla, K., Reddy, S., Rao, C., Kumar, S. and Venkareswarlu, B. (2010), 'Soil and water conservation works through National Rural Employment Guarantee Scheme (NREGS) in Andhra Pradesh – An analysis of livelihood impact', *Agricultural Economics Research Review*, Vol. 22, pp. 443–50.

Kazmin, A. (2013), 'India: Cash in hand', *Financial Times* (London), March 13, www.ft.com/intl/cms/s/0/20b56692-7c26-11e2-bf52-00144feabdc0.html

Kebede, E. (2005), 'Breaking the poverty cycle? Cash distribution and safety nets in Ethiopia', paper presented at meeting organised by the Overseas Development Institute (London), Nairobi, May.

Kenya CT-OBC Evaluation Team (2012), 'The impact of the Kenya Cash Transfer Program for Orphans and Vulnerable Children on household spending', *Journal of Development Effectiveness*, Vol. 4, No. 1, pp. 38–49.

Khandker, S. R., Pitt, M. and Fuwa, N. (2003), 'Subsidy to promote girls' secondary education: The Female Stipend Program in Bangladesh', Munich, mimeo, March, http//mpra.ub.unimuenchen.de/23688

Khera, R. (2011a), 'Revival of the Public Distribution System: Evidence and explanations', *Economic and Political Weekly*, Vol. XLVI, Nos. 44 and 45, November 5, pp. 36–50.

—(2011b), 'Trends in diversion of PDS grain', *Working Papers* 198, Centre for Development Economics, Delhi School of Economics.

Khera, R. and Nayak, N. (2009), 'Women workers and perceptions of the National Rural Employment Guarantee Act', *Economic and Political Weekly*, Vol. 64 (43), 24 October.

Kohler, G. (2014), 'Is there an Asian welfare state model?', Friedrich Ebert Stiftung Office for Regional Cooperation in Asia, March.

Krishna, A. (2007), 'For reducing poverty faster: Target reasons before people', *World Development*, Vol. 35, No. 11, pp. 1947–60.

Kumar, R. and Prasanna, R. (2010), 'Role of NREGA in providing additional employment for tribals and curtailing migration', in *National Rural Employment Guarantee Act (NREGA): Design, Process and Impact*, New Delhi: Ministry of Rural Development.

Leclercq, F. (2003), 'Education Guarantee Scheme and Primary Schooling in Madhya Pradesh', *Economic and Political Weekly*, Vol. XXXVIII, No. 19, May 10.

Lim, S. S., Dandona, L., Hoisington, J. A., James, S. L., Hogan, M. C. and Gakidou, E. (2010), 'India's Janani Saraksha Yojan, a conditional cash transfer programme to increase births in health facilities: An impact evaluation', *The Lancet*, 375, No. 9730, pp. 2009–23.

Lindert, K., Skoufias, E. and Shapiro, J. (2006), 'Redistributing income to the poor and the rich: Public transfers in Latin America and the Caribbean', Social Protection Discussion Paper No. 0605, Washington, DC: World Bank Institute.

Macours, K. and Vakis, R. (2008), *Changing households' investments and aspirations through social interactions: Evidence from a randomised transfer program in a low income country*, Baltimore: Johns Hopkins University Press.

Mahamalik, M. and Sahu, G. B. (2011), 'Identification of the poor: Errors of exclusion and inclusion', *Economic and Political Weekly*, February 26.

Mahaptra, R. (2011), 'Kind to cash', *Down To Earth*, New Delhi, February 1–15.

Marmot, M. and Wilkinson, R. (1999), *Social Determinants of Health*, Oxford: Oxford University Press.

McCord, A. and Farrington, J. (2008), 'Digging holes and filling them in again? How far do public works enhance livelihoods?', London, Overseas Development Institute, *Natural Resources Perspectives*, No. 120.

Mehrotra, S. and Mander, H. (2009), 'How to identify the poor? A proposal', *Economic and Political Weekly*, Vol. 44, No. 19, May, pp. 37–44.

Miller, C., Tsoka, M. and Reichert, K. (2006), 'The impact of the Social Cash Transfer Scheme on food security in Malawiu', *Food Policy*, Vol. 36, No. 2, pp. 230–38.

Misra, U. and Ramnath, N. S. (2011), 'Are direct cash transfers better?', *Business.in.com*, 21 March 2011, http://business.in.com/article/briefing/are-direct-cash-subsidies-better/23422/0

Molyneux, M. (2006), 'Mothers at the service of the new poverty agenda: Progresa/Oportunidades, Mexico's conditional transfers programme', *Social Policy and Administration*, Vol. 40, No. 4, August, pp. 425–49.

Mukherjee, N. (2005), 'Political corruption in India's Below the Poverty Line (BPL) exercise: Grassroots' perspectives on BPL in perpetuating poverty and social exclusion', *Development Tracks in Research, Training and Consultancy*, New Delhi.

Mullainathan, S. and Shafir, E. (2013), *Scarcity: Why Having Too Little Means So Much*, London: Allen Lane.

Nanda, B. (2012), 'The Ladli Scheme in India: Leading to a lehenga or a law degree', Miranda House, Delhi University, http://www.ipc-undp.org/pressroom/files/ipc126.pdf

Narayan, D., Pritchett, L. and Kapoor, S. (2009), *Moving out of Poverty: Success from the Bottom Up*, New York: Palgrave Macmillan.

Narayanan, S. (2011), 'A case for reframing the cash transfer debate in India', *Economic and Political Weekly*, Vol. XLVI, No. 21, 21 May, p. 43.

Narula, M. (2012), *Emerging Issues at Secondary Level: Focus on Private Schools in Madhya Pradesh*. National University of Education Planning and Administration, Occasional Paper No. 42.

NCAER (2014), 'Well-being of the older population in India 2004–05 and 2011–14: India Human Development Survey Fact Sheets', presented at the *Roundtable on Caring for the Elderly in India: Challenges for a Society in Transition*, NCAER, New Delhi, April 2.

O'Keefe, P. (2009), *People with Disabilities in India: From Commitments to Outcomes*, Washington, DC: The World Bank.

Ortiz, I. and Yablonski, J. (2010), *Investing in People: Social Protection for All*, Manila: Asian Development Bank.

Orton, I. (2010), 'Reasons to be cheerful: How ILO analysis of social transfers worldwide augurs well for a basic income (with some caveats)', paper presented at the *13th International Congress of the Basic Income Earth Network*, São Paulo, Brazil, 30 June–2 July.

Pani, N. (2011), 'Cash transfers can be inflationary', *Business Line*, 2 August.

Prabhu, K. S. (2009), 'Can conditional cash transfers work in rural India?', *Wall Street Journal*, 15 July. http://online.wsj.com/news/articles/SB124695317824004689

Prasad, S. (2013), 'Lots of glitches to iron out in India's cash transfer scheme', *Inside India*, May 6, www.zdnet.com/lots-of-glitches-to-iron-out-in-India-cash-transfer-scheme-70000114906/

Ramaswami, B., Murugkar, M. and Kotwal, A. (2013), 'Correct costs of the Food Security Bill', *The Financial Express*, September 2, http://www.financialexpress.com/news/correct-costs-of-the-food-security-bill/1156251

Ravaillion, M. (2007), 'How relevant is targeting to the success of an antipoverty program?', World Bank Policy Research Working Paper 4385, Washington, DC: The World Bank.

Ravi, S. and Engler, M. (2008), *Workfare in Low-Income Countries: An Effective Way to Fight Poverty? The Case of NREGS in India*, New Delhi: Indian Business School.

Roy, I. (2011), '"New" list for "old": (Re-)constructing the poor in the BPL Census', *Economic and Political Weekly*, Vol. 46, No. 22, pp. 82–91.

Saith, A. (2007), 'Downsizing and distortion of poverty in India: The perverse power of official definitions', *Indian Journal of Human Development*, Vol. 1, No. 2, pp. 247–81.

Samson, M., Lee, U., Ndlebe, A., MacQuene, K., van Niekerk, I., Gandhi, V., Harigaya, T. and Abrahams, C. (2004), 'Final report: Social and economic impact of South Africa's social security system', Cape Town, Economic Policy Research Institute Research Paper No. 37.

Saxena, N. C. (Chair) (2009), *Report of the Expert Group to Advise the Ministry of*

Rural Development on the Methodology for Conducting the Below Poverty Line (BPL) Census for 11th Five Year Plan, Delhi, Ministry of Rural Development, Government of India, August.

Saxena, N. C. (2010), 'Do targeted schemes and programmes reach the poor?', paper presented at the *International Seminar on Poverty* in Bihar, Patna, April 18–20.

Sen, A. (1995), 'The political economy of targeting', in D. van de Walle and K. Nead (eds), *Public Spending and the Poor: Theory and Evidence*, Baltimore: Johns Hopkins University Press.

Shah, M. (2008), 'Direct cash transfers: No magic bullet', *Economic and Political Weekly*, 43 (34), 23 August, pp. 77–9.

Shenoy, M. (2011), *Persons with Disability and the Indian Labour Market: Challenges and Opportunities*, New Delhi: International Labour Organisation.

Shivakumar, G. and Das, S. (2013), 'Cash transfer scheme for girls helps curb poverty in Odisha', *The Hindu*, December 5, http://www.thehindu.com/news/national/other-states/cash-transfer-scheme-for-girls-helps-curb-poverty-in-odish/articles5422620.ece

Shrinivasan, R. (2011a), 'Against the grain: Ration saga', *The Times of India*, 19 March, www.timescrest.com/society/ration-saga-5015

—(2011b), 'PDS: Reform or reject?', *The Times of India*, July 27, http://blogs.timesofindia.indiatimes.com/developmentdialogue/entry/pds-reform-or-reject

Sidhartha (2014), 'Finance, fertilizers and petroleum ministries to seek subsidy cuts', *The Times of India*, May 23.

Singh, A. (2014), 'In Madhya Pradesh, Dalit man building loo to save his marriage', *The Times of India*, January 6, http://timesofindia.indiatimes.com/india/In-Madhya-Pradesh-dlit-man-building-loo-to-save-his-marriages/articleshow/28453648.cms

Skoufias, E. and Parker, S. (2001), 'Conditional cash transfers and their impact on child work and schooling: Evidence from PROGRESA program in Mexico', *Economia*, Vol. 2, No. 1, pp. 45–96.

Skoufias, E. and di Maro, V. (2005), *Conditional Cash Transfers, Adult Work Incentives and Current Poverty*, Washington, DC: The World Bank.

Slavin, R. (2010), 'Can financial incentives enhance educational outcomes? Evidence from international experiments', *Educational Research Review*, Vol. 5, No. 1, pp. 68–80.

Soares, F. V., Perez Ribas, R. and Osório, R. G. (2007), 'Evaluating the impact of Brazil's Bolsa Família: Cash transfer programmes in comparative perspective', *IPC Evaluation Note No. 1*, New York, United Nations Development Programme, International Poverty Centre.

Soares, S. (2007), 'Conditional cash transfers in Brazil, Chile and Mexico: Implications for inequality', Brasilia: UNDP, International Poverty Centre Working Paper No. 35.

Standing, G. (2011a), 'Behavioural conditionality: Why the nudges must be stopped', *Journal of Poverty and Social Justice*, 19 (1): 27–38.

—(2011b), *The Precariat: The New Dangerous Class*, London: Bloomsbury.

—(2011c), 'Give cash some credit', *The Indian Express*, 28 May.

—(2012), 'How to make cash transfers work', *Indian Express*, December 17, www.indianexpress.com/news/how-to-make-cash-transfers-work/1046254/0

Standing, G., Unni, J., Jhabvala, R. and Rani, U. (2010), *Social Income and Insecurity: A Study in Gujarat*, New Delhi: Routledge.

Strandberg, N. (2001), 'Conceptualizing empowerment as a transformative strategy for poverty eradication and the implications for measuring progress', paper presented at United Nations Division for the Advancement of Women Expert Group Meeting on 'Empowerment of women throughout the life cycle as a transformative strategy for poverty eradication', 26–29 November, New Delhi.

Tabatabai, H. (2011), 'The basic income road to reforming Iran's price subsidies', *Basic Income Studies*, Vol. 6, Issue 1, August, pp. 1–23.

Taleb, N. N. (2012), *Anti-Fragile: How to Live in a World We Don't Understand*, London: Allen Lane.

Thaler, R. and Sunstein, C. (2009), *Nudge: Improving Decisions about Health, Wealth and Happiness*, New Haven: Yale University Press.

The Hindu (2013a), 'The Food Insecurity Act', *Business Line*, August 30.

—(2013b), 'India's food conundrum', May 11. http://www.thehindu.com/opinion/columns/Chandrasekhar/indias-food-conundrum/article4705855.ece

Times of India (2013), 'Build toilets first and temples later, Narendra Modi says', October 3, http://timesofindia.indiatimes.com/india/Build-toilets-first-and-temples-later-Narendra-Modi-says/articleshow/23422631.cms

UNDP (2013), *The Human Development Report, 2013*, New York: United Nations Development Programme.

UNICEF (2011), *The Situation of Children in India: A Profile*, New Delhi: UNICEF, May.

Varma, S. (2013), 'Tribals lose land, forced to become farm workers', *The Times of India*, November 10.

Virmani, A. (2013), 'India's problem is malnutrition not food security: Public health (not cereals) is the solution', *Economic Times*, February 4,

Weigand, C. and Grosh, M. (2008), 'Levels and patterns of safety net spending in developing and transition countries', Social Protection Discussion Paper No. 0817. Washington, DC: The World Bank.

Winterbottom, J. and Bhardwaj, M. (2013a), 'India increases food subsidies as prices remain high', Reuters, May 13, http://in.reuters.com/article/2013/05/13/food-security-bill-cost-analysis-idINDEE94C09J20130513

—(2013b), 'Cheap food plans to cost more than budgeted: adviser', Reuters, May 13, http://in.reuters.com/article/2013/05/13/food-security-bill-cost-analysis-idINDEE94C09J20130513

World Health Organization (WHO) (2011), *World Report on Disability*, Geneva: World Health Organization.

Index

AAY *see Antyodaya Anna Yojana*
abortion 17
Above Poverty Line (APL) 58, 84, 85, 86, 87, 187
Accredited Social Health Activists (ASHAs) 100, 104, 105
Adivasi 177
adult-to-child ratio 54
Africa 26
    cash transfer schemes 97
agewans 104, 163
agricultural labour 146–7
agriculture 137
    investment in 64
Ahluwalia, Montek Singh 6, 200
AIDS *see* HIV/AIDS
Akshaya Patra 116
alcohol 96–7
America, United States of (USA) 15
anganwadi centres 16, 43, 44, 89, 92–4, 95, 162, 163, 177
    records 93
anganwadi workers 16, 95, 169
animal husbandry 143, 146, 147, 193
ANMs *see* Auxiliary Nurse Midwives
Annual Status of Education Reports
    2009 125
    2012 117
Antyodaya Anna Yojana (AAY) 84, 85, 86, 88, 109, 151, 187, 192, 197, 198
APL *see* Above Poverty Line
ASHAs *see* Accredited Social Health Activists
assets 69
Auxiliary Nurse Midwives (ANMs) 16, 100, 104, 105
Awareness Days 37–8
Awareness Visits 195

babies 94
Bangladesh 27

bank accounts 38–9, 40, 62, 166–7, 168, 189, 211
    women 169, 170
banks 38, 62, 170, 211–12
basic goods and services 22, 137
beds 80, 81
Below Poverty Line (BLP) 4, 5, 6, 10, 11, 12, 58, 84, 85, 86, 87, 88, 109, 187, 192, 197, 198, 209
benefits *see also* pensions 3, 4, 10, 15, 18, 196, 197, 213
    maternity 16
Bhilami 118
Bihar 6, 39
Bolsa Família 12, 21, 28–9, 90, 109, 150
bonded labour *see also naukar* system 138, 146, 151
borrowing *see also* loans 59–60, 69–70, 202
    distress borrowing 60
boys 57, 96, 125, 126, 128, 141, 162, 163, 165
    education 119, 120, 122
    nutrition 94
    ratio to girls 160
    teenage 121, 123
BPL *see* Below Poverty Line
Brazil 14, 25, 27
    Bolsa Família 12, 21, 28–9, 90, 109, 150
bribes 16
budgetary cuts 211
bureaucracy 211

Cambodia 27
case studies 44, 50
cash line 10–19
cash transfers *see also* conditional cash transfers 3–4, 5, 10, 13, 18, 19–29, 32, 37, 47, 84, 90, 115, 168, 175, 197, 210–11
    administration 24
    Africa 97
    arguments against 19–22

arguments for 22–9
  Kenya 97
  Latin America 99
  Namibia 99
casual labour 145, 146, 173, 193, 201
CCTs *see* conditional cash transfers
censuses
  2002 181
  2011 72, 74
chemists 107
Chhattisgarh 7
child development 81
child labour 27, 29, 116, 140–2, 154, 155,
    165, 201
Child Labour Act 1986 140
childbirth 100
childcare 141
children *see also* boys, girls *and* teenagers
    13, 18, 20, 44, 72, 83, 101, 139
  diet 89–90
  eating habits 115
  education 115–36
  health 27, 72, 100, 126
  immunization 99, 105, 109–10
  nutrition 27–8, 90, 92–6, 97, 126
  underweight 95
  weight-for-age 92–6
child-to-adult ratio 54
China 12
choupals 176, 210
chronic debt 59–60
cigarettes *see* tobacco
clothing 130
collectives 153–4
commodity line 5–8
Community Surveys 43–4, 45
conditional cash transfers (CCTs) *see also*
    cash transfers 3, 14, 15, 17, 25, 27, 28
conditionality 13–18, 115
Constitution 1
cooking 76, 77
corruption 6, 16, 21, 83, 205
credit 59, 69, 91, 202
crises, financial 65–9

Dalit 177
Datoda 118
days of work 144–5
DBT *see* direct benefit transfer

debt 47, 49–56, 57, 61, 64–5, 99, 111, 113,
    138, 154, 185, 186, 191, 203
  chronic 49, 59–60
  monopsony debt 52
debt bondage *see also naukar* system 50,
    57–9
debt burden 56
Delhi 32
dependency 20–1
Dhanlaxmi scheme 17
diet 28, 89–90, 99, 130, 199
  children 89–90
Dignified Work Principle 2, 201
direct benefit transfer (DBT) 4, 6
disability 54
disabled 181–94, 198, 199, 202
  discrimination 182
  farm work 187
  healthcare 184
  hospital treatment 184
  school attendance 183
  women 185
  work activity 186–7
discrimination 182, 183
disease 72, 73
  resistance to 99, 101, 102
distress borrowing 60
distress migration 9
District Primary Education Programme
    116
doctors 43
  Bengali 100
  private 107, 108, 109
domestic violence 177
donor agencies 31, 209
door-step banking 39, 211
dowries 18
drainage 178

earnings 171
eating habits 89–90, 115
  children 89–90, 127
Ecological Constraint Principle 2
economic activity 138, 139–40, 142–3
  women 143
economic citizenship 23
economic growth 137–55, 158, 159, 174,
    196, 200–1, 210
economy 1

education 25–7, 28, 115–36
    boys 119, 120, 122
    girls 119, 120, 122
Education Guarantee Scheme 116
education services 22
eggs 90
elderly 101, 179, 181–94, 198, 202
    benefits 188
    discrimination 182
    food 189
    healthcare 190–1
    nutrition 189
    pensions 198
    work 193
elections
    general election of 2014 196
electrification 76
emancipation 202
energy 76–7, 189
entitlement 33
entrepreneurship 64, 68, 149, 203
environment 2
equal opportunities 3
ethical values 2
evaluation process 40–2
exploitation *see also* super-exploitation 52,
    69, 203

families 18
fans, electrical 80
farm work 201
farming *see also* agriculture 49, 138, 146
FCI *see* Food Corporation of India
fertilizers 77, 150, 153
    subsidies 206, 208
FES *see* Final Evaluation Survey
Final Evaluation Survey (FES) 40, 42–3,
    45, 54, 56, 59, 60, 61, 62, 63, 64, 65,
    71, 76, 78, 86, 93, 96, 102, 105, 107,
    109, 110, 119, 126, 129, 133, 134,
    139, 141, 144, 152, 164, 166, 168,
    171, 184, 187, 189, 197
    questionnaire 59
financial crises 65–9, 186, 192
financial inclusion 63, 212
financial liquidity *see* liquidity
financial stress 65
fish (as food) 90, 96, 153–4
fish farming 153–4

fishing 96
food *see also* nutrition 5–6, 8, 9, 89, 90,
    103, 104, 135, 162–4, 182, 199
    buying 56
    elderly 189
    production 201
    storage 201
    subsidies 7, 84, 86, 196, 197, 206
Food and Civil Supplies Department 11
Food Corporation of India (FCI) 7
food insecurity 102–4
food markets 91–2
food poverty 83, 91
food security 84
Food Security Act (FSA) 4, 8, 83–4, 209
Friedman, Milton 48
fuel 77, 85
    subsidies 207, 208

Gandhi, Mahatma 3, 202, 213
gender 161
gender discrimination 15
gender equality 9, 18, 159, 160, 172
general election of 2014 196
Ghodakhurd 118
girls 14, 15, 17, 27, 96, 116, 124–5, 126,
    128, 136, 141, 162, 162, 198, 199
    education 119, 120, 122
    healthcare 165–6
    marriage 160
    nutrition 94
    Odish Girls' Incentive Programme
      (OGIP) 26
    ratio to boys 160
    schooling 27, 164–5
    teenage 121, 122, 123, 125
    teenage pregnancy 136
globalization 65
gold *see also* jewellery 62, 168
government agencies 31
grain 84, 85
gram sabha 9
Gujarat 11
gwala relationship 57, 151

harvest season 59, 141
hazards 65–9
health 27–8, 72, 81, 99–113, 154, 184, 199,
    200, 210

children 27, 72, 126
  elderly 190–1
  improving 102–4
health centres 16, 100, 101
health insurance 99, 100, 110
health poverty 101
health services 10, 21, 22, 104–5
healthcare 1, 3, 104–13, 127, 199, 200
  behaviour 104
  borrowing 110–13
  disabled 184
  girls 165–6
  private 105, 109, 113, 213
  privatization 107–9
  spending 110–13
HIV/AIDS 21–2, 32
hospitalization 106–7, 111
  expenses 112
  men 107
  women 106, 107
hospitals 101, 105, 106
  private 105, 107, 109
hours of work 144–5
housework 141, 143
housing 60, 71, 77–80
  materials 77
  repairs 78–9
human capital 14, 25
human rights 14
humanitarian relief organizations 23

ICDS *see* Integrated Child Development
  Scheme
IES *see* Interim Evaluation Survey
illness 63, 64, 102, 127, 133, 135, 184,
  198
  treatment 103
immunization 16, 109–10
  children 99, 100, 105, 109–10
income, earned 139
indebtedness *see* debt
Indira Gandhi *Matritva Sahyog Yojana*
  15
Indonesia 100
Indore District 35, 45, 141
inequality 24–5
infant mortality 43, 160
infants 94
inflation 22

infrastructure 1, 3, 8
Integrated Child Development Scheme
  (ICDS) 95
intelligence tests 49
interest rates 55–6, 59, 70, 112, 169, 173,
  202
Interim Evaluation Survey (IES) 40, 42,
  43, 45, 54, 61, 62, 65, 71, 103, 110,
  119, 125, 128, 141, 151
investment 64, 146
IPE Global 26
irrigation 76, 149–50

Janari Suraksha Yojana 5
jewellery *see also* gold 62, 168

Kenya 97
kerosene 85
Keynesian economics 22
Kotkasim 39, 210

labour line 5, 8–10
labour market 147
labour migration 138–9, 154
labour supply 137
Ladli Laxmi scheme 17
Ladli scheme 17
land ownership 125
landlords 49, 50, 57, 58, 59, 146, 203
landowners 50
Latin America 3, 12, 20, 25, 26, 27, 28,
  115, 150
  cash transfers 99
latrines *see also* toilets 71–5, 198
Lauderdale Paradox 48–9
lentils 90
libertarian paternalism 15
Life Insurance Corporation 207
lighting 76, 77, 189
liquidity 49, 63, 64, 71, 78, 113, 203, 212
livestock 146, 147, 148, 176, 201
living conditions 71–81
living expenses 60
living standards 149
LMPs *see* local medical practitioners
loans 50, 52, 55, 58, 59, 112, 169–70,
  173–4
local medical practitioners (LMPs) 100,
  107, 109

Mahatma Gandhi National Rural
  Employment Guarantee Scheme
  (MGNREGS) 8–9, 10, 188, 192,
  198, 208, 209
Malawi 15, 17
Malaysia 100
malnutrition 72, 162, 163
Manitoba 100
manual labour 145
market economy 48
markets 190
marriage 160
  teenage girls 123, 136
mass media 211
maternal mortality 43, 100
maternity benefits 16
means-testing 5, 11, 12
measles, mumps and rubella (MMR) 110
meat 90
media 211
medical expenses 60, 99, 111
medical practitioners *see also* doctors 99,
  100
medical shops 106, 107
medical treatment 63
medicine/medicines 64, 99–113, 135, 166,
  184, 185, 199
  costs 99
  elderly 191
Mexico 15, 24, 25, 27, 29, 94
  Oportunidades 12, 24, 25, 29
MGNREGS *see* Mahatma Gandhi
  National Rural Employment
  Guarantee Scheme
Mid Day Meal Scheme 116, 117
Midline Evaluation Survey 42
midwives 100
migrants 18, 33
migration
  distress 9
  labour-related 138–9, 144, 154
  school-related 134, 139
  seasonal 138
milk 91, 148
Millennium Development Goals 24
Ministry of Human Resource
  Development 122
Ministry of Rural Development 11
MMR *see* measles, mumps and rubella

mobile phones 80
Modi, Narendra 74
money 48, 49, 52
moneylenders 49, 50, 52, 60, 64, 69, 173,
  203
monopoly 52
monopsony debt 52
monsoons 38
mortality
  maternal 100
  rates 181
mosquito protection 81
Most-Vulnerable-at-the-Centre Principle
  198
mothers 92, 118, 125
mukhiya 9

Namibia 21, 24, 25, 28, 29, 32, 99
  school attendance 26
National Commission for Enterprises in
  the Unorganized Sector (NCEUS)
  34
National Council of Applied Economic
  Research (NCAER) 8
National Development Council 7
National Family Health Survey of 2005–6
  177
National Sample Surveys (NSS) 11, 34,
  126, 150
naukar system *see also* debt bondage
  57–9, 138, 151–3, 154, 155, 201,
  203
NBA *see Nirmal Bharat Abhiyan*
NCAER *see* National Council of Applied
  Economic Research
NCEUS *see* National Commission for
  Enterprises in the Unorganized
  Sector
Nepal 100
Nicaragua 32
Nirmal Bharat Abhiyan (NBA; Total
  Sanitation Campaign) 72, 74, 75
non-ration shops 91
NSS *see* National Sample Surveys
nutrition *see also* food 27–8, 83–97, 154,
  162–4, 199, 210
  boys 94
  children 27, 97, 126
  disabled 183

elderly 189
girls 94

Odish Girls' Incentive Programme
    (OGIP) 26
OGIP *see* Odish Girls' Incentive
    Programme
Oportunidades 12, 24, 25, 29
own-account work 145, 193, 201
    farming 146

padi (rice) 83
Paine, Thomas 20
Painian Principle 20
panchayats 178, 210
    secretaries 43
Panthbadodia 135
Paternalism Test Principle 2
patterns of expenditure 44
PDS *see* Public Distribution System
pensions 4, 10, 198
pesticides 150
PFES *see* Post-Final Evaluation Survey
PHCs *see* Primary Health Centres
philanthropists 209
Philippines 100
PL *see* poverty line
Planning Commission 6, 7, 11, 200
ploughs 150
Population Census of 2011 72, 74
Post-Final Evaluation Survey (PFES) 40,
    43, 75, 91, 106, 179, 185, 193
poverty 2, 24, 205, 208
poverty card system *see also* APL, AAY
    and BPL 88-9, 167
poverty line (PL) 11, 34
poverty traps 5
pregnancy 15-16, 17
    teenage 136
prejudice 181
Primary Health Centres (PHCs) 100, 101,
    105, 106
productivity 72, 137-55
public deficits 211
Public Distribution System (PDS) 5-6,
    7, 8, 10, 11, 84, 86, 88, 162, 187-8,
    197, 208, 209
public expenditure 8
public health 72

pulses 90, 91

questionnaires 40-1, 42, 43
    design 41
    FES 59

rainy season 77, 85
Ramesh, Jairam 74
ration shops 6, 7, 36, 83, 85, 88, 91-2, 187,
    190, 197
rationing 9
rations 11, 85-6, 209
    storage 86
Rawls, John 2
RBI *see* Reserve Bank of India
relief organizations 23
religion 40, 73
Reserve Bank of India (RBI) 212
rice 83, 84
Right of Children to Free and
    Compulsory Education Act 117
Rights-not-Charity Principle 2
risk-taking 51, 52, 212
roads 36, 38, 74
Rozi-Roti Adhikar Abhiyan Delhi 8
Rural Development, Ministry of 11

Safai Vidyalaya 74
Sahavada 133
sanitation 71-5, 177-8
sarpanchs 9, 43, 178
Sarva Samriddhi Yojana 116
saving/savings 47, 60, 61-5, 73, 110, 168,
    169, 191, 203
    forms of 62-3
    uses 63-4
Saxena Committee 11
'scarcity mindset' 48-9
scheduled castes and tribes 1, 13, 26, 45,
    88, 89, 111, 118, 120, 123, 126, 127,
    129, 130, 136, 171, 199
    teenagers 124
scholarship schemes 116
schools/schooling 1, 2, 3, 10, 17, 21, 35,
    115-36, 139, 140, 142, 198, 199,
    200, 201, 210
    absenteeism 127, 128
    attendance 25, 26, 116, 118, 122,
    125-8, 165, 199

costs 119
disabled 183
drop-out rates 25, 26, 116, 117, 123, 200
enrolment 117, 122–5, 160, 164, 165
fees 26
girls 162, 164–5
grades 118
hostels 134
international literature on 124
performance 122, 128–30
private 117, 130–3, 213
privatization 130–3
records 129
registers 127–8
registration 122–5
religious 118
spending 119–22
teacher absenteeism 17, 132, 164, 165
transport 120, 134
uniforms 120, 128
Security Difference Principle 2, 3, 29, 198, 213
seeds 150, 153
Self-Employed Women's Association (SEWA) 3, 14, 18, 32, 33, 35, 36, 37, 38, 39, 40, 42, 44, 45, 54, 61, 63, 72, 76, 95, 104, 107, 111, 119, 120, 123, 125, 126, 128–9, 132, 133, 134, 139, 141, 148, 151, 158, 159, 161, 162, 163, 164, 166, 167, 168, 170, 172, 173, 175, 176, 177, 178, 198, 202, 203, 205, 207, 209, 211, 212, 213, 214
village leaders 43–4
self-rule 202
septic tanks 75
SEWA *see* Self-Employed Women's Association
sewing machines 149, 151, 175
shocks 65–9, 110, 113, 154, 182
shopkeepers 6, 43, 50
smallholdings 138
smoking *see* tobacco
social insurance schemes 206
social justice 198–202
social policy 2
social services 19
Society for the Elimination of Rural Poverty 207

South Africa 26, 29
soybean 92
Sri Lanka 28, 100
stress, financial 65
subsidies 7, 8, 23, 69, 84, 85, 91, 187–8, 196, 197, 206, 209, 210
fertilizers 206, 207, 208
food 206, 207
fuel 207, 208
Sulabh 74
super-exploitation 50
Swadeshi Principle 3, 29, 137, 147, 201, 203
Swaraj and Self-reliance Principle 3, 29, 201, 202, 203

Tamil Nadu 7
targeting 11–12
TB *see* tuberculosis
Teacher Perception Survey 118
teachers 44, 117, 118, 127
absenteeism 17, 132, 164, 165
teenagers *see also* boys, children *and* girls 123, 124, 125, 142
education 121–2, 123
television sets 80
temples 74
Thrift and Credit Cooperative Society 37, 168
Titmuss, Richard 24
tobacco 96
toilets *see also* latrines 123, 177
Total Sanitation Campaign *see also* *Nirmal Bharat Abhiyan* 72, 74, 75, 198
tractors 149
transport, personal 80
tuberculosis (TB) 32
tuition, private 117, 119, 133–4, 200

underweight 95
UNDP *see* United Nations Development Programme
unemployment 154
UNICEF *see* United Nations Children's Fund
Union Ministry of Drinking Water and Sanitation 74
Unique Identification Card 6

United Nations Children's Fund
(UNICEF) 37, 74, 93, 195
United Nations Development Programme
(UNDP) 32
United Progressive Alliance (UPA) 4, 208,
210
universalism 13
untouchability 177
UPA *see* United Progressive Alliance
USA *see* America, United States of

vegetables 91
voter ID cards 167

wage labour 142, 143, 144, 145, 146, 147,
201
wages 9, 201
water
drinking 75–6
sources 75–6
Weakest at the Centre Principle 3
weight-for-age (children) 92–6, 199
welfare 198–200
welfare state 3
welfare system 19

wells 149
wheat 83, 85, 88, 89, 90, 91
WHO *see* World Health Organization
women 9, 15–16, 18, 28–9, 38, 44, 45,
61–2, 73, 76, 143, 154, 157–80, 193,
198, 202
bank accounts 169, 170
childbirth 100
citizenship 158–9, 162
civil rights 176–8
disabled 185
domestic violence 177
economic activity 143
economic citizenship 172–6
emancipation 159, 179
employment 28–9
financial citizenship 166–72
hospitalization 106, 107
mortality 43
political rights 176–8
work 145, 150–1, 172
Women and Children, Department of 16
World Bank 14, 181
World Health Organization (WHO) 28,
93, 181